PHI[illegible]
ADAMS

The Ideas Man:
A Life Revealed

PHILIP LUKER

JoJo
PUBLISHING

Phillip Adams
The Ideas Man: A Life Revealed
Philip Luker

Published by JoJo Publishing
First published 2011

'Yarra's Edge'
2203/80 Lorimer Street
Docklands VIC 3008
Australia

Email: jo-media@bigpond.net.au or visit www.jojopublishing.com

Author's email address: Philip.luker@internode.on.net

JoJo Publishing
Editor: Ormé Harris
Designer / typesetter: Chameleon Print Design
Cover image: The front page photo of Adams was taken by Bob Finlayson of News Ltd at the Abbey Restaurant, Glebe, Sydney, in November 1999.
Printed in China by Everbest Printing

National Library of Australia Cataloguing-in-Publication entry

Author:	Luker, Philip.
Title:	Phillip Adams : the ideas man : a life revealed / Philip Luker.
ISBN:	9780987073464 (pbk.)
Subjects:	Adams, Phillip, 1939-
	Authors, Australian--Biography.
	Journalists--Australia--Biography.
	Motion picture producers and directors--Australia--Biography.
Dewey Number:	070.92

"He's been around the media for decades, he looks more like a priest than a radio jock, he talks proper, he has an amazingly retentive memory, he's accessibly cerebral, he wears his biases on his skivvy, he polarises opinion and opinion-makers, he applies historical perspective to his views and discussions, he attracts by far the most significant interview subjects from around the globe to his program, he probes and banters with them as an equal, he gets himself properly briefed on the detail, he gives his subjects time and space to be discursive and therefore, often, illuminating, he breaks all the rules of talk radio, he is an Australian institution and an international-calibre broadcaster who would distinguish the airwaves of any radio station anywhere. He is Phillip Adams."

— Eric Beecher in *The Reader* in December 2003

About the Author

Philip Luker did an Arts course at Sydney University and then became a newspaperman on the Sydney *Daily Mirror, The Sun,* the *Daily Telegraph, The Australian Financial Review* and the London *Daily Mail.*

He backpacked (before the word was invented) through 48 countries and was the first Australian journalist to get into Communist China, in January 1956. The articles and photos he sold, including a cover story in *Time* and a front-page series in all US Hearst newspapers, paid for the rest of his world trip, during which he travelled right through North, Central and South America and Africa. At Los Angeles Airport he met Marilyn Monroe on her way to marry Arthur Miller — she held on to his hand while he thought of as many questions as he could.

Back in Australia and wanting to run his own business, he successively launched, published and edited four management newsletters, *Foodweek, Inside Retailing, Greenweek* and *Mediaweek*, all of which concentrated on controversy and personalities and all of which are still being published by others. He wrote and published the books *How to Handle the Green Revolution* and *Inside the Food Industry.*

He returned to Africa to interview Australian doctors and nurses working for Medecins Sans Frontieres and, back in Australia, continued to interview MSF volunteers returning home and had a hundred stories published about them.

Luker lives in Sydney with his wife, Margaret. One day he wrote to Phillip Adams to ask whether he would co-operate over a biography. This book is the result.

Acknowledgements

Phillip Adams always received me at his Sydney office with courtesy, a cup of tea and a willingness to talk about his professional life, anecdotes, experiences and beliefs. He seemed to believe I had agreed not to delve into his private life. He never asked me to agree and I did not do so, either verbally or in writing. Adams said in his original letter to me, "I would not be happy with a heavy emphasis on my private life." This book does *not* heavily emphasise his private life.

Did he believe that, after working as a journalist for fifty years, I would not try to find out about his private life, just because he didn't want me to? Any worthwhile journalist who is refused information from one source tries to find it from another. My first duty in writing this book is to its readers, to tell them as full and honest a story as I can about Adams the man as well as Adams the journalist and public intellectual. Presumably, Adams' first duty is also to his readers and listeners. Ironically, most information about his private life came from his own mouth in a National Library oral history he gave me written access to.

Irina Dunn worked hard at finding me a good publisher and found one in Barry Dorr and his partner Jo. Their company, JoJo Publishing, worked swiftly and expertly to arrange the publishing and marketing of the book after it had been skillfully edited and managed by Ormé Harris, designed by Chameleon Print Design, and proofread by Merryl Scott.

The nineteen prominent people whose phone numbers Adams gave me as friends who might give me information and insight into him all agreed to do so, and I met all except two of them personally: Hugh Mackay, Peter Best, Peter Faiman, Matt Noffs, Brian Monahan, Lyle Dayman, Bruce Petty, Fred Chaney, Alan Snyder, Ranald McDonald, Carmen Lawrence, Philip Nitschke, Jim Soorley, Dick Smith, Bob Brown, Mark Aarons, John Cain, Barry Jones and Bob Ellis. Chris Bullock, the former executive producer of *Late Night Live,* told me how it operates and I watched it go to air twice. My conversations with these twenty people were always enjoyable and often very funny. All twenty were obviously fond of Adams but also mentioned his human frailties. I owe them my sincere thanks.

I contacted Paul Keating, Mike Rann, Anna Bligh and Bob Carr without help from Adams but they also were willing to talk about him. Only one of all these people, Bob Carr, asked me to tell him what I would quote from him. Only one person, John Howard, swiftly declined to meet me about Adams and there is no need to wonder why. Bruce Shapiro, *Late Night Live's* US correspondent, told me how he has enjoyed talking with Adams every week for twelve years. The willingness of all these associates to talk about him shows the warmth of his people relationships.

Adams told me he would leave it to me to contact some of the 'hostiles' as he calls them, and I did so: Bob Hawke, Alan Jones, Gerard Henderson, Philip Ruddock, John Brennan, Miranda Devine and Piers Akerman.

The National Library's Manuscripts Department gave me access, with Adams' permission, to the 500 boxes of letters and emails listeners and readers have sent him over almost forty years, and the library's Oral History Collection gave me access, again with Adams' permission, to its verbatim record of the two-day conversation Margaret Chalker had with him. *The Weekend Australian Magazine* gave me permission to reproduce extracts from his columns and Penguin Books gave me permission to quote from books of his columns where it holds the copyright. Bob Ellis, James Woodford, Alan Ramsey and Ashley Hay gave me permission to quote from *Late Night Live* sessions where Adams interviewed them.

The book could not have been written without continued support from my wife Margaret and daughter Trish Luker. Thank you all. I enjoyed my contact with you and enjoyed the research and writing.

— **Philip Luker**

To Margaret

'Some enchanted evening, when you find your true love,
When you see her call you across a crowded room,
Then fly to her side and make her your own,
Or all of your life you may dream all alone.'

— from the 1949 Rodgers and Hammerstein
musical *South Pacific*

Contents

Chapter One: **A Crowded Life**

Phillip Adams is a public figure who has generated his fair share of controversy and many people dislike him and his views. His office is tucked away in a pink building in a back street of Paddington in the Sydney eastern suburbs. It is lined with pictures and books and filled with antiquities — the largest private collection of antiquities in Australia. In contrast to the exterior of the building, this is undeniably a man's office, huge, untidy, dusty and gloomy, with no sign of a woman's touch. The carpet is rumpled. At the back of the office are a toilet and a very small, dark kitchen with no sign of food.

Apart from a brief chat by phone the previous day, when he warned me that 'several people have wanted me to co-operate with them over a biography and I have always declined', this was our first conversation. I can't help but wonder why he invited me to visit if he didn't really want me to write about his life. Perhaps he was ambivalent about the idea but, whatever his motives, he greeted me with a handshake and a soft smile at the front door and invited me to come inside and sit down. He sat behind his huge desk and listened politely as I introduced myself, outlined my journalistic experience and described my plans for the biography.

'Now,' he said, once I had finished, 'I've been asked to do this many times before and I've always said no.'

'Why?'

'I have a busy life,' he replied, 'and I believe my columns and my program reach a far wider audience than a book could.'

I began to explain my reasons for wanting to write a book about his life and why I thought it needed to be written. He put up some arguments against it. He said, for example, that his first wife, Rosemary, insisted in their divorce contract that he must never discuss her or their marriage with anyone. He suspected that their daughters would side with their mother and refuse to meet me. And he did not want to talk about his personal life. In my fifty years as a journalist, many, many people have said they would not tell me anything but I have ended up finding out quite a lot about them. For almost an hour we conversed, and then, suddenly, he said, 'All right, I'll do it.'

I stopped talking, nonplussed. This was not what I expected to hear after his considerable attempts to dissuade me. But before I had a chance to say anything else, he began talking about his childhood while I frantically took notes — his change of heart was entirely unexpected, and I had not brought my tape recorder.

* * *

Like most Australians, my first impressions of Phillip Adams were drawn from his ABC Radio National program *Late Night Live* and his *Weekend Australian Magazine* column. But Adams' on-air manner of cultivated intimacy only hints at the man behind the public persona.

I was attracted to his laidback style, which seemed at odds with his otherwise intense personality. He makes each listener feel he is talking solely to them, while his interview guests are made to feel that they are the most important people in the world. His language is in a colloquial but well-bred Aussie style and he has such a brilliant mind and computer memory that he can grasp whatever subject his guests raise.

I always liked the way he could mask a robust ego behind a humble front and display his huge knowledge with an earthy Australian lingo. I also appreciated the fact that most of the people he interviews on *LNL* are more interesting than the subjects of other print and radio interviews. Not only that, but Adams lets them finish their sentences rather than talking over the top of them — and that's rare.

Few Australian journalists have been as prolific as Adams. He has written about three million words in books, newspapers and magazines; and he's spoken many more words than that as host of *Late Night Live*, four nights a week for twenty years. But these words don't describe his personal regrets or indicate his weaknesses. They hint at his joys but don't provide the details. It's the details that I'm interested in as his biographer.

In spite of this background, he has never published an autobiography. More surprising, for a man whose hallmark is the conversational interview, is his reluctance to speak with prospective biographers. But this attitude makes me all the more determined to get to know the man who, despite leaving school at fifteen, is so comfortable conversing with academics, authors and other experts on subjects ranging from wombats to nuclear science.

He has known eight Australian prime ministers and most of the state premiers since the 1960s; he has grasped ideas (his specialty) from the arts, culture, commerce, agriculture, the law, media and science and stored what he has learnt in a magnificent brain which, even now he is past seventy, works almost 24 hours a day.

Along the way, Phillip Adams has crossed paths and occasionally come to blows with some of Australia's most prominent people: politicians, ad-men, film directors, business leaders, broadcasters and media tycoons. The list reads like a who's who of Australia — and includes former prime ministers Paul Keating and Bob Hawke, current and past state premiers Mike Rann, Anna Bligh, Carmen Lawrence, John Cain and Bob Carr; psychologist Hugh Mackay; cartoonist Bruce Petty; ex-*Age* publisher Ranald McDonald; film and television director Peter Faiman; actor Barry Humphries; composer Peter Best; media tycoons Kerry Packer and Rupert Murdoch; former federal ministers Barry Jones and Fred Chaney; writers and commentators Bob Ellis, Mark Aarons and Gerard Henderson; entrepreneur Dick Smith; Professor Robert Manne; and Adams' former advertising agency partners Brian Monahan and Lyle Dayman — an extraordinarily diverse list, reflecting the life of this unique Australian.

This book is a record of my conversations with these people and with many of Phillip Adams' friends and critics, who share their memories and reflections on his life and career and offer candid observations and criticism. The critics include Bob Hawke, Philip Ruddock and Alan Jones. I also draw on interviews with Adams in which he characteristically stirs the possum over how to elect an Australian president, why voters have become more conservative, how companies indulge in paedophilia and where Melbourne is different from Sydney. My interviews with him also provide rare glimpses into his personal life and his thoughts on his own career.

I condense extracts from a selection of *Late Night Live* interviews that showcase his skills as an interviewer, from Hazel Hawke talking about her life before and after Bob to Miriam Margolyes telling how the cruel adulterer Charles Dickens saved fallen women. I also examine the responses of ordinary Australians to Adams' columns and radio programs in some of the tens of thousands of letters he has received and which are now stored at the National Library in Canberra.

Which takes me back to where I first began to know of Phillip Adams — *Late Night Live*, where his ability to turn a sophisticated and intricately researched interview into a casual, friendly conversation showcases the qualities that have remained constant throughout his busy life and eclectic career. It seems appropriate to reflect on his life through the words of those who know him best as well as making many observations of my own.

Here then is Phillip Adams, a man of conversations and ideas.

Chapter Two:
Childhood Notions of Death

'I used to have this strange feeling of falling upwards through the galvo roof. There were searchlights in the sky, like fire, because it was wartime. I was lying on a brass bed in a little sleepout at the flower farm my grandparents ran in Melbourne. I lay there, having the feeling of falling upwards, through the roof, through the pine trees, up and up through the clouds, into eternity. I was appalled by the idea of something that went on and on forever, equating it with the notion of death.'

Even at the age of five, an awareness of mortality drove Phillip Adams. 'It was the greatest fear of my life, and it was a result of isolation. So I yelled out, "Phillip Andrew Hedley Adams, 798 High Street, East Kew, Victoria, Australia, the British Empire, the Southern Hemisphere, the World."'

Sixty-six years later, Adams is still pedalling at the same frantic pace, with the spectre of his mortality pursuing him. 'It gives me a sense of urgency to do all I possibly can in the miserable time span allotted after deducting the hours when I'm too young, or too old, or asleep, or on the dunny. The other factor is survival, coming out of my unpleasant childhood and the need to escape it. Off I go on another day. Life's been a whole series of days.'

* * *

Phillip Adams was born on July 12, 1939, just as the curtains were going up on World War II. He entered the world in Maryborough in central Victoria, where his father Charles was the Congregational minister. Charles and his wife Sylvia lived in a drab little weatherboard manse with a tennis court of buckled asphalt, beside a dull-looking brick church. It was hardly inspiring to young Phillip, let alone to his mother. Nor even to his father — it seemed all members of the Adams family were unhappy with their lives.

Glancing around Adams' Sydney office, I realise how far he's come from the little boy whose miserable childhood of neglect, hardship and abuse by a hated stepfather seems drawn from the pages of *David Copperfield.* I asked him what he remembered of his early life.

'My earliest memory, aged two, was looking up at the sky, which I thought was on fire, flames everywhere.' Adams' eyes wandered off as though he was playing back the scene in his head.

'I could see the flames through the peppercorn trees,' he continued, 'and I remember waddling in fear towards the manse and pulling open a battered flywire door to find my father, who told me not to worry because it was only lightning. My father was a petite, shiny little Englishman who not only polished his shoes frantically but even polished the soles. He had come to Australia aged fifteen after being rejected by his mother, who had worked in vaudeville with Charlie Chaplin as a juggler and seal-trainer.' Having lived such a colourful life, no wonder his grandmother was disappointed with her boring, somewhat obsessive son.

'What about your mother?' I asked.

'She was extraordinarily pretty. She told me later it upset other women in the church. She was depressed about living off my father's very low wage. I don't doubt she would have pushed and shoved him into enlisting in World War II as an army chaplain.'

Once his father was off to war, his mother 'immediately got a job in the rationing service, which gave her liberation, a chance to meet other men, and a wage. She left me, aged three, with my maternal grandparents, Bill and Maude Smith, who raised me on their little flower farm in East Kew in Melbourne for most of the next ten years.

'My mother was to me like a fairy in a Disney cartoon. She used to arrive at the farm and take me on bike rides. My father was a strange, distant man, who used to post me coconuts from the war, with my name and address on them — a common thing for fathers serving in the Pacific Islands to do for their children back home. The coconuts were my strongest memory of my father. At times also, Father would come home and be enormously emotional with me, which puzzled me because he was almost a total stranger, as was my mother.

'I rarely saw either parent and, when I did, it wasn't really successful. I remember my father, in uniform, arriving at the farm, taking me by the hand and walking me up High Street, East Kew, for my first day at East Kew Primary School. I remember crying all the way and not wanting to be left there. I didn't understand what my parents were up to or where they were. What I did understand was that I was living with my grandparents on a little flower farm at East Kew.'

* * *

Bill Smith and his identical twin brother Fred grew flowers commercially on four acres of land that, these days, is covered with faded brick-veneer houses in suburban Melbourne. All that remains of the farm where the brothers grew violets, chrysanthemums and poppies for the Queen Victoria Market is a street name, Violet Grove. The farm had a draught horse, an old plough and an outside toilet. Adams' grandparents were incredibly poor. Aged four or five, Phillip didn't realise he was poor until he went to school in handmade clothes and felt humiliated next to his better-dressed schoolmates. Living in a little sleepout at the farm, he lay in his old brass bed wondering whether there was a god and what colour dead would be. He agonised over these questions night after night.

It would not have been surprising for young Phillip to grasp at a comforting fable or to believe in God to give him peace, but he found he couldn't believe what he was told in religion classes at school. He thought it was nonsense.

'The important thing about this,' he told me, 'was that I had never heard the words "eternity" or "infinity". I had never read a book and I had no-one to talk to about it. People later assumed it was a reaction against my father's Christianity. It was nothing to do with that. I hardly ever saw him.'

Adams is well known as an atheist but said he didn't reject God at this early time of his life. 'He was never in contention,' he explained. 'My objection was that, whenever religious teachers at school told me there had to be a God because there had to be a beginning of everything, and God created everything, I would ask, "And who created

God?" I once asked my grandmother and she boxed me on the ear, the only time she ever hit me. I realised I was on to something. It was the most important moment of my life, from which everything else followed.'

To have had such a realisation and lived by it all these years displays a steadfastness usually available only to those raised in the church. 'Everyone agreed there wasn't an ending, because they believed they would go to either Heaven or Hell. Equally, to me, it seemed there couldn't have been a beginning. No end, no beginning, no need for God. I realised life just was, or wasn't, and didn't need an explanation. It certainly didn't need a god, because a god explained nothing. A god simply shoved the questions back.

'I grew up embarrassed by religion. I couldn't believe that other people really believed. Any human must feel awe when they look up at the stars or contemplate what it is all about. But I couldn't believe God created it. In school you go from studying water, what floats or doesn't float, and then, in religious class, Jesus walks on it. And these days at *Late Night Live*, I sit down with scientists who claim they can co-exist with Christianity's funny mythology, written by people who knew nothing about the world and thought the Sun went around the Earth, and who had no vision beyond the horizon, and believed stories about a virgin birth. All these were stories in exactly the same category as stories by Hans Christian Andersen, but not as funny.'

By his own reckoning, the loneliness of being isolated from his parents and living with his grandparents made Phillip an extraordinarily solemn, strange little character. One memory he recounted to me captured his state of mind neatly: 'My grandfather Bill and his twin Fred had been gold miners in Western Australia and started the flower farm together,' Adams explained. 'When Fred died, Bill and Maude sold Fred's house and it was pulled on a truck up High Street, East Kew, to become the Kew Cemetery caretaker's house. I can never forget seeing the house moving along the street to the cemetery. It was as if the house was being buried along with Fred.' For an already melancholic child, this event would seem much more dramatic. Clearly, it has still not lost its resonance with Adams.

* * *

Those early years on the flower farm have had a lasting impact. While his grandparents made little conscious attempt to educate young Phillip, he nonetheless learned a lot sitting at the kitchen table in his grandparents' weatherboard house. Their influence can be seen in many of his core values: from his close relationship to the land to his grandfather's strong, earthy, working-class sense of justice.

'My grandfather was gruff and distant, with the simplicity of a bushie,' said Adams. 'He gave me a sense of physicality. I used to watch him ploughing the fields with his huge draught horse, using the same kind of plough as the Egyptians used thousands of years ago. Off Grandpa would go, the plough bucking through the earth. He would let me stand between him and the plough, in the arch of his arms and with my little hands on the plough. To me, Grandpa was a giant of a man with a giant of a horse. I remember the sense of the physical and the smell of manure. It was a very elemental and simple world. No clock. Grandpa would tell the time by the sun.'

Clearly, though, Bill Smith was more than just a simple bushie. Adams remembers watching and listening as his grandfather propped a copy of *The Age* up on a sauce bottle and read aloud an article about "The Long March" in China, declaring that the poor Chinese deserved a better life.

'Grandmother was immensely caring. The food at home was incredibly simple, such as mutton kept in an ice chest, dripping on toast and a few vegetables they grew, such as beetroot. The house had electricity but my grandparents were too poor to have even a vacuum cleaner. They had a carpet sweeper. A horse and cart came in summer with ice for the ice chest and in winter with wood for the fire in the hearth. A baker delivered bread.

'The only electrical gadget they had was a radio, and we listened to the serials and the hit parade. Grandpa had never owned a watch; he had a clock won at cricket, on the mantelpiece, with a big brass key. I thought it was the most wonderful thing in the world and Grandpa promised he would leave it to me when he died. My school friends' parents had cars, which were still fairly unusual in Australia before television changed everything in 1956. I would sit on the kerb doing what many children did, writing down the numberplates of cars and trams as they passed.'

Adams evokes an Australia that is familiar to many of his generation but, for all the harkening back to 'simpler times', it is obvious that his life wasn't simple. His parents were absent and he was questioning his very reason for being alive.

From the time Phillip could read, his lifelong, desperate need to read developed quickly — he even learned to read *The Age* upside down across the table from his grandfather. He quite liked Biggles books, and The Billabong Books by Mary Grant Bruce, a series of Australian stories for children. So, despite his physical sense of isolation, he clearly connected to stories and to words. Only he knows how valuable they were to him, then.

Cultural and intellectual life in Kew in the 1950s was pretty typical of the rest of the country and, for young Phillip, consisted of an occasional comic stolen from the local newsagent or swapped with his friends. His favourites were Batman and Superman. Once a week, on Saturday afternoons, he went to the Rialto Cinema in Kew to see Tom and Jerry cartoons, Batman and Robin serials and Tarzan movies starring Johnny Weismuller. A shilling bought a ticket and an ice cream.

Later Phillip's grandparents took him to the posh Greater Union Cinema, which had American and sometimes English movies but never Australian ones. The only history he learned was American; the only indigenous people he saw were 'Red Indians'. His entire cultural experience was American. He and his mates even re-enacted Tarzan films in the gumtrees along the Yarra riverbank.

One of those mates was his best friend from school, Johnny Sinclair, who lived in a posh house over the side fence from the Smiths' farm. Johnny was Catholic, so on their morning walk together to school, Phillip would turn left to the state school and Johnny would turn right to the Catholic school. In Phillip's eyes, the Catholic school contained stark, frightening, bat-like creatures called nuns, who put the fear of Christ into him whenever he saw them. Phillip would join other boys from the state school chanting, 'Catholic dogs stink like frogs jumping out of hollow logs' and Johnny and his schoolmates would chant, 'State, state, full of hate'.

Adams remembers, 'We'd scream abuse at Catholics at a time when, at our parents' instigation, the division between Catholics and Protestants was immense, deep and bitter, and took generations to ebb away.' Then, at the end of each day, Phillip and Johnny would walk home together and play.

Despite this unusual friendship, Adams had a genuinely rough time at school. There are few places on earth crueller than a playground, and he was bullied because of his poverty and his sombre demeanour and melancholic manner. Put simply: he was different, and his difference made him a target. He was picked on because he wore funny clothes that Grandma had made him. He rode to school on a grotesque, rusty bicycle that an uncle had given him, and was mocked by the other boys who rode new Malvern Star bikes. He never mastered sport and to this day has no interest in it; when it came to team selection at school, he was never picked.

Adams remembers vomiting with fear some mornings, so strongly did he dread going to school, and not only because the other children bullied him. One teacher took a similar delight in tormenting him. By his own account, however, Adams was not entirely innocent and he remains ashamed of the fact that he joined in attacks on 'refoes' — refugee children from Europe. 'We'd pick on them and tell them to go back,' he said. Phillip's torment at school was hardly alleviated by his home life. If he hoped to find refuge there, it was not offered.

* * *

Any illusions that the end of the war might signal the return to a more normal family life were quickly shattered. 'My mother dumped my father when he came home during the war,' he said, 'and my father was thrown out of the Church because he had a drinking problem. I have terrible memories of being dragged around one day by my mother, the next day by my father, and being told I would have to go to court. There, a judge would ask me which of my parents I wanted to live with — a terrible question.

'My mother told me, "You're going to choose me," and my father told me, "You're going to choose me." I remember the feeling of desperation. How could a child make such a decision? Children are still being asked that question. The decision was made for me: I stayed with my grandparents until I was nine or ten. But as Grandpa Bill grew old and ill, he and Maude had to sell their farm. To complete the picture of his David Copperfield childhood, Adams described how his grandparents were swindled out of their land by a Uriah Heep-like businessman. 'A dignified, corrupt estate agent, who converted it into thirty building blocks, sold them to his mates in a fake auction and Bill and Maude were robbed.'

Then Adams made an important discovery. 'By this time, I had read all the children's books in the Kew Library branch near the farm and the librarian took me up one step into the adults' library and gave me John

Steinbeck's *The Grapes of Wrath*. Reading it made me realise how the weak are pushed around by the strong, as my grandparents had been.' And as the young Phillip had been by his parents.

The political instinct suddenly came alive in Phillip Adams when Steinbeck's ideas led him directly to the Australian Communist Party. He found his way to the banks of the Yarra River, where amateur orators used to speak on Sundays, as they did in The Domain in Sydney. On the Yarra bank were the Catholic Evidence girl, the Evangelicals and a screaming, red-haired fellow who went off to become a big player in the British National Front. And there was the Communist Party. Aged fourteen, Phillip began to turn up regularly to listen to their members' pronouncements. He remembers tugging at a communist speaker's jacket and asking how he could join the party. The speaker was amazed, not only because Phillip was underage for membership but also because, in those McCarthyite days, no-one asked to join the Communist Party. Nonetheless, a couple of members took Phillip's name and he was allowed to join.

* * *

After Phillip's mother remarried he moved in with her and her new husband, Michael Bourke. Phillip's grandfather was a proud, dignified and taciturn man, but on the day Phillip left, the boy could see that the older man was trying not to cry. Bill gave Phillip a ten-shilling note.

Phillip thought Michael Bourke looked like Alf Garnett, the mean-spirited bigot of the English comedy *Till Death Us Do Part*. Michael was, of all things during the war, a furrier, with an office in Bourke Street in the heart of Melbourne. Instead of fighting in the war, he was making money from selling fur coats. But to the ex-wife of a weak church minister, Bourke, with his black Studebaker and his fur coats, was glamorous. Phillip saw him differently.

'He was a psychopath, the most appalling creature, and for the next five years, my life was hell. Not just for physical abuse: the occasional outbursts of violence were almost cathartic and released tension. It was his mental torture of my mother and me, and it meant I couldn't sleep. I still remember rushing, in my pyjamas, into my mother's bedroom to try to protect her from the crazy, arrogant, sick, silly, sad man.

'On one particularly bad night, my mother and I ran from the apartment, me in my pyjamas and dressing gown and my mother in a nightie and dressing gown, and went to the local pictures to hide. You can imagine how embarrassed we were, dressed like that. On the screen appeared a sign: "Mrs Bourke wanted at the manager's office". We waited in our seats, hoping Michael would go away, and later went home because we had nowhere else to go. This was long before the days of women's refuges. In any case, my mother would have been too ashamed and embarrassed to admit that she, as a cotton mill's personnel officer, had any marriage problems. She was by then earning more than Michael, whose business had collapsed.'

Looking at this highly accomplished man before me, I wondered at the path he had taken. To listen to him talk about his stepfather, it was clear that these memories were strong, perhaps constant. It was almost as if his stepfather's ghost was at his back, still chasing him down the street. I wondered if anyone who has experienced such a thing ever loses the feeling of terror — do they ever feel they can escape, in either space or time?

'I remember trying to murder my stepfather when I was about eleven — it was highly ineffective. Michael was shaving with a cut-throat razor. I waited until the razor was at his throat and rushed at him, but it didn't even nick him. The only good thing about the continued horror was that it made me determined to survive and brought me and my mother much closer together.

'One day, when I was fourteen, I heard Michael abusing my mother in the bedroom. I rushed in and pushed Michael with such velocity that he flew over the bed into the Venetian blinds, which forever showed the impact.

'My mother had previously, in case of emergencies, put a change of clothes for me in a little suitcase that Michael used for his Masonic Lodge material. She told me to run away, which I did. I ran down the road towards Montmorency Railway Station, pursued by Michael trying to run me down in his Studebaker. I ran into the bush beside the road and arrived at the station in time to catch a train to the city to go to my father.

'At the next station, Greensborough, Michael's face appeared at the train window. He dragged me out of the train and started screaming and hitting me, surrounded by a menacing crowd of onlookers. Typically, Michael quickly changed his tune and became loving and apologetic, and offered to drive me to my father's place. I remember telling people on the station, "Don't let him take me. Don't put me in the car with him". But the people let Michael drive me away, although as soon as he got into the car, he started punching me again. I jumped out of the moving car and hit the roadway, and Michael drove off.'

Phillip went back to the station and caught another train to the city but, by the time he arrived, his father Charles had given up waiting. He found his way to St Kilda, where Charles lived with his new wife. Charles had told Phillip that she looked like the film star Yvonne De Carlo, so Phillip looked forward to meeting her. When he arrived at the house, Phillip heard screaming and found that 'Yvonne De Carlo' was trying to kill his father with a pair of scissors. Phillip knocked her unconscious and down she went with the scissors. So for the second time in a day he saved a parent.

Charles raced outside and jumped in his little car, Phillip taking the passenger seat. Both of them heaved in terror. Charles turned to his son and asked, 'Will you go back into the house and get my wallet?' Adams has never forgotten those words. And he did it: he went back into the house to make his scissors-wielding stepmother hand over his father's wallet. But he saw the truth: his father hadn't had the guts to try to rescue him from Bourke and now he didn't have the guts to get his own wallet from his wife.

Phillip described what happened after this torrid episode. 'I moved back to my grandparents on the farm. I hoped Michael, who had always denigrated me and told me I was an idiot and would never achieve anything in life, would live long enough to be proved wrong. I would have loved him to see the endless parade of preposterous cars I bought as my wealth increased.

'But when I was in my early twenties, Michael had a heart attack and died. My mother phoned me to say how thrilled she was. She had never had the courage to leave him because of the social stigma that was still, in those years, attached to broken marriages. I went over to my mother's house and lit the backyard incinerator and my mother and I burnt every one of Michael's belongings. At the funeral, people came up to us to say what a wonderful man he was, what a pillar of society. We could hardly keep a straight face.

'Later, my mother married a wharf-crane driver. He treated her well, although my snobbish mother was ashamed of him. She gradually pulled herself together but all her life she denied that she had experienced a terrible marriage to Michael. Later, when I started writing about him occasionally in my Melbourne *Age* columns, my mother always denied it had really happened. On her deathbed, she begged my forgiveness for subjecting me to Michael as a stepfather, and poured out more stories of his brutality, as our secret, because she had never wanted anyone to know and she saw it as her failure. Of course, I forgave her. I knew it had been much worse for her than for me.'

* * *

After the incident with the scissors Phillip saw less and less of his father and continued to live with his grandparents while he attended Eltham High School in Melbourne. The school playground was 'a seething hotbed of sexuality', he told *Australian Playboy* in January 1980. The school made a desperate attempt to segregate the sexes and every afternoon the students were bussed to Eltham Station, where the girls were supposed to travel in the front of the carriage and the boys in the back.

Phillip told the magazine: 'The more reckless boys would crawl along the running board for moments of rapture, but the real trick was to hide in the long grass and miss the first train. The second train was the most extraordinary travelling orgy. Amazingly, I don't remember one instance of pregnancy, despite the experiments. I well remember that my first attempt at sexual congress was behind the toolshed at Greensborough Railway Station. Dylan Thomas said that, to him, women were a blur below the waist. I was similarly ignorant, but I know that the few rather uncomfortable moments when my knees became embedded with gravel were inconclusive. The young lady was extremely contemptuous of my performance and she put me off more experimentation for some considerable time.'

At his grandparents' house, Phillip sat in his little room and wrote and wrote. He covered the walls and ceiling with pictures from newspapers and magazines, things that would transport him away from his room in time and space, such as pictures from the ancient world. He wrote for the high school magazine and his contributions were praised by a couple of teachers.

One of these teachers was so impressed that she decided to give Phillip a leg up. Her husband took Phillip into the city and introduced him to 'Jimmy' Haughton James who, with partner John Briggs, ran the advertising agency Briggs and James. As soon as he could, legally, at the age of fifteen, Phillip walked out of Eltham High School into his first job — a job in the super-creative world of advertising that would set his direction for life.

Chapter Three: **Supping with the Devil**

On his first day at Briggs and James, Phillip, acting as delivery boy, had to take a naked female plaster dummy on a tram. You can imagine his embarrassment. At just fifteen years of age, his job was mostly to deliver printing blocks to production houses on a bicycle. He was also writing for the communist *Guardian.* So he was in the furnace holds of capitalism by day and trying to undermine capitalism by night. Meanwhile, Jimmy James took an interest in young Phillip; he was amused by Phillip's Communist Party membership. Jimmy was keen to raise understanding of modern art, design and photography, and in the 1940s he had edited *The Australian Artist.* In the 1950s he took Phillip Adams down the road to show him art in the National Gallery of Victoria.

No-one taught Phillip advertising; in fact, no-one taught Phillip anything. He just had ability and learned as he went along. Phillip benefited from the meritocracy of advertising: no-one cared which side of the street you came from and you needed no formal qualifications. You just had to be able to do the job. So Phillip's advertising career soon took off and he wasn't delivering printing blocks on a bike for long.

* * *

Most advertising agencies in Australia in the 1950s were Australian-owned and staffed by creative eccentrics. Phillip is just one of several well-known people who worked in advertising in those days — individuals who went on to help shape Australian culture in the second half of the twentieth century. They included Donald Horne, Leo Schofield, Bruce Petty, Peter Carey, Fred Schepisi and Richard Walsh. Phillip was one of several Communist Party members who worked in advertising at the time, although Phillip and many others quit the party after Russia crushed the Hungarian Revolution in 1956, when Phillip was seventeen.

Others who had good jobs in advertising kept their party membership quiet — in contrast to Phillip, who even now often mentions his brief membership in print or on air, to give himself a touch of notoriety. The Communist Party of Australia was dissolved in 1991 when it had fewer than a thousand members, but the Socialist Party of Australia renamed itself the Communist Party and still publishes *The Guardian* from its office in Surry Hills in inner-city Sydney.

Even Labor Party members kept their membership quiet. The Labor Party often had difficulty getting ad agencies to run its campaigns or finding announcers to broadcast its voiceovers because the announcers were required by law to identify themselves at the end.

Television was launched in Australia in 1956 and soon afterwards Phillip found himself running Briggs and James' television department; some of his staff were twice his age. Bruce Petty had been drawing cartoons for *The New Yorker, Punch* and *Esquire*, and he and Phillip started making television commercials together. Phillip switched agencies and joined Paton Advertising, which was run by elders of the Toorak Presbyterian Church. At that time, Brian Monahan, a businessman with a background of selling ads in *Time*, and Lyle Dayman, an artist with advertising experience, owned and ran the small agency Monahan and Dayman and their market research consultant recommended that they hire Phillip as a copywriter.

Brian and Lyle were impressed by Phillip's creative ability and not only hired him as copywriter and creative director when he was only in his twenties but — to make sure they didn't lose him — gave him an equal partnership in the agency, which then became Monahan Dayman Adams (MDA), with just a handful of staff.

'Straightaway the agency went ahead in leaps and bounds because of Phillip's brilliance,' said Brian Monahan as he sat opposite me in his South Yarra terrace.

His wife had just brought us coffee and cakes, and as she was leaving the room I asked her if she had found Adams attractive; so many women did and do.

'He was not my type,' she said.

'He's an insomniac,' said Monahan of his former colleague, 'and sometimes he'd work all night. He's got such an intellect that, unlike others driven by physical exercise or something else, his brain drives him. It doesn't stop for a minute. Maybe he can't stop it going so fast. He often said that it annoyed him that people used so little of their brainpower. Perhaps he was out to show he wasn't going to waste a minute. Like a brain athlete, he was training his brain all the time.'

According to Monahan, Adams is a sincere person with empathy for those less fortunate than himself. His interest in others is also genuine. Monahan saw evidence of this in the way Adams was always helping people in the office with their personal problems. He was the father confessor and the agency's unofficial resident psychologist, sought out by executives and staff for help with their personal problems. Brian Monahan said he himself had once sought Adams' personal advice about a problem. Almost paradoxically, however, Adams was fairly antisocial and going to an office cocktail party was his worst nightmare.

'But some of the girls in the office had an eye for him and would melt in his presence,' Monahan commented, smiling. 'He could hypnotise women with his intellect and he enjoyed their company and they enjoyed his. He was selling himself all the time. Now he says he despises advertising, which is a bit rough as he was in it for a long time.' Perhaps Adams was being deliberately provocative when he used the word 'despise'.

A few days after my meeting with Brian Monahan, I got a phone call from Phillip Adams.

'I don't think I should talk to you any more,' he said abruptly.

'Why not?' I said, unsure if he was joking.

'Brian Monahan says you asked him about me flirting with girls in the MDA office.'

'Come off it,' I responded. 'He only said you flirted. He didn't say you had affairs.'

There was something that sounded like a grumble on the other end of the phone. We talked for a little while longer and I convinced him to keep meeting me.

* * *

With Adams on board, MDA started to attract bigger clients such as Qantas, Westpac and Myer. It soon became Australia's third biggest agency after George Patterson and John Clemenger. The partners moved the office to the Melbourne advertising heartland of St Kilda Road and increased their staff to twenty.

Adams wrote copy for these large corporate clients but his real brilliance was as a creative strategist and salesman. He understood the psychology of products and markets. He could analyse problems and come up with strategies to solve them. He could talk about almost any product from cosmetics to tyres; his brain was already programmed with information that others would have to spend days researching. And he could sell anything.

Lyle Dayman told me, 'He was an idea-a-second man and he was good at selling his ideas to clients. His biggest role was to get big accounts for us and keep them happy. One of the reasons we did so well was because none of the three of us was a typical adman. We weren't bull artists, and people believed us.'

In the 1970s, Barry Humphries, as Edna Everage, did a television commercial created by Adams called 'Guess Whose Mum's Got a Whirlpool', which was so memorable that it was revived for Mother's Day in 2009, starring Bert Newton, Molly Meldrum and Dave Hughes, each portraying their own mothers and paying tribute to the original Edna Everage ad. Adams told me, 'I originally came up with the slogan when driving from the Malley's factory that made Whirlpool washing machines at Auburn in Sydney to Mascot airport. My inspiration was the "Guess Which Twin Has a Toni" slogan, which I had seen on trams as a child. Malley's didn't really like the ads and wondered whether Barry, in drag, advertising washing machines, was a good idea. But the campaign sold an awful lot of washing machines, and gave Barry, who was having major problems with alcoholism, a much-needed infusion of cash.'

* * *

In spite of Adams' well-known left-wing views, he got on well with clients. Brian Monahan said, 'We used to have arguments about politics and religion at the office, the only trouble being that he was better at quoting sources. I had a strong leaning to the Liberal Party, Phillip to the Labor Party and Lyle was in the middle of the spectrum. I was Catholic, Lyle had no strong religious views and Phillip was atheist. At one time we had to put a line down the centre of the office because Phillip and I were preparing opposing advertising campaigns.'

Advertising agencies in those days were havens for interesting, creative people. Monahan Dayman Adams provided a wonderful environment for its staff. Even now, more than thirty years later, people tell Brian Monahan that their time at MDA was the happiest and best of their working lives. The agency's engine room was the bar. You could help yourself to a drink at any time and there was no charge. You would find people there until early morning and they would still have their work ready by 9 am. Many of its staff went on to have tremendous careers in films and other creative industries. But Adams didn't drink at the bar. In fact, he hardly ever drank. After work, he'd go straight home.

The MDA partners, their staff, clients and other invited guests such as politicians and media personalities also had regular office lunches together — but only for about ninety minutes and fuelled by mineral water, which was replacing wine at business lunches. Adams was the life of the party, holding forth with political anecdotes.

Board meetings were also a lot of fun. Phillip would occasionally seize the opportunity to lie down on the couch and look as if he was asleep, but at a strategic moment would make a pertinent comment. Lyle Dayman told me, 'Phillip sometimes actually fell asleep during board meetings, although I have to admit that I used to relieve the boredom myself by drawing sketches of the other board members.'

At this time, Adams was doing a great deal in his life, such as writing columns for *The Age*, which riled some of MDA's clients, while others found his views challenging and entertaining. He was also making films and working on government committees.

The partners were earning big money, which made left-winger Adams feel guilty. He started to despise the advertising business that was making him wealthy and expunged his guilt by planning campaigns for the good of society. In 1975, he conceived the 'Life. Be in it' campaign for the Victorian Department of Youth, Sport and Recreation. Graphic designer Alex Stitt brought the campaign to life with cartoon characters, particularly a lethargic, beer-bellied, middle-aged couch potato called Norm. The Victorian Government launched the campaign in 1975, initially urging people to get out and get exercise, although later the campaign was expanded to promote quality of life.

By 1977 the campaign had become national, supported by all Australian governments, and fat, middle-aged Norm became such an anti-hero cult figure that he took part in the 2001 Sydney Centenary of Federation Parade. The Macquarie Dictionary of Slang describes Norm as 'an average citizen addicted to watching sport on television'. In 1981, federal funding for the campaign ended and 'Life. Be in it' became a not-for-profit company. You can send Norm an email at www.lifebeinit.org to find more about it and suggest how Australians could become more active. Perhaps the campaign should be modernised and stepped up as it is now 35 years old and many Australians have never seen it.

Another legendary campaign, devised by Adams in 1980, was 'Slip! Slop! Slap!' for the Victorian Anti-Cancer Council. Peter Best, who wrote the music for the original commercial, told me that the slogan was originally 'Slip! Slop! Shove!'

'But,' he said, '"Slip" (on a shirt), "Slop" (on sunscreen) and "Slap" (on a hat) preserved the "Sl" sound each time.'

And so another widely recognised slogan sprang from the frontal lobe of Phillip Adams. Like 'Life. Be in it', 'Slip! Slop! Slap!' went national and has been adopted by all state cancer councils. Both campaigns were usually screened free of charge as community service announcements. 'Slip! Slop! Slap!' was also used in New Zealand and Canada. The cartoon characters were again created by Alex Stitt, with Sid as an animated seagull. The ad has become Australia's longest-running commercial.

For another government initiative — planning a national campaign for disabled people — Adams spent a day in a wheelchair to experience what it was like to be disabled. He told me, 'I learned more about being disabled in that day than ever before or since. I was sitting in an Adelaide office with other people planning the campaign when a man in a wheelchair came in. "Get in the chair," he told me, so I did. "Now go downstairs and see what it's like." So I did. At the lift, I could hardly reach the button and the lift doors nearly closed on me. Downstairs, there were steps leading to the street.

'I might have been at Niagara Falls,' Adams said. 'I cheated and got out of the wheelchair and walked down the stairs, so people stared and me and probably thought I was trying to fool them that I was disabled. Then on the footpath, there weren't ramps at the kerbs like there are these days and I had to get out of the chair again. It was an amazing day, but I learned what it is to be disabled and it helped us plan the ad campaign.'

Adams undertook more and more 'do-good' campaigns because he enjoyed using advertising to do things other than sell products. The origin of one campaign was the fact that few women were presenting for breast-cancer examinations and research found they feared that neither they nor their men would be able to cope with a breast operation, in the same way that men feared losing their penis. Women complained that when they found a lump in a breast, their doctors often brushed it off. So a breast-cancer campaign planned by Adams and others used drama to show men how to treat women's anxieties, friends how to be supportive and doctors how to be understanding.

But not all the memorable campaigns were for not-for-profit organisations. Every time Adams sees the Qantas slogan 'Spirit of Australia' he remembers giving birth to it; now he wants to take it back because he says Qantas doesn't deserve it.

* * *

As global brands reached Australia and started to dominate sales, their advertising agencies bought local agencies and began to dominate billings, which made it harder for local agencies to pick up anything except the crumbs. About eighty per cent of ad bookings were taken by international agencies, which made MDA's success and continued growth even more remarkable. The agency that had started in one room generated an extraordinary client list and opened offices not only in all Australian capital cities but also in London, New York, Chicago, San Francisco, Hong Kong, Singapore and Auckland. Adams counteracted his feelings of guilt for working on commercial campaigns for global brands by planning social engineering campaigns against racism and smoking.

In 1974, when he was only 35 and still at MDA, he said in the first of two oral histories recorded by the National Library, 'Advertising is a despicable, irritating, shallow sort of business, but I think its history will be interesting. I think it's going to eventually be used as an educational force against consumption, against the very things it's been used for in the past.

'In a sense, what is advertising? It can be used to persuade people that racial prejudice is bad just as easily as to sell detergent. It can be used, as it is in America, to discourage consumption just as simply as it is used to encourage it. *Sesame Street* uses advertising technology for educational purposes — short spans of attention, lots of colour, and lots of technique as in television commercials — to keep people interested.'

Adams' criticism of advertising must have made his partners and workmates squirm and point out that he made a lot of money from it. He continued in his oral history, 'Advertising has to be cleaned up and the sooner the better. I'd like to see stringent government regulations not only on cigarettes but also on alcohol and some other products. I am against advertising being used in politics because it is dangerous. Although I've done a number of political campaigns, I've also lectured and written against applying advertising techniques to politics. I'd like to see Australian laws preventing political advertising, mainly because it makes parties so vulnerable to business interests funding the campaigns. It's not the case in Britain, where there is televised free political program time but no such thing as televised political advertising. That approach should be followed here.'

By the early 1980s, Phillip was sick of the ad industry and exhausted not only from it but additionally from film-making, writing columns — even if he enjoyed the activity — and sitting on many Victorian and federal government bodies. In 1983, MDA's partners floated the agency on the stock exchange, then bought Alan 'Mo' Morris and Allan 'Jo' Johnston's Mojo agency, which had made the ads 'Put Another Shrimp on the Barbie', 'C'mon Aussie, C'mon', 'I Feel Like a Toohey's' and Paul Hogan's 'Anyhow, have a Winfield'. In 1989, Mojo-MDA, with billings of $500 million, received a takeover offer from Chiat-Day of Madison Avenue, resulting in $A77 million being spread largely among the three partners.

Brian Monahan bought a cosmetics business. He thought it would be a simple marketing exercise to crank up the brand, Natural Glow. He didn't understand the manufacturing, distribution and retailing problems but later found a CEO with industry knowledge and the brand, now called Natural Glamour, is sold in all Kmart and Priceline stores and several thousand chemist shops. Lyle Dayman bought a farm at Yea in Victoria and later returned to his home state of South Australia, where he has a house on the beach at Somerton Park. He paints landscapes and streetscapes for his own pleasure and his paintings are sold in local galleries.

Adams' campaign, in columns and in the Labor Party, against televised political ads led to the Hawke Government (1983-91) banning any commercials of less than two minutes' duration so that parties could not 'hit and run'. The networks were also required to give free time during election campaigns. Adams and his supporters were pleased that they had actually changed the laws, but then the High Court overturned the laws on the grounds that they were against free speech.

Adams has maintained friendships he made in his thirty-five advertising years, particularly with Peter Best, Brian Monahan and Bruce Petty. Peter Best told me Adams wrote an email to him a little while ago that said, 'Here we were, two old lefties who put a lot of time and energy into helping advertisers get richer — talk about supping with the Devil. But we had fun in advertising and when it ceased being fun, we both got out.'

Chapter Four:
Having Fun Making Films

Phillip Adams told me during one of our hour-long sessions at his office at Paddington in Sydney, 'I bought a clockwork movie camera for sixty quid, but it was useless.' We were discussing his first forays into film-making, which sprang from his experiences making commercials at the Melbourne advertising agency Briggs and James in the early 1960s. He and a colleague, Brian Robinson, wondered whether, if they could make commercials, could they make movies? A few loonies and brave souls were experimenting with film; why shouldn't they join them? They had to put up their own money, of course — hence the sixty quid expenditure.

'The camera ran for twenty seconds and then stopped,' Adams continued. 'So you could have no shot longer than twenty seconds. And we couldn't record sound. We edited literally with scissors and sticky tape. We had no gear and when we needed light interiors, we would borrow emergency lighting from road gangs. And when I say "borrow", I mean we borrowed it and took it back later, hoping no-one had noticed.'

With the most primitive equipment, Brian and Phillip started to make a feature film. It cost them six thousand dollars, took six years of their spare time and was the story of a love affair between a kindergarten teacher, Jill, and a bikie tow-truck driver, Jack — a story in nursery rhymes with a voiceover reading the rhyme.

It was launched in 1970 and called *Jack and Jill: A Postscript*. The proposition was that, simply by using nursery rhymes and stringing them together, they could make a feature film. It opened with a voiceover, Phillip's then wife Rosemary, saying 'Mary, Mary quite contrary', and you saw a statue of the Virgin Mary. Then with 'How does your garden grow?' the camera zoomed out to reveal a cemetery. Every nursery rhyme told part of the story. Adams told me, 'Bugger me, the film won the Grand Prix at an international film festival, a modest one, the Adelaide-Auckland Film Festival, but nevertheless a kosher film festival.'

Jack and Jill was the first feature film to win the Australian Film Institute Best Film award. Years later, in his oral history for the National Library, Adams called *Jack and Jill* 'an abysmal thing, greatly embarrassing to look at in retrospect but with a lot of innovations, both in the way it was put together and the narrative style of using nursery rhymes.'

It was the first of fifteen feature films that Adams made or helped make in the sixties, seventies and early eighties, mostly as executive producer or producer. Amongst these films were *The Naked Bunyip, Hearts and Minds, The Adventures of Barry McKenzie* (released in 1972, directed by Bruce Beresford and the most successful Australian film up to that time), *Don's Party* (1976); *The Getting of Wisdom* (1978); *Lonely Hearts* as executive producer (1982); *We of the Never Never* as executive producer; *Grendel Grendel Grendel* as producer (1981); and *Fighting Back* as executive producer (1982).

Many other people had tried in vain to revive the Australian film industry after its succession of booms and slumps since the 1906 *Story of the Kelly Gang* became the world's first feature film. Adams saw a great opportunity when John Gorton became Liberal prime minister in 1968; Gorton was also the minister for the arts. Adams didn't know Gorton, but his friend the quiz champion and then schoolteacher Barry Jones did, for the oddest reason. Jones had the first open-line radio program in Australia and also a low-rating program on Channel Seven called *Encounter*. He managed to have Gorton appear on both programs and it gave Gorton's role as prime minister a degree of credibility. One thing led to another: Gorton smiled on Barry Jones as his lucky rabbit's foot and Jones' reward was to be invited to The Lodge. Gorton loved American westerns, but he was also worried about foreign ownership and selling the farm, and Jones and Adams saw this as their way in.

So they pedalled John Gorton an argument that America was gobbling up Australia's national identity, which indeed it was. Gorton bought it and also bought Jones' and Adams' idea that the government should forget financing opera houses or art galleries and instead help create an Australian film industry.

Gorton agreed to send Jones and Adams off on a six-week world trip in December 1969 to study film industries, with the Liberal MP Peter Coleman accompanying to keep an eye on them.

* * *

It was Adams' first overseas trip. He and Jones went to Tokyo then Moscow, Warsaw, Berlin and Prague and met Peter Coleman in Stockholm. Peter had refused to visit any communist country as he thought his editorials in the right-wing magazine *Quadrant* had made him personal enemies with communists, although (Adams said in the oral history) it was actually because Coleman thought he might catch communism like a virus.

In Moscow they visited film schools accompanied by a Soviet-provided interpreter, Vladimir Schmidt, who spoke English with a US mid-western twang. He had learnt English from a mid-western woman who had developed an unrequited passion for Lenin in the 1920s; he said his ambition was to visit Minneapolis or Kansas City and ask, 'Where's the john, Mac?' and not be detected as a foreigner. Senator Eugene McCarthy from Minnesota, who had challenged Lyndon Johnson for the Democratic presidential nomination in 1968, was also staying at the Hotel National in Moscow and was amazed at Vladimir's accent. Vladimir revealed himself as a dissident who typed up poems by politically incorrect writers such as Pasternak and bound them. Jones and Adams wondered whether he was an agent provocateur trying to entice them into an anti-Soviet act.

One icy night Jones and Adams drove in a rented car to see the Bolshoi Ballet but they skidded on the ice and ran into the back of a taxi. A crowd gathered, the traffic police arrived and they were told to follow them to a police station to be interrogated. The prospect of seeing the Bolshoi faded as they waited and waited, until an officer in gold braid appeared and made a phone call to someone who probably had even more gold braid, repeating, 'Touristi Avstraliski'. Barry Jones intervened and said, 'Nyet touristi, apparatchiks!' He thought 'apparatchiks' meant 'bureaucrats'; instead it turned out to be a magic word, because apparently the police thought they were Communist Party officials. They were given broad smiles and coffee and allowed to go.

In Prague they made the serious mistake of wearing Russian fur hats as they trudged through the icy streets; it was just a year after Soviet tanks had crushed 'the Prague spring'. As Jones recounts in his autobiography, *A Thinking Reed* (Allen & Unwin), a group of sullen youths closed in on them. They waved their passports and were allowed to continue. In Warsaw they met Jerzy Toeplitz, who had been dismissed as rector of the famous Polish Film School in Lodz. They regarded him as the best available candidate to run their proposed Australian film school. In those days of the communist secret police, he was worried about surveillance at Adams and Jones' hotel and suggested they walk in the street. They walked at length and when they returned to the Hotel Bristol, Adams' hotel key was not at the reception desk. They raced upstairs (said Jones in *A Thinking Reed*) and could hear a phone ringing in his room. They persuaded a housekeeper to open the door and found it had been ransacked. Probably the ringing phone had been a warning from the lobby to the thieves to clear out. Jones' room was untouched. In a slow interrogation by the police, Adams had to answer questions on a document such as his mother's name, date and place of birth, while the thieves escaped.

In Los Angeles, they had lunch twice at Ma Maison, where they were reliably told Orsen Welles was an habitué. But their lunches were on his days off. Jones said in his book, 'Welles was a talismanic figure for both of us — bearded, overweight, frequently frustrated but always aiming at the universal.'

In all, Adams and Jones visited nineteen film schools and Peter Coleman twelve. Jones and Peter Coleman had a blazing row for a time and wouldn't talk to each other, so Adams would sit in a car with them and Jones would say, 'Tell Coleman such and such', and Coleman would say, 'Tell Barry so and so'.

* * *

Adams and Barry returned with a proposition to put to Prime Minister and Arts Minister Gorton. Adams wrote the one-page report, which began with a piece of deliberate plagiarism from the American Declaration of Independence: 'We hold these truths to be self-evident. It is time for Australians to see their own landscapes, hear their own voices and dream their own dreams', with the establishment of a small film industry to interpret the national identity, producing ten to fifteen feature films a year, intensely local and culturally specific. The resulting films turned out to be *Strictly Ballroom* and *Priscilla Queen of the Desert* — films that didn't need studios or a lot of infrastructure but had a certain cheek and vibrancy about them. The report suggested that the government establish an experimental film fund for would-be young film-makers, a national film and television school, and a film bank.

The report asked Gorton for $100,000 and he agreed to provide it. But he was soon out of office, replaced by Billy McMahon and succeeded as arts minister by Peter

Howson, who proceeded to de-Gortonise everything. On ABC Television's *This Day Tonight*, Adams called Howson 'a pain in the arts' and noisily resigned from the advisory committee. It worked like magic. Billy McMahon, who had succeeded Gorton as prime minister, rang Adams the next morning, grovelled, said Sonia sent her love and similar rubbish and promised to restore the plan, which gave Adams and his supporters breathing space until Gough Whitlam was elected prime minister in 1972 and put a lot of money into reviving the film industry.

Reserve Bank Governor H C 'Nugget' Coombs taught Adams that if a prime minister or political leader is also made arts minister, the arts world has no trouble getting action and money, so Adams promoted that idea successfully to Gorton, Whitlam and others. Initially Whitlam planned to make Senator Doug McClelland minister for the media and arts, and McClelland told Adams he planned to dismantle structures that Adams had set up, such as the Australian Film Development Corporation, and would not set up a film school. He was also uncomfortably close to the Hollywood film industry.

Adams said, 'Nugget and I begged Gough not to give Arts to Doug but to keep it for himself because it's always better for the arts to be run by a prime minister or premier than by a junior minister — you get much more done.'

Adams wrote to Whitlam urging him to keep the arts ministry for himself. Whitlam did so and made McClelland media minister. Adams went on: 'Doug never forgave me. But we had Gough in our corner, which meant we had the film school and all the other things we had talked about to John Gorton.'

While Whitlam was wondering what to do with the arts, Adams got a phone call from Peter Ward, an offsider to Don Dunstan, the then South Australian premier, asking Adams to come to Adelaide to talk about film. Adams went to Adelaide and was ushered into Dunstan's huge office, with a conversation pit almost out of sight of the desk. Dunstan came swanning towards Adams dressed in a safari suit and held out his hand, on which was a huge turquoise ring. Adams didn't know whether to kiss the hand or shake it. 'It was offered in a cardinal sort of way,' he told the National Library, 'so I think I actually bobbed the knee and put lips to ring.'

Don Dunstan told Adams he wanted him to live in South Australia and develop a state film industry. Adams declined to move but suggested that Dunstan's government form a state film corporation, have it look as if it was making documentaries for the government but actually make feature films. Dunstan thought it was a good idea and said he could get the funds approved, so the South Australian Film Corporation was born. Adams helped recruit some of the staff and soon the corporation made *Sunday Too Far Away* and *Picnic at Hanging Rock*.

So then other state governments had to have film corporations — NSW Premier Neville Wran in his state; Dick Hamer in Victoria; even Tasmania had one for a while; Queensland had one but the man who the premier, Joh Bjelke-Petersen, appointed to head it robbed the corporation blind and ended up in jail, along with his wife.

Despite such missteps, Australia went from being one of the hardest places in the world to make films to one of the easiest. For a few glorious years, several federal and state bodies were lavishing money on film-makers.

* * *

In the late 1960s Adams was given a few thousand dollars by the ex-racing driver and tyre magnate Bob Jane and made *The Naked Bunyip*, a film about Australian sexual morays, starring Graham Blundell. Blundell played a young reporter who rushed around Australia asking people about their sex lives. The film had contributions from such well-known people as Malcolm Muggeridge, Norman Lindsay, young Harry Miller and young Barry Jones. For the first time in Australia, interviews with prostitutes were shown in a film. The film included scenes of full frontal nudity, lesbians kissing, a topless woman, descriptions of back-yard abortions, a gang rape and a doctor talking about anal and oral sex — a lot for Australians in 1960-70s to accept in a film.

It started off three and a half hours long, but the one-armed chief Commonwealth film censor, Russell Prowse, came to Adams' aid ironically by insisting on many cuts, even a scene showing lesbians talking to each other, in spite of the fact that, at the same time, the Savoy Cinema in Melbourne was screening a film about lesbians. Adams pointed this out to the censor, who said, 'They're European lesbians. We're not going to have that sort of thing here.' It was great for publicity and Adams made the censor's cuts as obvious as possible by showing an animated bunyip, drawn by Peter Russell-Clarke, dancing across the screen every time the censor had made a cut. Adams said, 'In the 1960s in this wide, brown land, we had about the most repressive censorship in the Western world. So one of the reasons we made *The Naked Bunyip* was to stretch beliefs over sexuality, because it was starting to be debated, certainly in the Northern Hemisphere. There was another issue: The film industry was as dead as sexuality.'

In 1970, Adams screened *The Naked Bunyip* — now reduced by 45 minutes and the recipient of lashings of publicity generated by the censor — to great applause in halls and theatres, for example, the Palais, in cities and towns because the cinema chains had no faith in Australian movies. The film opened at the Palais Theatre in Melbourne, the biggest cinema in the country. It was packed to the rafters. The most popular parts of the film were the missing parts. The censor was off his face about it. He became very, very angry and threatened Adams and his friends with all sorts of legal problems. Barry Humphries decided to hold a press conference to cash in on the situation more. He told the press that the censor would have given his right arm to have been there — perhaps he had lost his arm through over-zealous film cutting. 'These were not the kind of comments that would endear us to Mr Prowse,' said Adams. 'We couldn't afford to promote the film but Mr Prowse came to its aid by banning a lot of it.' Adams and Barry Humphries made the best of the publicity and the showdown accelerated the collapse of film censorship.

The censor again helped Adams and his backers to get publicity when in 1972 they screened *The Adventures of Barry McKenzie,* and Barry Humphries (who, as Edna Everage, starred in the film with Barry Crocker) poured petrol on the fire by again making speeches saying '... the chief censor told me straight from the shoulder ...'

Adams tried to get the film screened by Hoyts or Greater Union cinema chains, both of them foreign-owned and avoiding Australian films like poison, and suffered the same fate as he had with *The Naked Bunyip.* So Adams and company screened *Barry McKenzie* in public halls and independent cinemas starved of films by the distributors. Barry Humphries and he again had a wonderful time organising the publicity and the film took off like a rocket — it was the first Australian film to gross a million dollars, the first commercially successful Australian film for thirty years and the first to be seen as a success overseas since World War II. In the film, produced by Adams and directed by Bruce Beresford, Barry McKenzie (Barry Crocker), the extreme embodiment of Ockerism, sets off to England accompanied by a small inheritance and Aunt Edna (Barry Humphries) to get a cultural education. Aunt Edna, of course, later became Dame Edna Everage and is still going strong. Barry McKenzie is fond of beer, Bondi and beautiful sheilas, and gets drunk and vomits (often), is ripped off (more often) and insulted by effete Englishmen (constantly). He is exploited by record producers, religious charlatans and the BBC.

Adams believes that if it hadn't been for the interest *Barry McKenzie* created, many Australian film classics would never have been made. In London, *Barry McKenzie* took off as audiences understood the anti-ocker humour, although it failed in the provinces. In Adelaide, where Adams had hired a cinema to screen *Barry McKenzie*, he and Barry Humphries arrived to find a hundred ockers dressed as Barry McKenzie forming a wedding-type arch of beer spray from a hundred cans. Adams invented a character called Carlo, who claimed to be an earnest film buff and wrote letters to *The Age* attacking the character Barry McKenzie and saying he was an insult to proper film-making.

* * *

'They were funny days,' Peter Best said when I met with him at my home. He had met Adams when Best was writing advertising jingles at Monahan Dayman Adams; he wrote the music for *Jack and Jill* and *Barry McKenzie*. From ad jingles to films was a steep learning curve for both of them. Best later wrote the music for *Muriel's Wedding* and *Crocodile Dundee*. *Crocodile Dundee* made a lot of money for him.

He said that for twenty years Adams had been suggesting they go and live alone on a tropical island with no phones and write a musical together. Well, perhaps there would be just a few phones.

'I knew he'd never have time to live on a tropical island and even if he did, he'd spend most of his time on the phone sorting out someone else's problems,' Peter said. 'So we've never written a musical. It's a pity.'

Best described the birth of *Barry McKenzie*: 'I was at Sydney University and Bruce Beresford was there also. I went to London in 1970 and ran into Bruce at a party and he told me he was trying to get the *McKenzie* film up. He was going to go back to Australia to try to get some funds. I told him to talk to Adams because he was a whiz at that sort of thing. So Bruce and Phillip got together, Phillip got the money and asked me to write the music. Bruce and Barry Humphries both wanted someone with a lot of experience. Phillip kept pushing for me. I'd written the song, *The Adventures of Barry McKenzie*, which became a hit in the end.

'Phillip rang me and said, "Barry's having dinner at your place tonight."

'I said, "Is he?"

'He said, "You'd better go out and get some food."

'So Barry came to my place on Port Phillip Bay, where there's a lot of smelly seaweed. Barry came in and said, "There's a terrible smell in here."

'I said, "There was no smell until you arrived."

'Then I played him my song and he was really excited. Barry rang Bruce and said, "Peter Best has to do the music." I also did the music for the sequel, *Barry McKenzie Holds His Own*.'

Peter Best said Adams' contribution to Australian films was bringing people together, raising funds from governments and corporations, producing ideas and suggesting things for people to discuss.

'He's an amazing facilitator,' Best told me. 'I've never known anyone who spends so much time and energy trying to help people. He finds it hard to say "no" to people who ask him to launch a book or join a committee. But he also finds it hard to follow through because he's always trying to do too much. I've never known anyone who works so hard. He never has any time off. I'd go crazy. In films, he also had an extraordinary amount of trust. He didn't interfere with me at all. Some producers are not only hands on but also lips on and teeth on. Phillip saw his job as choosing a team, then letting it go.

'Some people in the film business have become quite bitter because Phillip has promised to help them and has tried to help, but because he hasn't come up with what they wanted, they have become cross with him. His family life was so bad when he was a kid that he turned inwards on himself. I went to boarding school from age seven to ten and that turned me inwards, too. I've known Phillip for forty years and we're good friends, but we don't live in each other's pockets.

'At the time when Phillip went to Kerry Packer and asked for some money to make *The Getting of Wisdom*, a lot of people were doing disgusting things over tax concessions, such as being paid $5 million in producer's fees for a film with a budget of $8 million. Phillip could see it would wreck all the things and the people he stood for. He cared for the people who wanted to make films, not for the people who wanted just to make money. If the film industry was a car factory, the federal government would come up with an impressive lot of money to support it,' Best told me.

'If you look at a film like *Crocodile Dundee*, you couldn't calculate how much money it has made for Australia. The French Government charges a fee for every ticket sold and uses that money to support its own industry. If we added twenty cents to every ticket sold, we'd have a lot more money to make films with. Also, if you look at the statistics for French, American or British films, they have more failures than successes, just as we do. Our problem is that, for a country with a serious film industry, we have the smallest audience.'

After his conversation with me, Peter Best went to have lunch at Adams' house in Paddington, Sydney. Not knowing what lunch Adams would come up with, he took his own loaf of bread with him.

* * *

Peter Faiman is another of Adams' friends who first met him in the 1960s. He was a junior director at Channel Nine Melbourne and Adams used to come in with his Monahan Dayman Adams partners to watch the agency's commercials being made.

'Phillip was very affable, curious, supportive, approachable and respectful of me,' said Faiman when I interviewed him at my Sydney home. 'He was a kid trying to do his best. He was the creative communicator of MDA. His main contribution to Australian films was his "can-do" attitude and total support for the creative people and the stimulation he gave everyone. He created the idea from the ground up, touted it, brought people together as producer, encouraged them, gave them the vision and the can-do, and promoted it all from nothing to realisation. It was his inspiration that drove the films.'

Peter Faiman later rose through the Nine Network ranks, directed the *Paul Hogan* and *Don Lane* shows, directed *Crocodile Dundee*, started the FX TV network for Rupert Murdoch in New York and directed the opening and closing ceremonies of the 2000 Sydney Olympic Games.

'Phillip encouraged me throughout my career,' said Faiman, 'including *Crocodile Dundee.*' With an $8 million budget, it took $45 million in Australia and A$400 million in the United States in its first year (1986), more than any other Australian film, before or since.

'He always gave me his point of view and feedback on my shows,' Faiman continued. 'That's very important in the creative process because you get slammed so often. It's so intense and so public. It's always been a tremendous factor in our friendship to have him giving me insightful understanding of what I'm doing and stimulate my mind. In return I've clued him into a lot of insider information on the film and television industries because his curiosity makes him want to know the information and the trends, why things work or don't work and what the public is thinking.'

Despite Faiman's glowing review of Adams' skills, not everything Adams touched worked out the way he planned. In the 1970s he had a passion for bringing three-dimensional (3D) television to Australia. Adams told me, 'Ranald McDonald, managing director of the Melbourne *Age,* and I used Kerry Packer's money to do experiments for weeks. We had a creative, exciting time and 3D TV worked on a technical level. The next hurdle was to get it to work on a cultural level. There needed to be 3D goggles in every Australian home and we felt this was possible. But the main problem was that Kerry Packer couldn't see the 3D effect because one of his eyes had been damaged by polio when he was a boy. So he backed off and 3D television didn't eventuate in Australia at that time.'

* * *

In 1976, four years after *Barry McKenzie* was launched, Adams was the producer and Bruce Beresford the director of *Don's Party*, the film adaption of the David Williamson play of the same name, about a Labor cheer-squad celebrating before a 1969 federal election victory that didn't eventuate.

In his oral history for the National Library in Canberra, Adams said Beresford told him that there are probably no more than twenty film actors in the world who are bankable (including several Australians) and every producer tried to sign up at least one. It was the same with other film crew. Don McAlpine, the cinematographer for *Barry McKenzie*, has since shot fifty other Australian and American films, including *Moulin Rouge, Mrs Doubtfire, Down and Out in Beverly Hills, Puberty Blues, The Club, Breaker Morant* and *My Brilliant Career.* Adams' point is that Australian films struggle but Australia's contribution to American films is vast. Australians are happy to see Australian actors doing American accents in major US films. Adams has always dreaded Australia becoming the Hollywood back lot that it has become: sequels of *Star Wars* and *Superman* being made in Australia — films which otherwise have nothing to do with Australia.

Australians have always loved seeing themselves on television but are diffident about seeing themselves on a big screen. Television is like looking in a mirror and seeing yourself reflected but film is a big window and Australians have always preferred a big American window. They are 'iffy' about their own industry and have to be cajoled into seeing Australian films apart from those that say flattering things about us, such as the mystical *Picnic at Hanging Rock* or the patriotic *Gallipoli.* They don't like films that criticise their own country. They like films about people winning, not losing, as do the characters in many Australian films. Just as *Barry McKenzie* kicked down the door for other

Australian films, film did the same for other arts, such as theatre — the number of Australian plays professionally produced has multiplied.

Adams believes the film driving force is not the writers or film-makers but the Sidney Nolans, Arthur Boyds and other Australian painters who showed there was an Australian look, light and energy. But in spite of the gains, only 3.8 per cent of Australian cinema takings in 2008 came from Australian films, down from 4.0 per cent in 2007 and 4.6 per cent in 2006.

America has one anti-hero, Woody Allen. That's his job. Australia produces dozens of Woody Allens in wry, oblique and offbeat films. Australia has made film after film about innocent country boys like *Barry McKenzie* going to the big smoke, either Sydney, London or New York. Australian films are pro-life — exuberant and happy. But these days the films that people enjoy are highly energetic, powerfully visual, often quite vulgar, naive and very likeable, said Adams. Australia is also one of the great documentary nations. America doesn't make many of them. If you look at pay television in Australia, some docos are Australian with American voice tracks.

* * *

Phillip Adams was chairman of the Australian Film Institute, the Film and Television Board of the Australia Council, the Australian Film Commission and Film Australia. More than anyone else, he revived the Australian film industry in the 1970s. His biggest regret was the damage that the 10BA tax concessions did to Australian films. The concession, introduced in 1981, allowed investors to claim a 150 per cent tax concession and to pay tax on only half of any film income. Adams said in his oral history it didn't matter if the film was ever shown, so long as it was actually made, the investors got their tax cut. 'Australian films will not survive without a government subsidy of one sort or another, preferably straight subsidies, not corrupting tax concessions.

'We have, de facto, a nationalised film industry,' he said. 'But apart from America and India, every film industry in the world requires heavy government subsidies. The difference in film-making is that the subsidy is more democratically applied. The money that subsidises a seat at the opera, ballet or theatre in Australia is quite staggering. For a much more modest investment, film reaches an infinitely greater number of people here and overseas.'

Adams told me, 'Paul Keating was the last prime minister to promote the arts, not because he was arts minister but because of his personal interest. Australian films have always been a creature of government because of our small market — basically, they need the help. They didn't regain prominence after the seventies because there was no great pressure from either the government, the industry or the community for it to happen. In fact, while the worst things overseas film-makers say about each other's products is that they are "interesting", Australian film-makers have a mean-spirited mentality and like to knock each other's work.'

The main problems Australian films face are Australians' preference for American films, lack of finance, and scant access to film screens: Hoyts, Greater Union and Village Roadshow operate about 90 per cent of Australian screens and keep 70 per cent of total takings, the remaining 30 per cent being shared by film-makers and distributors. Australian films not backed by Hollywood studios are screened in only about 10 per cent of Australian cinemas. The only way Adams got distribution of *Barry McKenzie* and *Don's Party* after the cinema chains had knocked them back was by hiring town halls or even buying independent cinemas with federal money, when Gough Whitlam was prime minister.

Adams devoted twenty years to Australian films and these days is disgruntled that most Australians still prefer American films and do not demand good Australian ones but often denigrate the oily-rag ones they see.

'Jesus,' he told me, 'ninety-nine per cent of American films are appalling.'

'Australians don't buy Arthur Boyd paintings of American landscapes but never hesitate to patronise Hollywood films — often acted in or photographed by Australians and made in Australia.' He said Australian film-making peaked in the Whitlam era, after Barry Jones and he persuaded Gorton to press the right buttons. Adams used to tell federal governments that Australian films would increase tourism and trade, and they did. When the government found out that Australian exports of rutile to Venezuela had skyrocketed, it found the reason was that the importer had seen *Picnic at Hanging Rock*.

The last films Adams produced were *Lonely Hearts* and *We of the Never Never* in 1982 and *Abra Cadabra* in 1983. He acted as a radio announcer in *Dallas Doll* (1994) and as the voice of God in *Road to Nhill* in 1997. But after that he walked away; he had done his dash.

Chapter Five: **The Phillip Adams Enigma**

Phillip Adams is perhaps the most remarkable person in Australia — a man remarkable for his brain and for his achievements, a chaotic man who masks his robust, well-deserved egotism behind a humble front and his massive knowledge behind earthy Australian lingo. He denies he has an ego, even though everyone has, but he doesn't want to admit it.

Adams only very rarely introduces himself on his *Late Night Live* program five nights a week on ABC Radio National and the reason is probably because he expects everyone to know. Once in 2008, he said on-air that the ABC had asked him to say his name on-air so he would do so, twice a year. He said it then, 'This is Phillip Adams,' but it was the last time he did so that year. There seems to be quite a struggle between the ABC and Adams. Early in 2009, the ABC inserted an introduction to *Late Night Live* in which an announcer says, 'This is *Late Night Live* with Phillip Adams — ideas and opinions from around the world.' A few evenings later, 'with Phillip Adams' disappeared, I suspect at Adams' instigation, although he won't talk about it. At the start of almost every program since then, Adams has had cracks at the anonymous announcer and nicknamed him 'Horace' until in January 2011 Adams said on-air that Horace had left the building in disgrace after a scandal and been replaced by his twin sister 'Doris'.

The psychologist and social researcher Hugh Mackay told me at his home in Exeter, in the New South Wales Southern Highlands, that Adams is playing a quirky game by not announcing himself. Obviously most *Late Night Live* listeners know who the presenter is and Adams would be intrigued if the few listeners who didn't know wanted to know. Adams told me he doesn't know why he doesn't say who he is; he just doesn't want to and he would hate to sound like the ex-2UE (and current 2SM) announcer John Laws, who had 'massed choirs singing his name — quite grotesque'.

I tackled Adams over the fact that many of his friends say that, in spite of his humble façade, he has a robust ego, even though justified. He was so upset about it that he sent me an email: 'Ego? Total twaddle. Just the opposite. I find it embarrassing to say on air, "I'm Phillip Adams" ten times an hour, so I don't say it at all. For much the same reason, I find it excruciating to listen to myself. I've hardly listened to a *Late Night Live* rebroadcast in twenty years. Three cheers for radio allowing a degree of anonymity, which I far prefer.' But I'm sure Adams would not react kindly if the ABC disguised his voice so much that people really didn't know who was talking.

Adams is self-deprecating and sounds humble; he has a big ego but doesn't sound egotistical. There is a paradox in his engaging sense of seeming not to take himself seriously and a whimsical edge to what he says, whether he's taking the piss out of himself or out of others. What has made him an outstandingly successful adman, broadcaster and columnist is that he enigmatically both simplifies and exaggerates. Hugh Mackay said, 'That's one of his tools. He exaggerates a person's significance when interviewing them and the person realises the joke. But while exaggerating, he also simplifies. You see the person or the point more starkly. He's bright and funny, capabilities that give him the ability (and also, to his mind, the licence) to exaggerate.'

Phillip Adams is also an enigma in the way that he knows he is far more intelligent than average but constantly plays humble on-air, although — another enigma — not in print. His brain wows academics but he talks at everyone's level, and in far more Aussie tones and using far more Aussie expressions than most Radio National presenters. When in 2008 he talked about the world financial crisis, he said his listeners are 'much smarter than I am'. And in fact he does not know, or claim to know, much at all about finance and economics and rarely has studio guests to talk about them, although he has more such guests now than before the crisis. He also liked to point out in one *Late Night Live* broadcast in 2010 that, in twenty years, he has had only two programs on sport.

Matt Noffs, whose grandfather, the Reverend Ted Noffs, founded the Wayside Chapel in Sydney, told me when I met him at a Bondi Beach café, 'It's bizarre. Everyone loves his personality and his character, his deep velvet voice that comforts them. It's a voice of reason and incredible intelligence. His brain wows academics but he talks at everyone's level. Phillip is inclusive, which stands out especially in Sydney, where people shut others out of their lives. I've got many Sydney friends who believe that if you exclude people, it's cool. Phillip brings people in, like a favourite uncle. Listeners wonder, "What's he going to say now?"'

Adams is still amazed by what he has done in his life, while at the same time continuing to pedal hard in case he falls off the media landscape. Peter Best, the music composer of several films that Adams produced in the 1970s and '80s, thinks Adams still has the feeling of, 'Pinch me, I'm dreaming'. Many times, Adams has said to him, 'Isn't it amazing what the two of us have done, Pete?' Peter Best has known Adams longer than almost anyone I spoke to about him.

But no-one I spoke to has known him as long as Bruce Petty, who at 81 in 2010 is ten years older than Adams and used to eat sandwiches with him at lunchtime in the Melbourne Botanic Gardens when they worked for rival advertising agencies in the late 1950s and '60s. Bruce Petty is an eminent cartoonist with a bleak, cynical sense of humour; he is still drawing doodle-bomb cartoons for *The Age*. He told me at his home in Rozelle, Sydney, 'I listen to *Late Night Live* regularly and Phillip is amazed himself how well he's got on.' Another enigma: 'Even though he despises the commercial world, he gets on well with the people in it.' Yet another: 'A part of him is shy and reclusive but he has no trouble connecting with people of large intellect.'

A few years after eating sandwiches with Bruce Petty, Adams took off to fame and fortune in the ad world after Brian Monahan and Lyle Dayman hired him as a copywriter. Brian Monahan told me at his home in South Yarra, 'I used to spend my weekends playing golf, Lyle Dayman used to sail his yacht and Phillip would work at his desk.' Monahan used to ask Adams how he, as a socialist, could drive around in a red Ferrari and Adams would reply, 'Everyone should have one.' The Ferrari was the first of a battalion of expensive classy cars that left-winger Adams bought while he generated accounts and money for Monahan Dayman Adams.

Even after Brian Monahan has known Adams for more than forty years, he still seems mystified by him. In fact, many people feel intimate with Phillip Adams but no-one really knows him. In friendships, he skips like a stone over the water and Adams admits he does not have great talent for friendship. I'm sure it's mainly because many of his friends are overawed by his brilliant mind. Significantly, his two best friends, Paul Keating and Barry Jones, also have brilliant minds. Phillip Adams likes to be the life of the party but doesn't go to parties, and enjoys telling that to others. He's charming to everyone, but as soon as he wants to end a conversation, he does so abruptly, and like his friends, I have many times been on the receiving end of that abruptness. He does not start his emails with, 'Dear ...' One of his oldest friends — they have agreed to speak at each other's funerals — is the eccentric left-wing writer Bob Ellis, who told me he feels unworthy to interrupt whatever Adams is doing, and Adams ends their conversations whenever he wants to. Ellis gives advice to politicians whether they want it or not. But I wanted his advice and knowledge about Adams. He told me, 'Phillip on *Late Night Live* takes you to a high perspective of the world. It's a sort of mateyness or comradeship where you go on a journey of the mind together, not too far from the sermons his hated father preached. It's no accident that some great communicators like Enoch Powell, David Frost and Francis James had parsons as fathers. You sit there as a little boy and watch your father with a hundred people behind you, and you pick up a few tricks.'

Phillip Adams is also good at taking credit for past achievements. He takes credit for great shifts in civilisation and repeatedly tells his listeners and readers that he warned them about global warming more than twenty years ago. Like many other people who fear the effects, I wish that not only Adams' listeners and readers but also politicians, who are supposed to lead us, had acted on his advice twenty years ago.

Adams is always a bit premature. Like Peter Ustinov, he looked fifty when he was twenty-two and stayed that way, except that he lost more hair. He is impatient to a fault and his attention span is about forty-one seconds, after which he looks over his shoulder at someone else in the room, or at the door, so he can escape. He very rarely drinks liquor, and I suspect the reason is that he never wants to lose control over his mind. Another mystery is how he manages to do all he does, at his age, on a minimum of sleep. He's an insomniac. Bob Ellis said, 'Phillip has never learnt to sleep, and it's a great affliction. Wayne Swan, Kevin Rudd and Mike Rann have also never learnt to sleep. It gives you more time to do things but also makes you more paranoid, more jumpy and more indecisive.'

Another enigma: Adams is humble but strident in his opinions, a charming person who doesn't try to be social. He is best either one-on-one or addressing a large crowd, not a large social group. In his advertising life, he had to be gregarious but writing is a solo job. Peter Faiman, a film and television director, who has known him since the 1960s, told me, 'Phillip is a loner and enjoys being one. Both of us like one-on-one chats or small groups. Phillip is as much a listener as a talker and that's been an essential part of our friendship. He has tremendous mental capacity and an extraordinary memory but he doesn't use his magnificent brain against you.' But sometimes Phillip Adams is a smart arse, and a few times I saw evidence of it in our regular conversations over three years when, in spite of what Peter Faiman said, Adams wanted me to realise he has a superior brain. I never doubted it.

In spite of getting to know him quite well, I didn't once feel I could take the mickey out of him or crack a joke at his expense. He doesn't react well to criticism or jokes about himself, which I believe is a large reason why he has refused many other biographers' requests for co-operation — he fears what they might write. Maybe he thought I was too nice or straight a person to write uncomplimentary things about him. I have just tried to paint an honest picture.

Gerard Henderson, executive director of the Sydney Institute and a weekly columnist in *The Sydney Morning Herald*, told me at the institute's heritage terrace in Sydney, 'With Phillip, everything is laughable except Phillip Adams. He jokes about everyone, but the minute you make a joke about him, he gets upset. He gets upset at me mainly because I laugh at him the way he laughs at everyone else, which you're not supposed to do. I get criticism all the time and I don't know what I'd do without it. Many journalists are thin-skinned, especially Phillip, and I think he is insecure. Many journalists also have large egos and Phillip is no exception. If you read or listen to him, he's always talking about himself and how well he's succeeded in spite of his hard childhood. There's always this self-regard. He is like a priest in a pulpit. When I used to go to Catholic Church as a youngster, the priest would get up in the pulpit and state the faith and the congregation would say, "Amen". That's what Phillip does.' Gerard Henderson also had many complimentary things to say about Adams and stressed that he was commenting on this aspect of Phillip only because I asked him to.

Some of Adams' listeners and readers would give him full credit for staying left-wing while the Labor Party has moved to the centre; others would say he is clinging to old views of the world that have become redundant. The collapse of communism in many countries and the failure of socialism in others was a retreat from significant policies campaigned for by the left since the 1850s. The left finds it easy to define what it is against but much of its policy is still platitudes because no-one seriously believes socialism, as distinct from social welfare, will return. Many Americans think social welfare is socialism. They are entirely different concepts.

Mark Aarons, journalist and author and son of the late Laurie Aarons, the most notorious communist in Australia's history, is a true believer in the Labor Party but is one of the few who would admit that the left does not have a vision of what it could be in the future and that Adams is a victim of that as much as anyone.

Mark was a Communist Party member from 1969 to 1978 and in 2010 published *The Family File* (Black Inc) about his family, particularly his father, who, Mark said, was the most spied upon person in Australia's history. Page by page, Mark read 20,000 pages of records that

ASIO (Australian Security Intelligence Organisation) had collected about Laurie, who died in 2005. Mark obtained the pages from ASIO by fax, with only the sources obliterated. I well remember my own mother, a Sydney North Shore Liberal, cursing Laurie Aarons as an evil person when I was a schoolboy in the 1940s. An ASIO executive, who was in charge of a 30-year investigation into Laurie, wrote to Mark to say he wholeheartedly agreed with what Mark had written about injustice.

In contrast to Mark's comment that Adams clings to redundant views, former West Australian premier and Australian Labor Party president, Carmen Lawrence, told me on a visit to Sydney that Adams is in front of some sections of the party: 'His left-wing views are ones that can be implemented and that is an important thing about his contribution — it is realistic as well as idealistic. At the same time as I was campaigning for a more humanitarian approach to asylum-seekers, Phillip was raising the issue in his columns. The Labor machine has moved right but Phillip has stayed left. He doesn't make you think he is better or smarter than he is, but on the other hand he likes to hold the floor,' said Carmen. 'You wouldn't be able to do a job like his without having an ego, but his self-depreciation is real.'

I believe Adams' self-depreciation is his way of creating warmth between himself and his guests and listeners. He once told me, 'I'm amazed by how little I've done,' but this is really the humble front he shows to people. He is actually surprised by how much he has achieved — more than most of the pillars of society, business or government. Some of his weeks, even in recent years, are much busier than almost any other seventy-plus person could handle.

For people who believe in the stars, even Adams' star sign is enigmatic: Cancer. The Universal Psychic Guild says most Cancers are bundles of contradictions. They are compassionate and caring with family and friends but can cut to the bone with ever-changing moods. They are eccentric on the one hand but insecure about how others see them. Phillip Adams has these characteristics.

Chapter Six: **The Good Guy and the Flip Side**

Even Adams' critics regard him as a good guy, but some of both his supporters and critics say his personality has a flip side. For example, he is a champion name-dropper. Another Philip, Philip Ruddock, who argued with Adams on-air and in print several times when Ruddock was immigration minister and attorney-general in the Howard Liberal government, told me at his electorate office in Berowra, on the northern outskirts of Sydney, 'Adams and I have always had a civil relationship. He's always treated me well when he's interviewed me. You couldn't fault his behaviour and his approach is professional and appropriate. He lets me say what I want to say, whereas some other radio people, such as Alan Jones, push their own views and talk over you.'

Based on the thousands of listeners' and readers' letters and emails to Adams that I read at the National Library in Canberra, almost as many people dislike his views as like them, but no-one I spoke to, or whose letters I read, said he is bad tempered, although two said he sometimes becomes nasty when crossed — and I experienced that Adams' emotion myself. He has a genuine concern for people and wants to contribute to a better world. The only problem for several of his friends is that he is impatient and abrupt. He has no time for pleasantries or chitchat — to his mind, it's a waste of time.

He is a kind person and a softie. During one of the hour-long meetings we had at his office in Paddington, Sydney, he fixed me with his sapphire blue eyes and described an incident when he was at East Kew primary school in Melbourne. A local preacher used to come to the school every week and drone on about the bible. Phillip didn't believe a word of it. He told me, 'At the end of the year, the preacher said he wouldn't be back the following year. It was obviously a health issue — he looked dreadful. He told the class it would comfort him if any boys could stand up and say they accepted God as their personal saviour as a result of his teaching. The whole class froze. I knew my father conducted similar lessons in schools and I stood up out of sheer sympathy for the preacher.' Even as a schoolboy, Adams could not only sum up the situation but had a huge feeling for others.

But he has a dark side, and one example of it is his tendency to overplay it. He is funny, engaging and effective, but overstating things is a flaw. Hugh Mackay told me he wonders whether Adams slightly exaggerates his own importance. 'I don't detract from his importance,' said Mackay. 'He has been a towering figure in Australian cultural life. But sometimes he overstates his contribution. And in spite of his openness, he is very prejudiced, politically, religiously and culturally.' These are very human characteristics. Mackay once said, 'I can't imagine anything more tedious than a perfect person, especially if it was someone who also demanded perfection from me.'

Hugh Mackay has had personal experience of Adams the good guy. When Mackay divorced, Adams was concerned and kept in touch with him more closely than before. Adams' concern for people, both broadly and personally, is not always recognised by people who don't know him. People think he's clever, influential and knows many people in high places but it's not widely understood that he has a great warmth for people.

The best way to make the world better and nicer, unless you are the US President, the Pope, Oprah Winfrey or Rupert Murdoch, is to do whatever you can, or use whatever pulpit you have, to persuade people — not to become good, because that would be pretty futile — that there are things they can do to make the world a bit nicer, and to do them.

Peter Best, the music composer, told me, 'Under John Howard, Australia became a much meaner place. It is possible for politicians — and Paul Keating did it — to bring out the nicer side of the national psych. Phillip has been plugging away at that for as long as I have known him (about forty years) but a really cruel trick he's played on me a number of times — and I'm sure he's played it on others — was when he was a partner in the ad agency Monahan Dayman Adams. He'd get me to come and meet a really big client the agency depended on for survival. He would say, "Everybody, this is Peter Best. He's a genius." And I wouldn't dare say anything for the whole meeting.'

Adams' home compound at Hawthorn in Melbourne was amazing in those years — he kept buying houses next door to accommodate artifacts he had bought around the world. He had a huge lake and one time when he was ill, Peter Best and his wife Cherry bought him a remote-controlled boat so he could sit by the lake and frighten the ducks with it. Best told me, 'What happened to Phillip as a child was awful and the scars made him bitter in many ways. He didn't like my own father and thought he was jealous of me. Phillip told me, "Just get rid of him, Pete. Tell him to piss off. That's what I did." I replied, "I actually like my dad," and Phillip said, "Well, if you like him, that's okay." He's never forgiven people who were bad to him when he was a kid. It has affected many of the ways he feels and things he does. His childhood comes back to him often. You always wish you could rewind the video of life.'

The weaknesses Adams admitted to me were: 'A short attention span, never producing a great master work, being like a little Chinese juggler twirling bamboo sticks to keep all his plates in the air at once, a weakness for a cup of tea, and not being gregarious, which is a great problem for my family because I have no small talk and spend a lot of time alone and prefer it that way.' He also acknowledges the criticism that he sometimes tap-dances with issues instead of dropping depth charges. 'The truth is that, because I was never properly educated, I was never taught discipline.'

Adams doesn't look after himself; he never exercises and is overweight. He eats hardly anything when he is in Sydney although Adams' partner Patrice Newell is a good cook and they grow most of the food they eat at their farm: beef, lamb, honey, olives and vegetables of all sorts.

Several of his friends and I have told him that to keep his mind active, which he certainly does, is great, but he should also keep his body active. He hasn't taken any notice and that will count against his health in the long run.

Adams is passionate about people although a self-proclaimed anti-social but enjoys the attention he gets when, for example, he chairs ideas festivals. He naturally revels in the spotlight when something he says or does makes headlines. When in August 2010 he got Kevin Rudd to give him his first major interview after the Labor Party backroom assassinated him and appointed Julia Gillard as Prime Minister, the interview received massive coverage in newspapers and on television and radio.

For a public intellectual who has made a long and well-publicised contribution to Australian media and politics, Adams acts, when he achieves a significant impact, like a cadet journalist getting his first story in print. He emailed me after the interview, 'KR (Kevin Rudd) reckons I've saved the election — and his career. Mark Scott (ABC managing director) is thrilled. RN (Radio National) is enraptured by the public and media response.' Adams usually overstates reactions to what he says and does. Unfortunately for the Labor Party, the interview did not save Labor in the election, which resulted in a hung parliament and Labor staying in government only with help from independents.

Gerard Henderson, executive director of the Sydney Institute and one of Adams' arch rivals, told me all media commentators receive letters; other people might get hundreds a year but Adams says he gets ten thousand, 'which seems a bit high. I don't know if anyone cares how many letters he gets but it's pretty self-indulgent to talk about the number. However, Phillip definitely has a fan club and they all love him. If I knew how to get a fan club, I'd get one myself.' It's probably a question of Gerard and Adams' personalities — Gerard's fans probably like him; Adams' fans love him, particularly the women.

Paul Keating has said there are lovers and haters. Phillip Adams is a lover. People like him because he invites them into his heart and mind. Matt Noffs told me, 'The rudest thing about him is his abrupt phone calls and emails. If I phone him, he answers, "Yup?" and if he has finished wanting to talk to you, he just cuts in and hangs up. I've started to act the same way — people tell me I now don't say goodbye on the phone. It's amazing how much time it saves!

'I'm sure Phillip is an arsehole at times. Another dark side of him is that he likes to drive expensive cars. And sometimes he promises to do things for people and doesn't get around to them.' Aged 31 in 2010, Matt Noffs is only half the age of most of Adams' friends, which makes his perspective of Adams particularly interesting. He told me some of his Adams experiences: 'He showed me how to choose my battles wisely. For example, I wanted to get stuck into the Reverend Fred Nile (a bible-bashing New South Wales politician) because I thought he was an ignorant bastard. But Phillip said everyone would make up their own minds about Nile no matter what I said and I would only exhaust my energy. He was right.

'I told Phillip I was terrible at writing but *The Village Voice*, a local newspaper in Maroubra, Sydney, wanted me to write a regular column. Phillip said reading and writing go together like a horse and carriage and told me to read a lot, so I did — even a dictionary — and I felt my mind was opening up. It made me feel better when I found out that Phillip's spelling is as bad as mine.'

Matt Noffs was named in *The Weekend Australian Magazine* in 2009 as one of the next hundred leaders in Australia and also by *The Sydney Morning Herald's (Sydney) Magazine* as one of the top hundred most influential people in Sydney. With no political experience, he decided to take part in the 2007 federal election. The Labor Party asked him to be in its campaign and Malcolm Turnbull, the Liberal MP, took him for a walk at Bondi early in 2007 and outlined what he would like Noffs to do. Turnbull told him the Liberals would lose the election but he would take over the leadership, both accurate predictions. After the Liberals got back into power, Noffs could 'take over youth affairs'. It sounded wonderful and some of his friends told him he could be a Trojan horse in the Liberal Party and change it. He phoned Adams and told him what had happened and Adams said, 'Be here tomorrow at 10.30am.' He got there and Adams advised him very strongly not to join the Liberals: 'They're not a political party; they're a state of mind. Don't join either party. Your grandfather (Ted Noffs) was influential because no-one could pigeonhole him. He was a multi-partisan, so he could put pressure on anyone and any party. Look what I do. I might be a Labor Party member (he was then) but I'm never beholden to any party or anyone.'

Another example of how Adams and Matt Noffs have worked together was early in 2009 when Noffs set up the Street University at Liverpool in Sydney as a division of the Wayside Chapel to give disadvantaged young people with nowhere to go a place where they can explore ideas outside a tertiary institution. He asked businesses in south-west Sydney, which has huge drug and alcohol problems, for help to buy a warehouse for $1.5million. He told me, 'I thought I was kidding myself. I went to the federal government and it gave me a small sum. Phillip said he would write a column about it and in the end he wrote three and raised $100,000 from his readers.' Now at the Street University young people attend free lectures from experts on subjects such as sociology ('Shit You Can Wrap About'), identity, maths, literacy, basic science, making speeches, writing CVs, art and graphic design, and business.

Adams is a sincere person, skilled and devoted to trying to improve people's lives. He hates injustice and hates authority being used for its own sake and many *Late Night Live* programs expose injustice. For example, the programs for the week from August 2 to 6, 2010 included interviews with: a Cambodian woman whose parents were murdered by the Khmer Rouge; two people who described Indian corruption and shoddy building work in preparing New Delhi for the 2010 Commonwealth Games; ex-Prime Minister Kevin Rudd about how he was sacked; an African American who spent forty-four years in Louisiana state prisons; and three South Africans about the first democratic elections there in 1994.

In spite of the seriousness of *Late Night Live*, Adams enjoys the program and uses his sense of humour to lighten it. His character is passionately engaged. His aim is to discover ideas, to analyse them and to discuss events, trends and issues. Mark Aarons, the left-wing writer, told me, 'Phillip is an engaged, even chaotic person, which I love about him. He appeals to a section of society that is engaged with ideas and wants to be challenged by information. He has a passion to explore ideas and to talk with people doing things beyond the headlines. Not that he is uninterested in current affairs, but he is particularly interested in the trends and what the future holds. When I was working on the original ABC Radio *Lateline* program in the 1970s, Phillip was playing an important part in developing the Australian film industry and he would appear on *Lateline* to talk about films and the need for cultural expansion.

'It was an exciting time, with the Whitlam government putting a lot of money and effort into culture. But I didn't meet Phillip until 1989, when he had moved to Sydney and interviewed me for his late-night 2UE program about my first book, *Sanctuary! Nazi Fugitives in Australia* (Heinemann). The session was a dialogue and occasionally a monologue from Phillip.'

Being humble is a broadcasting technique, but Phillip's love of people is completely genuine. Most people I interviewed about Adams mentioned this point directly or by example.

Barry Jones, the former international quiz champion, Hawke government minister and close friend of Adams, said, 'You can cure people of dengue fever or you can try to cure the swamps where the mosquitoes live — that's what Phillip tries to do. He wants to create an environment where people don't suffer. His primary role has not been to create policy but to encourage, goad or persuade people to take up particular issues.' Like Adams, Barry Jones has a brilliant mind but unlike Adams, he has no people skills. I waited for him outside his unattended Melbourne University office for an hour after our appointed meeting time and was about to give up when he arrived and apologised. I could tell he didn't like me, or my questions about Adams. Other people I have spoken to about Jones told me they have the same problems with him. Despite the reluctance that was seeping out of Jones like a vapour, I made the best out of meeting him because he is one of Adams' best friends.

He told me, 'I talk to Phillip by phone and we exchange emails several times a week but we see each other only a few times a year because I live in Melbourne and he lives in Sydney.' I asked Jones his opinions of *Late Night Live*. Only an intellectual like him could give this response to such a simple question: '*Late Night Live* is a combination of an emotional and intellectual response to people of a particular demographic. Phillip's contribution and its consistency week after week reinforce his listeners' value systems. It is also a combination of predictability and unpredictability — if Phillip talks about a well-known person, you can predict the broad line but you might not predict the specifics that have just occurred to him. It means a lot to listeners, many of whom will say, "I'm glad I heard that because it reinforced what I believed".'

Miranda Devine, the controversial News Ltd columnist, also said that Adams' views in his columns and radio programs are predictable. Overall she was not complimentary of him — she said he is a talented writer who is entitled to his own opinions but uses a lot of hyperbole and exaggeration, possibly because he is from a fiction-writing background in advertising and films. 'He's preposterous but it's fabulous to have a writer like him, with talent and passion. He's like an old-style bleeding heart. He has genuine concerns but these are not rooted in reality and are based on vague notions. He's probably another bleeding heart who never really rubs shoulders with the great unwashed. His column writing can easily become stale, and it's dangerous as he's teetering on the verge of exaggeration. My bullshit detector often goes off when I read what Phillip writes. But he is fresh and energetic in his ideas.'

Miranda Devine knew me from when I published *Mediaweek*. In *The Sydney Morning Herald* (where she used to work) on December 6, 2007, she wrote about Adams: 'Here we go again. Smug white folks have reactivated the "Sorry" debate, demanding that our new political leaders demonstrate their non-racist bona fides by apologising on behalf of the nation for the "Stolen Generation." Phillip Adams writes in *The Australian* of "weeping with" members of the stolen generation and scorns Paddy McGuinness and co, who seem to prefer the term saved generation. Adams should go out to Brewarrina in Western NSW, where five-month-old Mundine Orcher was systematically beaten to death over four weeks by "culturally appropriate" foster carers. Harrowing would be a visit to the gravesides of any number of Aboriginal children beaten to death by their "carers" under the so-called watchful eyes of welfare workers reluctant to intervene for fear of creating another stolen generation.'

There is enough of the old leftie in Adams to want to change systems and the environment, without considering — as many current politicians do continually — whether the changes will gain or lose votes. He is very driven and gets through a prodigious amount of work, and that is important to him. He is a genuine person with empathy for less fortunate people and his interest in people is also genuine. On air, he talks about a lot of dreadful things happening on Earth in a way that is kindly to his audience, and he addresses his audience in an endearing way. He doesn't put people down (except a few arch enemies like the rival columnist Gerard Henderson) but adds familiarity and friendliness to an otherwise very trying world. Bob Brown, the Australian Greens leader, told me when I met him at his federal parliamentary offices in Sydney, 'As a compere, Phillip magically lightens a meeting but doesn't distract from the discussions, so you want to keep listening instead of going home and locking yourself in a cupboard. That's a great ability. Phillip is one of the great popular philosophers and intellectuals of Australia. He leads all the others.'

Significant praise.

Another person who, like Bob Brown, is often interviewed by the news media is Philip Nietzsche, Australia's most prominent and controversial euthanasia campaigner. He told me, 'You never feel you are walking into a minefield with Phillip Adams. I have been interviewed by many people who don't like me, and others who try to get some response that will attract media attention, but I never feel Phillip might trap me. You feel you are talking to someone interested in what you say. That's rare among interviewers.

'Phillip is a shining light in a bleak landscape of informed comment on contemporary social issues and he fills a unique place in broadcasting. I can't think of anyone else I want to listen to. It is rare that I'm not interested in his *Late Night Live* topics. When I switch on television current affairs, I often find I've got better things to do. I almost never think that when listening to Phillip's program. What stand out particularly are the people the program gets, and the regulars. You generate respect for what they say. Phillip has a humble approach when interviewing people who are full of themselves.'

It's probably a strategy to get the best out of people; it works and it's clever. Adams doesn't stand in their light. He enjoys what he does and sounds as much on the ball as ever, in spite of speaking a little more slowly as he has grown older. He could never just sit around. What drives him is his fantastic brain.

It is Phillip Adams' brain that amazes Professor Allan Snyder, director of the Centre for the Mind at Sydney University. Adams is a board member and the centre aims to help people harness their full creative capacity by studying what makes the mind work best. Snyder was born in the United States but is now an Australian citizen, and with typical American enthusiasm he went over the top about Adams: 'He's an incredible, remarkable man; he has a panoramic, universal mind and can explain anything. He can put a magnifying glass on anything and make it come alive. He understands the emotions, drive and rationale behind everything in politics. And he's the quintessential psychologist — he understands people's motives and passions perfectly.' What Snyder particularly likes about Adams is that he is interested in everything. Snyder himself is interested in what makes a champion and he finds Adams good to talk to about that because he says Adams is a champion himself, one who applies his champion mindset to one field and then to another. Snyder asked me, 'What's Phillip going to do when he grows up?'

On an enthusiasm for Phillip Adams scale of one to ten, Allan Snyder would score ten, in contrast to the News Ltd columnist and one-time Melbourne *Herald Sun* editor Piers Akerman, who scored none by telling me, 'Phillip Adams is not current. He represents a number of left-wing people who have enough money to be able to spout extreme views that have little or no relation to ordinary Australians' concerns. What he says is fine in theory but lousy in practice. He is a theoretical socialist. His views are outmoded. He would be laughed out of any circle except the backwaters of a former Soviet satellite which had not been reached by news of socialism's collapse. He is amusing as a museum piece.' Piers Akerman's statement said more about him than about Adams.

What the English poet Alexander Pope wrote in 1711 could apply to Phillip Adams: 'Great wits may sometimes gloriously offend and rise to faults that true critics dare not mend'.

Chapter Seven:
The Angry Old Left-winger

Phillip Adams has certainly influenced the Australian Labor Party but when I asked fellow left-wingers how much he has influenced it, for how long and in what ways, I received a wide variety of answers. He saw that Kevin Rudd could beat John Howard with policies only a few degrees to the left of Howard's ('Howard Lite') and recommended Rudd to lead the federal Labor Party before many party members had even heard of him. Then when Rudd grew too keen on running Australia by himself and with a kitchen cabinet, his popularity both inside and outside the party crashed and he was knifed in the back and replaced by Julia Gillard. Adams became really upset and quit the party. He had never been to a party meeting anyway. It was typical of the way Adams broadly supports many Labor Party policies but sensibly remains a maverick by attacking the policies he dislikes, although he rarely supports Liberal Party policies and the few liberals he interviews on-air about politics are 'small l' liberals. After the federal election in August 2010, he said on *Late Night Live* that he had voted Green. It was a sign of how much he — like many other left-wingers — has become fed up with the party's power-brokers and policies, or the lack of them.

Bob Hawke, who was one of Australia's most successful prime ministers (1983-91) with a great deal of help from

Treasurer Paul Keating, told me at his Sydney office, 'Phillip Adams is often a pain in the arse. Occasionally he says something that's worthwhile. With all the important things to read today, who would turn to Phillip? I'm not saying that in a nasty way. There's so much to read. I don't think he has made a significant contribution to Labor Party thinking. I was never close to him. Labor Party policies are made by the conferences, caucuses and executives. It's rare that an individual makes an impact. I'm not aware of a Phillip Adams idea taken up by the Labor Party that was not put up as soon as or earlier by other people. He has to give opinions every week and he must run out of ideas and get sick of it. That's evident in much of his writing.' I disagree with everything Hawke said about Adams except that some of his recent columns rake over old ideas looking for embers and need more fire in them.

Hawke was courteous but, aged eighty-one in 2010, seemed despondent, and was not as interested in Phillip Adams as in the fact that, in 1960, I was a junior sub-editor on the now defunct Sydney *Sun* when his wife Blanche d'Alpuget's father Lou was a senior sub-editor on the same newspaper. Adams had told me Bob would not see me, as they don't like each other, but I persisted and Hawke welcomed me with considerable disinterest. He said, 'I'm not a great radio listener. I never listen to Phillip on-air and rarely read his column. He is a person given to falling out with others. He and I had a falling out. I don't remember what it was about. I don't know and I don't care. Some people think he's a pompous pain in the arse, others tend to like him and others are indifferent. He's a non-event as far as I am concerned.' The spark that Bob Hawke had in office has left him as he has grown old.

In sharp contrast, Bob Brown, the Australian Greens leader with one of the most recognised faces in Australia, was brimming with vitality and praise for Adams when I interviewed him. Whatever you think of Green policies, Brown is respected and is a straight-shooter. He said, 'Phillip's contribution to the left side of Australian politics has been enormous. His policies are now much more similar to the Australian Greens' than Labor policies. Phillip has never courted the Greens but he's become a breath of fresh air in Australian political commentary, which has become materialistic — especially in the John Howard years — and supportive of the idea that everyone down on their luck is a bludger,' said Brown. Adams' listeners would include many Greens supporters.

Adams has a long history of wanting the Labor Party to once again become a great party of the left, especially in humanity and social justice. He is like a reformist priest wanting the Catholic Church to become a bastion of humanity. He still hopes something will turn up to make it again a party of 'the light on the hill' whereas in fact there is no hope for this, because Labor has moved too far to the right to take much notice of Adams, although some party members do. Bob Brown said Labor's movers and shakers are now Sydney and Melbourne boardrooms — 'we have a plutocracy of government by the rich.' Adams' flagrant atheism had been a great contribution to encouraging others to think for themselves. He had also been a maverick by bravely speaking out about the contradictions of religious dogma and this had been a remarkable contribution to Australian intellectual life over the past fifty years, when there had been very little of it.

The way that Adams loudly quit the Labor Party in June 2010, when Kevin Rudd was deposed, was an example of Adams as a left-wing political maverick. The image suits him. He was one of a number of people Rudd would phone for their opinions after he became Labor's federal leader but before becoming prime minister, so he played an important role as a sounding board for ideas that got Labor into power in 2007. In early 2009, Adams claimed to me that Kevin had phoned him eight times in vain over a period of a few weeks to ask him to quit writing his *Weekend Australian Magazine* column in protest at the way *The Australian* was running a vendetta against him. Each of the eight times, Rudd had not got through to him. I wonder about the eight times.

Adams' influence on the Labor Party has mostly been on individuals. His primary political role has not been to create policy but to encourage, goad or persuade people to take up particular issues. When he lived in Victoria, his influence was mostly on how to sell a policy because of his marketing skill. John Cain, the Victorian premier from 1982 to 1990, had direct experience of Adams' work for Victorian Labor and was keen to talk about it when I spoke to him at his office in the Old Treasury Building in Melbourne. He said, 'Phillip made a significant contribution to Victorian Labor politics in the 1960s, when Labor was down and out in every sense after the 1955 split' (which led to the rival Democratic Labor Party being formed). 'Phillip kept Victorian Labor going in those years. The party became an arrogant rump with no policies. Phillip went to Clive Stoneham (state Labor leader) and wrote two policy speeches, in 1961 and '62, as the source of ideas and traditional Labor policies and values.' (But the Liberals under Henry Bolte remained in power.)

Adams in those years was a keener Labor Party supporter than he is now that the party has moved right, following the voters. He was also impressed and even seduced by the trappings of the advertising world, where he first became such a success and also where he made a pile of money. It was his brilliant ideas and selling ability that made him an advertising wizard and he applied the same abilities to Victorian Labor Party policies and campaigns. When Labor won government in Victoria in 1982 as the state's first Labor government for 27 years, Adams gave it plenty of good advice because it was implementing a full agenda in difficult times. He helped write Labor's policy speech for 1985; Labor won again and John Cain was re-elected premier.

In those days in Victoria, when Adams and Barry Jones were very influential in getting John Gorton, who was Liberal prime minister from 1968 to '71, to recognise the importance of the arts, most Liberal governments paid little attention to the arts. Bob Menzies, the founder and still the father figure of the Liberal Party, did not want to interfere in the arts when he was prime minister from 1949 to '66. Adams, Gorton, South Australian Premier Don Dunstan and Gough Whitlam (prime minister from 1972 to '75) created an atmosphere where government had a role to play. John Cain told me, 'This was the time when political parties started to use focus groups and Phillip was good at interpreting the results. Even after he moved to Sydney in the late

1980s, he was influential in talking to opinion-makers.' Cain is still active in politics as an associate professor in Melbourne University's Political Science Department. He criticised current Australian politics: 'The parties are now less responsive to ideas and don't do the policy work they should. They depend on donations from lobby groups and others who want to win favours. Australian politics is going American-style. Phillip was right to recommend Kevin Rudd as Labor leader. Beating John Howard was a great achievement. Howard ran the most evil government Australia has ever had. It lost all sense of decency and proportion. Phillip said in *The Australian* that Rudd had the best chance to beat Howard. But I'm not sure that what Phillip — or any writer — says in a newspaper is influential. Phillip's main appeal is the breadth of issues he covers, his forthrightness and his worldwide contacts, many of whom we would otherwise not hear from.'

Even Gerard Henderson, The Sydney Institute's executive director and a person who Adams seems to dislike more than anyone except John Howard, admits that *Late Night Live* has a lot of talent and is a good program and that Adams is an able broadcaster who he listens to regularly, although not every night. At least he listens, which is more than most of Adams' critics do, whether they lean to the right like Gerald does or nowhere at all. But Gerard said Adams' columns are always predictable — you can tell what will be in them in the first paragraph. 'He is a successful columnist but his columns are essentially his opinions, whereas I put many facts and quotes in my columns. Phillip's positions are predictable as standard fashionable leftism, although he is a very successful product and he's done well. I don't feel resentful about him at all. He will be on Radio National until he wants to leave, and he's had a good run, four nights a week for twenty years. Radio National should share the spot around a bit, keeping Phillip but giving others a go, too.'

I can imagine Adams' reaction to that suggestion would be vitriolic and Adams does not have the same ambivalence to Henderson as Henderson has to him. They snap at each other in print and Adams' snaps seem more heartfelt than Henderson's. He said in his *Weekend Australian Magazine* column on February 24, 2007, 'My favourite adversary remains Gerard Henderson, hereafter poor Gerard. Or PG. I've known PG for decades, and approved of his early columns attacking "the lunar right". We fell out when I chaired an event at the Adelaide Festival of Ideas and introduced him somewhat lightheartedly. But Gerard is bereft of humour. His conservative colleagues don't take themselves so seriously. Constantly trying to outdo each other in the preposterousness of their public utterances, they become self-parodic when attacking such favourites as Robert Manne, David Marr, the ABC or me. It's all good fun, involving panto performances. Only PG seems to believe what he says in columns, on the ABC and in that strange magazine from his mysteriously-funded Sydney Institute.' The column droned on for a whole page and Adams' loyal readers would probably have preferred one of Adams' beautifully-worded stories about the animals on his farm. Adams and Henderson sometimes exchange terse emails. On June 5, 2009, Adams emailed Henderson, 'Gerard, would it be possible for you to stop, just for a moment or two, being such a humourless bore? Silly question. The average house brick is more amusing, the most pigeon-shit-splattered bronze statue of some long-forgotten 19th Century personage propped up in a public park less pompous than the Gerard who spends so much time and effort trying to keep himself on his pedestal. Big hug — Phillip.'

Adams tends to dismiss Henderson but certainly not the reverse. He told me Adams is a very polished presenter, that he chairs many conferences, that it's fun for him to have a go at Adams from time to time, he is not calling for his execution and he's glad he's around. He takes Adams very seriously indeed. Seriously enough to have observed him closely.

If Gerard Henderson is not a true believer in Phillip Adams, Carmen Lawrence certainly is. On a trip to Sydney from her home state of Western Australia, where from 1990 to '93 she was the first female premier in Australia, she told me, 'Phillip is always asking questions. He's driven by intellectual curiosity and wants to find how the world ticks and others' views of it.' I asked her whether she, like many intelligent women, finds Adams attractive. With caution that comes from a lifetime in politics, she replied, 'I find him an attractive person because what he does, he does well, engagingly and warmly. He allows others to speak freely, to tell their stories. He gets good people on his program, not just current celebrities. His producers dig out some of the best minds around the world.'

'Charming' is too weak a word for Phillip Adams, Carmen said. 'People often talk about his intellect and say he is a vigorous, thoughtful person and a provocative public intellectual. His brain attracts both men and woman but he uses it in a way that is not condescending. You wouldn't be able to do a job like his without having an ego, but his self-depreciation is real.' On this point, I disagree with Carmen. Adams uses self-depreciation to hide his justifiable egotism. Carmen Lawrence said, 'He is a "people person" who has always tried to influence policy by discussion, not by making recommendations to committees. And the good thing about *Late Night Live* is that it includes people of all stripes.'

A person of a very different stripe to either Carmen Lawrence or Adams is Alan Jones, who has the biggest radio audience in Australia as 2GB's breakfast presenter. I knew him from when I published *Mediaweek* and he told me at his studio he would not dump on Adams, then proceeded to do so. He even claimed Adams could not even call himself a broadcaster because his range of subjects is limited and he 'follows a very narrow path'. Adams had limited appeal and that would always be the case. It sounded an awful lot like 'dumping' to me. Alan's audience reaches about 486,000 New South Wales listeners a week; Adams' *Late Night Live* reaches 233,000 people a week in the five mainland state capitals and more than 350,000 when smaller cities and towns are included. In other words, not nearly as many people as Alan Jones.

Adams got stuck into Alan Jones' ethics in his book, *Talkback: Emperors of the Air* (Allen & Unwin): 'Jones makes no bones about being an opinion for hire. He is a salesman and entertainer, not a journalist, so he is not bound by the journalists' code of ethics. He has been likened to a secular priest.' (So has Adams.) 'His flock responds to his opinions, his interest in their concerns, his wholesome country childhood, his omniscient public image and his reassuring daily presence.'

Jones told me, 'Phillip didn't rate when we both broadcast on 2UE from 1988 to 1990 and he would never rate on commercial radio because its demands are not consistent with his talents — but that's not a criticism.' I doubt that Alan Jones would rate (or even get a job) on ABC Radio National. He continued, 'If I start talking about opera, I know that people will listen for only a few minutes and then switch off. Phillip takes a particular subject and then goes into some detail about it and there is a role for that, but not in general broadcasting. I don't listen to his program but I read many of his columns in *The Weekend Australian Magazine*. As a self-educated person, he's got a wonderful breadth of knowledge in his known areas and he has read widely, not necessarily on subjects that everyday Australians would identify with. His writing is more humorous than his radio work. He's got a lot to recommend him because there's an audience for his kind of stuff.'

But probably few people want to hear about Mahatma Gandhi having an erection at the age of sixty (and why shouldn't he?), which according to Adams himself in *The Sydney Morning Herald* on June 6, 1987, was what he talked about on his first morning on-air. Adams added, 'That tended to lose half the audience and three-quarters of the management.' John Brennan, the program director who, in sixty years in radio, discovered Alan Jones, and also John Laws and Stan Zemanek, gave me a good example of how Adams has a brilliant mind and has mixed with other brilliant minds but could not adapt to ordinary listeners' interests. Kerry Packer, who at the time owned 2UE, told the station to hire Adams as a presenter because he had heard him address a meeting. John Brennan, who was 2UE's program director at the time, asked Adams what was happening in his life and Adams told him the most important thing just then was the birth of a litter of beautiful Dalmatian puppies. Brennan continued the story: 'I said, "Terrific. Tomorrow, ask the listeners to name one of them." He said, "You're joking!" I said, "I know you think it's mundane but you will relate better to your listeners." When Adams asked his listeners to name one of the puppies, the switch melted. He was very surprised.

'He didn't stay long in breakfast because our average suburban listeners wanted presenters to speak out for them over their social and economic concerns and to explain complex issues. That's what commercial radio talkback is all about.' Brennan envied Adams' intellect and found him a genuine and understanding person with an encyclopaedic mind. He got to know Adams well enough to be invited to stay a weekend at his Elmswood farm. After Adams was switched from mornings to 8 p.m. (after Stan Zemanek), he took talkback calls on Monday, Tuesday and Wednesday nights and interviewed top people of all occupations on Thursdays and Fridays.

No-one has ever aroused Phillip Adams' anger as much as Stan Zemanek did. Stan used to name talk-back callers 'dickheads, numb nuts, half-wits, left-wing loonies and typical Labor voters' and in *Talkback,* Adams said Zemanek's style was like a wrestler's, his favourite callers were 'soft targets, the more drunk the better' and his show was a running joke. But in 1997, Zemanek's program topped Sydney evening audiences with 210,000 listeners — which says something about average listeners' intelligence. Adams was on the government-appointed committee that made Aboriginal singer Mandawuy Yunupingu Australian of the Year in 1992 and Zemanek told his audience the committee comprised 'arty-farty wankers'. Adams called Stan 'lecherous, an oaf and spectacularly incoherent'. But I couldn't call Stan to ask him for a rebuttal because he died of a brain tumor in 2007.

Adams' own evening audience rose to 52,000 and John Brennan said his talkback presentation improved. But he still found it hard to relate to ordinary listeners' interests. He was funny and outrageous, he said what he believed and didn't care whether you liked what he said or not. The listeners thought he was off the planet. His contract expired in 1990 and was not renewed. Luckily for him, Brian Johns, the ABC's managing director, phoned him and asked him to present *Late Night Live* — the luckiest phone call he ever received, because *LNL* suits him perfectly, he enjoys presenting it and in 2011 he will have done so for twenty years.

Brian Johns' call opened a new life for Adams, in which he could use his great interviewing skills not on commercial talkback callers concerned about the price of bread but on intelligent experts from around the world, in what has become Australia's literary magazine with an audience far greater than any intellectual publication. Part of his charm and skill is to make people he interviews think they are the most important people in the world, unless they are one of the people who have clashed with him in the past, like Bob Carr, who was New South Wales Labor premier from 1995 until 2005. Adams told me Carr would not talk to me about him. But as usual I persisted and Carr did talk to me about Adams, mostly but not entirely in praiseworthy terms.

He said that at times, and only at times, Adams' view of the world 'leads him into a smugness and predictability. I had to tell him that during the backlash against John Howard's approach to Wik (the High Court's decision on native title rights), he was broadcasting the same indigenous grievances and gripes night after night — there was no criticism of his own position or openness to fresh ways to deal with indigenous Australians' condition. That's one example, and it's a rare one, but on occasions like that you can — for a moment, and only for a moment — understand the right-wing reaction to left-liberal orthodoxy in Australia. Thank God and the ABC, Phillip is there and he is what he is, one of the jewels of ABC Radio National, a corner of the radio universe free of the cacophony of climate-change denials, rank racism, manufactured grievances and fake indignation that is the currency of commercial radio.'

At the same time as Adams got his break on Radio National in 1990, Jim Soorley, who was once a Catholic priest but is now a non-believer, won his first election as Lord Mayor of Brisbane, the biggest local government area in Australia, and became one of the few Australian politicians to raise their votes at three elections in a row. He was having dinner in Brisbane with Phillip Adams soon after Adams got involved in the Adelaide Festival of Ideas in the late 1990s. He is always a sucker for a good idea — he tells people to give him an idea and he can always find a million dollars to put it into practice. He told me, 'I asked Phillip to run a Brisbane Ideas

Festival every two years and the city council would fund it. Phillip said, "Done deal."'

Adams has been involved in the festival since the first one in 2000, not only chairing sessions but also coming to committee meetings. The state government now provides most of the funds but it was Adams' ideas and initiative that has made it happen. He has a deep-seated dislike of prejudice and ignorance and an appetite to know and understand issues; he is also an artist with creative energy and insight. You get a feeling when you listen to his program that here is a man who is gentle, searching for the inside of people he is interviewing. He has an incredible ability make them feel at ease.

Jim Soorley said, 'Phillip is driven by a search and a thirst for knowledge and by a sense of fairness and social justice, demanding that people throw away their prejudices' — a sentence that sums up the inner Phillip Adams better than any other spoken to me by his friends.

Who can tell what effect Phillip Adams' spoken and written words have had on Australian society? As the American historian Henry Brooks Adams wrote in his book *The Education of Henry Adams* in 1907, 'A teacher affects eternity; he can never tell where his influence stops.'

Chapter Eight:
Keating Pre-cooks Adams

Paul Keating's office is in an old, gloomy Georgian terrace in Potts Point on the borders of Kings Cross in Sydney; he and his secretary occupy the first floor. He is one of Adams' two best friends, the other one being Barry Jones. Adams had told me several times that Keating would not see me, but I persisted, and Keating's secretary sent me a letter saying when and where he would see me. He is one of the most complex, controversial politicians Australia has ever had. But his elitism upset ordinary Australians.

I was shown into his large, dark office and sat waiting for the man about whom so much has been written and spoken. I was almost startled when he slid silently into the room and shook my hand. I respectfully regard this accomplished man who left school at the same age as Phillip Adams: fifteen. A lot has happened since then. He served as a backbencher under Gough Whitlam; he was Bob Hawke's treasurer and then usurper as prime minister. He was the driving force behind the Hawke government's economic reforms and was invaluable as Hawke's treasurer because he was happy to be a maverick and to challenge accepted views. But he is probably best known as a witty and often venomous speaker who people either like or decidedly dislike. His arrogance was a large reason why the Labor Party lost in 1996 to the Liberals under John Howard, who is equally despised by Keating and Adams.

As we sat down in his office, he smiled softly and said, 'Phillip's been unwise to co-operate with you. I'm surprised myself that I agreed to see you. I normally send authors packing; you slipped through.' Keating was well aware of why I'd gone to talk to him and launched into a well-prepared monologue to prove it.

'Phillip has a compellingly progressive mind,' he said in the famous voice that once wielded words like a rapier during Question Time. Aged 66 in 2010, his voice is now more subdued. He continued about Adams, 'There is no element of reaction. The whole framework is one of enlargement, starting, of course, with the human spirit. Everything flows from that. No matter how the decades go on or what the issues are, Phillip always approaches an issue from the framework in his head. And the framework is progressive, so even as time progresses and changes, he progresses further. Even Phillip's prejudices — and we all have them — spring from that same approach.

'He is also a very attractive writer,' Keating continued in soft tones. 'He has a great facility with words and this is part of his power. Great writers are also great thinkers. No-one can write well if they don't also think well, because that would be immediately apparent in their writing. What happens with Phillip is that he has a great penchant for synonyms. He tries to paint in synonyms, finding similar things to contrast with, to tell a story. He has the ability to use vivid colours and thoughts in his writing. This comes, I think, from the fact that he has thought about most arguments beforehand. It means that his phrases and synonyms come pre-cooked. It's like turning out a high cuisine meal. A lot of the ingredients have been cooked over time and they are brought together with great facility.'

Paul Keating continued: 'Phillip's mind organises ideas and arguments and then intersperses them with colours. His mind can put charcoal on a canvas but also use pre-mixed colours and add them to the picture. This was why his columns read so clearly and visibly.

'Of course, many people would disagree with me. Conservatives disagree with Phillip vehemently but they would all give him — perhaps through gritted teeth — marks for consistency. The consistency is not rooted in prejudice; it's rather rooted in position. The position gets back to that progressing framework.'

Keating barely drew breath as he continued talking about Adams: 'He's had a substantial effect on the Australian community. The media tends to attract people from the right and not many people write from the moderate left. Throughout the barren Howard years, Phillip marked out a position every week. You can't do that by episodic flurries. You have to have a wider position. If you look through the barren years of the Howard orthodoxy, Phillip was perhaps the most obvious writer commenting from the centre and centre left. So his influence has been quite large. He has his ABC program and his Australian readership and he's been blessed with a very attractive, intimate voice. There is a relationship between him and his listeners. He also has the ability to stand back somewhat from the discussion yet the same ability to pull the threads out and follow — as any important interviewer does — the myriad of issues and to know a fair bit about them. He lets people talk. He doesn't dominate the conversation.'

I asked, 'Can you evaluate his influence on the Australian Labor Party?'

Keating answered, 'He gave the party a litmus background. It wouldn't take Labor people long to know if he believed they were on the wrong track. In countries like France and Britain there are colour standards and Phillip represents a standard — it's a standard in the colour way of the Labor Party, not the exact colour but the colour way, the general colour tone of the broad Labor Party. The Labor movement does not hang on Phillip's every word, but the political colour way he works in is broadly sympathetic to Labor. So although Labor people might not read what he writes every week, they would notice if he wrote things at odds with them and might ask themselves, "Is Phillip right? Is what he says worth considering?" So he is a litmus provider to the debate, particularly in the centre left.'

I knew, coming here, that I would be talking to one of the sharpest wits of the Australian landscape, a man capable of many interesting turns of phrase. I tried another question: 'How did Phillip stand in relationship to the party as it moved more to the centre?'

Keating replied, 'The party moved to the centre under me and also under Bob Hawke, but especially under me, well before Kevin Rudd, and Phillip was dubious of the rational agenda. He had to be intellectually charmed into the rationalist position. It's a measure of his mental dexterity that he understood how, for example, an open, competitive economy was better grafted to a traditional social wage and how an open, wealthier economy was better able to fulfill the obligations of that social wage. In other times, he might not have thought so and other, more rigid people of the left will never think so. He's burned them off because, simply, his mind is better.'

I asked, 'Did Phillip see how far-left policies would never appeal to Australians?'

'It's a matter of delivery. The first structurally important graft of elements of policy, which came to be known as the Third Way, started in Australia. I used to call it the Only Way. The First Way was trickle-down capitalism where private ownership is everything; the Second Way is state socialism, where there was no private ownership; but there had to be a better way. The Australian Labor Party in the 1980s and '90s broke the mould, and Phillip had the intellectual gymnastics to understand that. We had copycats. Tony Blair started talking about the Third Way, not knowing what it was; and the same with the Clinton Administration in the United States. But no-one did it as successfully as the Labor Government in Australia in the 1980s and '90s.

'Phillip barracked for it.' I am heartened to see that Keating still has the same brio that brought him to national prominence.

Did he support your policies?

'It's true he was pro my prime ministership but not at the start. As we went on a bit, I don't think Phillip expected me to legislate native title. Rather, like other people, they expected economic things from me, not the romantic end of the agenda. When he started to see bits of that, I think he realised there's something going on here.'

He's very keen on you now.

'We've got time now.'

Did he attack Howard too much?

'No. Howard was in many respects left alone. Not many people called the Howard template into question. Most journalists were in his favour, including, until the latter years, the Canberra Press Gallery.' Paul Keating and Phillip Adams cannot accept that many Australians are happy with mediocrity. John Howard knew it and it kept him in power for twelve years, although everything about Paul's prime ministership was directed at revolution and reinvention. Many weeks in *The Australian* from 2000 to 2007, Adams attacked Howard, who also aroused Keating to some of his most delicious quotes in Parliament, such as calling Howard 'a dead carcass swinging in the breeze ... a mangy maggot ... brain damaged ... a desiccated coconut ... araldited to his seat.'

How often do you listen to or read Phillip?

'I'm not a radio listener, not even *AM* or *PM* on the ABC. I find they interrupt my thought processes. I read Phillip's column in *The Weekend Australian Magazine*. Not every weekend does it bounce off the page, but it has a lot of bounces. The storyline, the colour of the words, the beauty of the words, the analogies and synonyms are there. He's an attractive writer, and also a sought-after speaker. I've never seen him disappoint an audience. It's never ordinary. The facility is there, the wordsmithing, the pre-cooked phrases, the pre-cooked thoughts, the compositional quality, and the showmanship it takes to put it across. He is also a charming person. "Charming" is not a word you throw around much, but you can with Phillip. He makes the person he's speaking to feel important. The subject he's got might not enthuse his imagination, but he makes a fist of it.'

How has Phillip's advertising and marketing experience helped the Labor Party?

'Some of the world's sharpest minds are in advertising – you've got to be smart to see the standouts, to pull the issues out and put them into a campaign. It never surprised me that he was a powerful force in advertising; also in films. He was very influential, when I was treasurer, in setting up the Australian Film Commission and in general support for the film industry. That's part of the Australian story. People who have a position, like him, influence you and ones who have thought-out positions tested over time are always valuable to speak to because they have a framework.

'Phillip's influence in the Labor Party has probably declined a little, but that happens to us all. You can't be a topical, fresh-faced person forever. The years wear you down and your complexion has a less rosy hue. You become more pasty. That's happened to him and to me. We see each other regularly and talk about local and world politics.'

Do any sections of the Labor movement criticise Phillip?

'Occasionally, if he offends someone. Most Labor people know he's a kindred spirit. He doesn't agree with everything Labor does or says and he has sympathies for the big mass party of the moderate left. But he's never toed the party line.'

Did he have any influence with Kevin Rudd as prime minister?

'I think he did. He has some contact with Kevin. I'm pretty certain Kevin would regard him as a sane character with a balanced view and would regard his counsel pretty well.'

What drives Phillip?

'A determination not to fall by the wayside, the compulsion to keep fresh and to keep his older mind current. And that means climbing over the issues and the facts and synthesising and distilling them as always. When you've been doing that for decades, it doesn't necessarily get harder but it's still laborious. Phillip suffers the labour for the benefit of remaining current.'

Why does he have so many listeners and readers, do you think?

'The two Fs: framework and facility. All facility and no framework, not worth listening to or reading. All framework and no facility, the same. You need both and he has both. He has the framework and he has the colour, the adjectives and synonyms, the story-telling, the precooked thoughts, the high cuisine. All good restaurants have the marinations going and the other ingredients going, and they bring them all into the grand presentation at the end. That's what Phillip does.'

An image of Phillip at a stove flashed into my mind. Given that I've never seen him make anything more complicated than a cup of tea, it was amusing.

How would you describe Phillip as a man?

'He's a softie to a fault. He should have said no to you and he didn't. He's a softie and, frankly, anyone with any brains is soft. What's the point of being hard? We're only here for a certain time. His neurons are running around at a great pace.'

Does he have any good or bad habits?

'He likes cars. His silhouette is a bit like the comic character The Little King.' Otto Soglow drew The Little King in 1931 in *The New Yorker* and from 1934 worldwide, until both Otto and the fat Little King died in 1975.

'Phillip's overweight,' Keating explains, in case I didn't understand the reference. 'But you can't exercise your way into immortality, and I think Phillip understands that. You can't exercise your way into not ageing. So he's not going to even try.'

What are his demons, then?

'You never quite know what people's demons are. I don't know what Phillip's are. I think if I had to say what his principle demon is, I'd say it's the threat of loneliness.'

I said, 'He likes being alone for some of each week.' I've both observed this and been told this by Adams himself.

'But he's not alone. He's got many friends. He's a person who would suffer greatly from loneliness.'

How do Patrice and Phillip seem as a couple?

'It's a partnership that has gone on for a very long time. And always well, in my observation.'

Phillip has had many successes. Has he had any failures?

'Phillip might like to have been elected to Federal Parliament, and he would have been good enough to have been. Given his attachment to the public realm, it's hard to think he might not have liked to be elected. He is a commentator more than a proselytiser. It's very hard to be a commentator. You're asked to comment on a whole lot of things because of the complexities of modern life, the flow of information, the frequency and velocity of events. To be a commentator of note today and to be able to stand your ground for decades is very difficult to do, and Phillip does it with élan. He is a great listener to audio books in his car. It's a lazy way of reading books, but as he drives for three hours each way between his nirvana in the Hunter Valley to his office in Paddington every week, it is far more absorbing than listening to the squalor of talkback radio. Phillip is an unusual person to be a rural burgher on a farm in the Hunter Valley. You'd expect him to be an urbane urbanite.'

Paul Keating extended his hand. As I shook it, I felt a sense of opportunity lost, not for my conversation with him, but for his role in public life. However you regard his politics, Australian public life has been more boring without him. He is currently a Visiting Professor of Public Policy at the University of New South Wales and he emerges from time to time to call politicians nasty things, making headlines. But I wonder if he'll ever take a bigger role again, or if he would even want one.

Chapter Nine: **Eight Prime Ministers Adams Has Known**

When next I see Phillip Adams, I decide to continue the prime ministerial theme. My conversation with Paul Keating has inspired me to find out what other prime ministers Adams has known and to dig around in that brain of his for some insights into the people who have shaped Australian history the most. 'So,' I begin once we're sitting down with cups of tea, 'prime ministers'.

Adams begins talking about John Gorton, who he said was clueless and incapable of spin but totally genuine. The day after Prime Minister Harold Holt disappeared while swimming at Cheviot Beach in Victoria on December 17, 1967, John McEwen, the deputy prime minister, said his Country Party would not remain in the Coalition if deputy Liberal leader Billy McMahon, Holt's logical successor, was made prime minister, because he didn't trust him. This put John Gorton, minister for education and science, into contention as Liberal leader against his main rival, external affairs minister Paul Hasluck. Adams' friend Barry Jones had already raised Gorton's credibility by interviewing him on his Victorian radio and national television show. Gorton was a larrikin and fond of a drink. He was also fond of attractive young women, which made him popular with the voters but not with the Liberal Party.

But he was elected party leader on January 9, 1968 and prime minister the next day. He invited Barry Jones to a sleepover at The Lodge to thank him and to talk about Jones and Adams' plans to revive the Australian film industry.

Adams told me, 'Barry told me that he was sitting with John by the fire at The Lodge and John said, "I don't know what to do about the Canadians. I've never liked Canadians."

'Barry said, "It's different there now because of Pierre Trudeau."

'Silence. "What's Trudeau?"

'"The new prime minister of Canada."

'"What happened to Lester Pearson?"

'"He lost his job."

'"Hang on," said John. "I had to sign a letter to this Trudeau bloke."'

Adams laughed at the memory, as I did. Pierre Trudeau was prime minister of Canada from 1968 to '79 and again from 1980 to '84, outlasting Gorton by many years. But Adams wasn't finished with the Gorton anecdotes yet.

'Another time, John was holding a press conference on an Asian tour when someone asked him what he would do about the general SEATO situation and John was heard to ask an aide, "Who the fuck is General Seato?"' Adams roared with laughter. SEATO was the South East Asia Treaty Organisation.

'Then there was the time when Barry and I visited John at his office in Parliament House. On his desk were signed photos of the Pope, Harold Wilson and another man with epaulets. I asked him who he was and he said,

"Fucked if I know." It turned out to be Prince Bernhard of the Netherlands.

'Gough Whitlam looked as if he should have been a Liberal prime minister and John a Labor one. That minced-up face of his was a good face.' Gorton's face had been mutilated when he served in the Royal Australian Air Force during World War II. 'I liked him all the more because he backed our film project. Barry and I would write speeches for him and I remained quite good friends because he was a strong nationalist and he hated the fact that we had sold the farm to foreigners. Also, he was a republican. He said the British wanted Australians to roll over on their backs so the Poms could trickle their tummies like a dog. His nationalism did him no good in his own party. The Liberals used his strong flirtations with Liza Minnelli and Ainslie Gotto against him, but their main aim was to get rid of him.'

At John Gorton's ninetieth birthday celebration in 2001, Adams was the only one there from the left. The Liberals despised Gorton but pretended they cared. Gorton told Adams he was quite enjoying the bizarre event, where people who loathed him were pretending to love him. John Howard spotted Adams and told the function how Gorton had associated with people who were not the Liberals' usual friends and one of those associations had led to the film industry.

'It was Howard's olive branch to me,' Adams told me. 'He kept offering them and I kept rejecting them. Soon after his birthday, John Gorton died.' The date was May 19, 2002.

'The Liberals don't have genuine affection for their ex-leaders, like the Labor Party has,' said Adams. 'Even when they're disasters, Labor loves them. You couldn't not like John Gorton. He was as rough as bags, immensely vague and didn't know what was going on, but totally genuine. He just didn't have any skill at spin. He wasn't a thoroughbred Liberal out of The Melbourne Club. It was the first time the club had lost control of who would be prime minister. In some areas, he was very progressive. In others, he was hopeless.

'The myth is that he used a casting vote to vote himself out of the prime ministership when he called a party meeting in March 1971 and a motion of confidence in his leadership was tied. The myth is just a myth. Under the party's rules, a tied motion is automatically defeated. Gorton said, 'That is not a vote of confidence, so the party will have to elect a new leader.'

* * *

After John McEwan retired as Country Party leader, his successor Doug Anthony told the Liberal Party that the veto against Billy McMahon no longer applied. So the Liberals elected McMahon to succeed John Gorton. McMahon, his wife, Sonia, and little 'Nugget' Coombs, the Reserve Bank Governor, mounted the stairs in Washington with Sonia's thigh flashing in the picture that went around the world. Adams wrote that it looked as if Snow White was down to her last two dwarfs. Soon afterwards, Tony Staley, a Liberal MP, came to Adams with a job offer from McMahon and Adams said, 'But I've just described your boss's wife as being Snow White down to her last two dwarfs.' Staley said, 'The PM thinks that's funny.'

When I ask Adams about it all now, he says, 'Billy as prime minister was a joke from start to finish, probably our most underwhelming PM, a non-event, but a cunning little bugger. Afterwards, he disappeared into the mists of time. Once when I was staying in the Sebel Town House in Sydney, all I needed was a nap.

'I told the switch, as a joke, "No calls, unless it's a prime minister." I literally collapsed on the bed and the phone rang.

'The reception asked, "What about an ex-prime minister?"

'I said, "Which one?"

'They said, "Sir William McMahon."

'I said, "Put him through."

'Bill said in his squeaky little voice, "Hello."

'I said, "Hello, Bill."

'Bill said, "Who's that?"

'I said, "It's Phillip."

'He said, "What can I do for you, Phillip?"

'I said, "No, Bill, you're ringing me."

'He said, "Oh, yes. I've written my autobiography, Phil, and I'd like you to read it."

'I said, "I'd be happy to do that, Bill, if you courier it to me."

'It arrived; I ran through it and saw how bad it was. Every prime minister's autobiography is self-serving, but Bill's was preposterously so. I rang him and diplomatically said, "Bill, it needs a really good edit before you submit it to a publisher." He didn't take any notice and submitted it to several publishers, all of whom knocked it back. I sent the one copy I had to Barry Jones and told him, "You'll love this." Barry agreed with me and then lost the copy. For years I asked him whether he'd found it, because I wanted to send it to the National Library, but he never did find it.'

McMahon stayed in Parliament until he was seventy-four and died of cancer, aged eighty, in 1988, twenty-two years before Sonia died, also of cancer, in 2010.

* * *

Gough Whitlam walked all over Billy McMahon in the December 1972 election and became prime minister in the first Labor government for twenty-three years. Adams had been one of his young supporters in the 1960s, when Whitlam was the Labor Party deputy leader under Arthur Calwell. Calwell was the end of an era and had to go. Even then, television was becoming a major factor in politics and Calwell was a bad joke on television, physically and vocally, whereas Whitlam was a gift from heaven.

When I asked Adams about this time he said, 'We all knew Calwell wouldn't win the 1966 election against the prime minister, Harold Holt. It was not ideology; it was presentation.'

Adams wrote a secret report to a Victorian Labor Party committee saying the party had to get Calwell out of the picture and suggested he be persuaded to ask Holt for an aircraft to fly him around the world seeing world leaders who supported Labor's anti-Vietnam War policy. While he was away, Gough Whitlam and Jim Cairns would put on a double act and run the election campaign. Calwell went along with it and teed-up the plane from Holt. Then one Saturday morning *The Australian* had a page one story, 'Secret committee says dump Calwell' and all the committee members were named, which was embarrassing as the atmosphere was still pretty McCarthyite. Calwell cancelled the trip and we were well and truly done over in the election. Adams thought Whitlam was pretty special, and of course he's not alone in that opinion: many Australians still feel the same way. Jim Cairns, the hero of the left, led the anti-Vietnam marches and decided he would have a crack at the Labor leadership, but only to give Whitlam a kick in the backside. He didn't want to win. He and the party knew he wouldn't win a federal election because he was too left-wing.

Adams told me, 'Cairns wrote a very feeble, incredibly polite letter to all Caucus members. Jim was, in fact, a very polite, decent human being. He was ill — and holding press conferences in his pyjamas was not a good look. I sat on his bed and rewrote the letter, making it angry. I took out every "Mr" before Whitlam, put in some really ugly, aggressive prose about Whitlam being pompous and arrogant, who the hell did he think he was and finished by asking, "Whose party is it anyhow? His or ours?" To everyone's astonishment, Gough won the leadership ballot by only three votes. He never forgave me and whenever they met, he would call me "Jim Cairns' campaign manager". He was so petulant, he never really spoke to Cairns again, even when Jim was deputy prime minister and treasurer. So when I think of Gough, I think how close Australia was to Whitlam not becoming prime minister — because of a letter I helped write. The greatest triumph with Gough was the arts.'

Adams once more told me about Nugget Coombs and his influence in having Whitlam, as prime minister, keep the arts portfolio and Doug McClelland look after media, thus allowing them to achieve all of the plans, such as the film school, once discussed with John Gorton (see Chapter Four).

He continued: 'Gough was magnificent in his first hundred days. There was always a quality of self-ridicule and self-mockery about him. When he says, "I'm the greatest", it sounds okay but not when it appears in print. Gough really believes he is the greatest. But he ran a shambles of a government, a lot of it because he was a great inspiration but not a great prime minister. He's spent the rest of his life trying to convince us that he was. I revealed in an *Australian* column that he planned the world's biggest state funeral for himself, down to the last item, like the mounted police having polished black boots. He had committees working on it, such as a music committee. He chose Centennial Park in Sydney for it, to accommodate the thousands of people who would come. In some ways he is preposterously over the top, in other ways he has a quality of amusement. He's hard not to like.

'He loves food and uses it as fuel — it doesn't matter what the food is — and when I did the breakfast program on 2UE, he'd come in if I provided breakfast for him. He eats massively. I also wanted to interview him for *Late Night Live* and I rang his assistant, who said, "Okay." So on the way I did a detour and bought a box of disgusting cakes and custard tarts. Gough was thrilled with them. His assistant went and got a towel and put it around Gough's neck. While he was doing the interview, he was scoffing the cakes. He looked like Mount Vesuvius erupting. It's amazing that Gough ever made it past eighty, because he does everything wrong. The wrong food, too much of it, and no exercise.' Whitlam was 94 on July 11, 2010.

It is well known that on November 11, 1975, John Kerr, who Whitlam had appointed governor-general, created Australia's biggest constitutional crisis by sacking Gough's government and appointing the Liberal leader Malcolm Fraser as caretaker prime minister.

* * *

'Malcolm believed, like Whitlam, Hawke and Keating, that he was born to rule,' Adams said. 'People say he's shy and that's probably right. He has no social graces and no small talk. To have dinner with him is agonising.'

Adams was invited to The Lodge, the prime minister's Canberra residence, while Malcolm was living there.

'He always took pills for back pain,' Adams continued, 'and I think they added to his grumpiness. And he liked to have a drink.' During the Fraser government Phillip was on the Advance Australia committee; the chairman was Jim Leslie, the boss of Mobil and later chairman of Qantas. The committee's job was to make Australians more patriotic and to make them buy more Australian goods. A survey commissioned by the committee found that people ran a mile from anything with 'Made in Australia' on it.

'I thought Malcolm should know this,' said Adams. 'But first we had to run it past Phil Lynch, the treasurer, who paled visibly when we told him, and said, "I'm not telling him. You tell him." So we went into a room and everyone from Jim Leslie to Phil Lynch was scared stiff at having to deal with Malcolm on the issue. In he came from lunch, grumpy. All the others looked as if they were hiding.

'So I said, "You're not going to like this, Prime Minister, and it's pretty grim." I read him some bits from the research.

'Fraser shouted, "You tell them that the Holden is as good as the Mercedes and the Ford Falcon is as good as the fucking BMW."

'I said, "No, you tell them. They won't believe it because they know it's not true."

'Everyone was terrified of this towering man. He was pretty hard to handle.

'The good thing about him is that he's always been terrific on race,' Adams said. 'That's why the Africans love him. The Centre for the Mind held a function in the Great Hall at Sydney University to coincide with the 2008 Beijing Olympics because Professor Allan Snyder, the centre's director, believes the same attributes as that make sporting champions make champions in any area. Only Allan could get Nelson Mandela there as the centre's Millennium Fellow. The protocol required me to introduce John Howard, the centre's patron, and Howard to introduce Mandela.

'An hour before the event, I got a phone call from Howard's office.

'"Do you really want to introduce Mr Howard?"

'"Of course I don't."

'"Yes, it would be a bit hypocritical, wouldn't it?"

'"Not as hypocritical as him introducing Mandela."

'So the line-up was rejigged, and I did a vote of thanks to Mandela. Lovely guy. At the drinks, Malcolm

Fraser, at the top of his voice, told me Howard's record on race, abandoning all rules of Cabinet confidentiality and directing the remarks at Howard, who became increasingly uncomfortable. Fraser said Whitlam had rung him when Fraser was prime minister and asked him to let in a pile of Vietnamese who had helped the Australian troops in Vietnam. Fraser said no-one opposed it except Howard, who protested against letting them in. It was perfectly consistent with his racial attitudes.

'In the ceremony at the university, the Vice-Chancellor asked me to get Fraser out, so I took him into the anteroom and we had a cup of tea. Malcolm became, next to John Hewson, the greatest Howard hater of all. He always supported my refugee campaigns. After Kim Beazley capitulated over refugees, Fraser effectively became the opposition leader on the issue.'

* * *

The man who succeeded Malcolm Fraser as prime minister was Bob Hawke, who led the Labor Party to victory in 1983. Adams knew Hawke much earlier.

'He was as drunk as a skunk when he rolled into the *Don's Party* film opening night,' said Adams about his first meeting with Hawke in 1976. 'He had to be virtually carried to his seat. By the time the film was over, he was back in command and took us to a party. He had so much physical resilience that he could drink enough to kill anyone else and still operate. I saw this same resilience at the Tax Summit, when, after Bob had stopped drinking and become prime minister, he invited people to Parliament House to discuss the future of taxation in Australia.

'It was where Paul Keating lost his GST — Paul was advocating it but by the end of the conference Bob, who always saw the writing on the wall, had dumped it. Paul was enraged. I was there to represent the arts but couldn't stay awake and was shown asleep on television. But dazzling Bob sat there chairing the summit for days because he's so physically disciplined. I've always been impressed by that ability. But he's always been a very naughty boy and that's legend.

'He has a genius for seducing even men — not physically, but constantly. He doesn't have blood, only testosterone. He invades your personal space. I've seen him work a room and have been on the receiving end of his sexual radiance plenty of times. He's just as skilled at seducing men as women and I've seen many high achievers with that ability.

'I've never been close to Bob,' Adams continued, 'but I thought he was pretty good at his job. Bureaucrats and members of his cabinet tell me he was the best prime minister at chairing meetings. He was the first among equals, he got things going and everyone got to talk — that's very rare. On the ethical level, he was mediocre. He threw a dinner party for Paul Keating, a French count and his girlfriend, and the actress Miriam Margolyes. It was one of those parties where everyone has to sing a song or tell a story and when it was the French count's turn he decided he would propose marriage to his girlfriend. So in front of everyone he proposed marriage and she's thrilled to bits. Next it's Miriam's turn and she said she'd do one of her acts of a Charles Dickens character.

She said, "How could I refuse this invitation? I was told the other guests would be two ex-prime ministers and a French cunt!"'

Hawke and Adams nearly had a fist fight in a VIP lounge at Sydney Airport after Hawke lost his job as prime minister. The story was that Hawke was involved in horse racing in Hong Kong. All Adams said in a column was that Bob Hawke always sticks up for the little man — in this case, the jockey. Hawke went ballistic when he saw Phillip at the airport, screaming obscenities and threatening violence. It must have been Phillip's final insult to him — Adams had been very pro-Keating and had said it was time for Hawke to go. Now, Adams told me, he and Hawke bump into each other occasionally when it's unavoidable, and they're pleasant.

* * *

It took two challenges by Paul Keating, private and public sniping and a recession to unseat Hawke and install Paul Keating as prime minister. Keating finally won in a party-room ballot on December 20, 1991. Hawke alone could not have reformed the Australian economy, but Keating alone could not have sold the reforms to the people.

Adams remembers Keating making an impression on him as far back as the early 1970s, when he heard him in a parliamentary broadcast as the MP for Blaxland in Sydney's western suburbs; Keating was still in his late twenties.

'He was good!' said Adams, reminiscing about the man I interviewed only days ago. 'I became intrigued by him, although I didn't entirely approve of his views because he came from the New South Wales hard right faction. As the years passed, he became more interesting. After he became prime minister, every year when I was chairman of the Australia Day Council, I'd go to Kirribilli House in Sydney, collect Paul and Annita and we'd go to Admiralty House next door for the Australian of the Year ceremony. Telstra, the sponsors, pitched a tent for the guests. Most years, we used to upset Alan Jones with our choice.

'One year, when I was writing *The Penguin Book of Australian Jokes,* I told the audience it contained quite a few jokes about Paul and we had gone into history and found they were originally anti-Hitler jokes, invented by a couple of Munich comedians who finished up in Dachau. That's the way jokes work — the costumes change but the joke continues.

'Paul smiled but Annita was livid. Later that day, we wandered down the Admiralty House lawns towards the harbour. Paul Kelly, of *The Australian*, was with us. The rest of the media were up on the hill with long-distance microphones and could pick up our conversation. As a joke I said loudly, "Rupert Murdoch is gay." Kelly nearly passed out. Paul Keating quite liked what he called my "fucking irreverence". So we had a rapport.

'I love the British MP Tony Benn's argument that politicians are either straight men, fixers or maddies, and I wrote a column allocating Australian politicians, such as John Cain and Nick Greiner as straight men, Neville Wran and Bob Hawke as fixers and Margaret Thatcher, Ronald Reagan, Jeff Kennett and Paul Keating as maddies — ones who really do things, whether you like what they do or not.

'The phone rang at the farm and Paul's voice said, "It's your mad mate here." He was delighted because that was the way he saw power — if you have it, you use it, which is why he thought Kennett was the only state premier worth feeding, because he used power.'

In 2007, ABC Radio National ran a poll to find out what listeners thought were the world's greatest speeches. Keating's 1992 reconciliation speech at Redfern Park in Sydney came third after Martin Luther King's 'I have a dream' and the Sermon on the Mount.

'I rang Paul to tell him,' said Adams, 'and he thought it was okay to come third after those speeches.

'He was in great pain after he lost, badly, in 1996 to John Howard, the person in Australia he most despised. He immediately resigned as Labor leader and from Parliament a month later (on April 23, 1996). After that he lost Annita, a calamity for him because he will go to his grave adoring her. They're not divorced, but she'd had enough of it. The Labor Party dumped him and tried to write him out of history as much as possible. People crossed the street if they saw him coming.

'His last disaster was Don Watson's biography on him, *Recollections of a Bleeding Heart*' (Random House), said Phillip. 'Paul regarded it as a personal betrayal and a gross misrepresentation of what was really going on. Paul's argument is that it makes him look like Hamlet on the battlements of Elsinore, a pale figure full of indecision. His version was, "Don wasn't at the meetings. I'd be there fighting all day and go home dead tired and listen to some music, and that was when Don would come in."

'Paul and I propped up each other for John Howard's twelve years in power. He'd come around and we'd talk and he'd tell his wonderful anecdotes. I have a huge affection for him and think the world of him. I asked him once, "What does it feel like to be the last Labor prime minister?", and I meant "last" because I couldn't see the Labor Party climbing out of the Howard years, which had so completely reshaped Australia.

'In Kevin Rudd's 2007 election campaign, Paul got more and more angry because Kevin was not taking his calls. I knew Paul would blow his stack in the middle of the campaign. So I rang Kevin and asked him to ring Paul. Then I rang Paul and said, "I think you might get a call from Kevin." But he didn't, and he went on *Lateline* on ABC TV and did them all over because he was angry about being marginalised. Then Kevin redeemed everything by making a fuss of Paul at his policy launch in Brisbane Town Hall.

'Paul was always annoyed that, after Bob Hawke left office, he made piles of money from racing and international gambling connections, Burma, China and so on. I was sitting in the Chairman's Lounge at Sydney Airport with a friend from Melbourne, and we compared notes about the states of mind of Paul and Bob, and my friend said, "Hawke's got no money. He does things on success fees but he's not having much success."

'I said, "Hasn't he got a building in the CBD?"

'"Yes," said my friend, "but it's mortgaged to the hilt."

'I thought, Paul would like to know this. So he rang him and asked if he would like some good news.

'Paul said, "Yes, I'd like some good news."

'I sang a little song: "Hawkie's got no money, Hawkie's got no money" and asked him where he was.

'He said, "I'm in Beijing and he's sitting opposite me." They were there representing different interests.'

I laughed, imagining Paul Keating looking like the Cheshire cat as he faced his old adversary.

Adams went on: 'I see Paul as the great brain, the most extraordinarily gifted prime minister we've ever had ... Any Canberra bureaucrat you ask who's observed prime ministers up close says Hawke was a dazzling PM at running meetings, getting across the briefs and understanding the politics, but Paul was the most exciting. He is the most complex and charismatic character of them all. He was a maddie and Hawke was a fixer. To me, Paul in those short years was astonishing.'

* * *

Phillip Adams was born fourteen days before John Howard, but they are separated by vastly different ideologies and agendas. Hearing Adams say a kind word about Howard is like hearing the English praise the French, or the reverse. But he surprised me.

'I saw John in the VIP Lounge at Sydney Airport one Monday morning after he'd lost the Liberal leadership in 1989 over his appalling interview with John Laws on 2UE, when he bucketed Asian immigration,' Adams said. 'The Labor Party was greatly relieved that he had lost the leadership, because it feared him. The whole Liberal Party was up one end of the lounge and Howard was at the other end because no-one was talking to him. People forget how out of it he was at that stage.

'We each made ourselves a cup of tea and I said to John, "Our blokes are terrified you'll get the leadership back."

'He asked, "Why?"

'I said, "They know how smart you are politically. They know you're not afraid of Keating and that's pretty rare because almost everyone else is terrified of Paul, much more than they are of Hawkie. They know you understand the Labor Party as an organism. If you ever get the Liberal leadership back, the ALP will be concerned."'

Just to balance the unexpected rosy hue, Adams then told me, 'When Howard won, and won big, I knew the first thing he would do would be to attack everything Paul had done, he detested Paul so much. Howard came into power not with an agenda but with a hit list. My first reaction was to resign from everything to do with the government because I knew anything I was connected with would get no funds or support. Paul had given me the wonderful job of building a national museum as chairman of the board, to be announced after the 1996 election, which Paul lost. I resigned soon after the election.'

Keating had also asked former Victorian Premier Joan Kirner and Adams to write a report for COAG (the Council of Australian Governments) on preparations for the 2001 Centenary of Federation celebrations. Committees from all the states signed it but Adams knew that the actions suggested in the report, which included reconciliation and the republic, wouldn't happen. Janet Holmes à Court chaired the national committee and 'Howard sacked her,' said Adams.

'If you didn't resign, you were sacked. I predicted that the new chairman Howard would appoint would be Dick Smith, who at the time was a mate of his, and I was correct. I thought it was outrageous. It was typical of the way Howard operated.'

The Great Purge went on. The whole Howard issue boiled down to the refugees, which he made into a crisis, because Australia had more illegal refugees coming in through Mascot and Tullamarine, dressed in suits, than it ever had arriving in boats. They'd come in on tourist visas and disappear. Howard whipped Australia into a frenzy over boat people, aided by his appalling surrogate Pauline Hanson. The Labor Party collapsed ethically and morally and Kim Beazley, the leader, fell over: that was when Adams knew he could never support him.

'My horror of Howard focused on his shameful manipulation of bigotry,' Adams said. 'When he ran for a second time in 1998, he was asked why and he said something quite extraordinary. He said, in effect, "To prove my legitimacy to Robert Manne"' (Professor of Politics at La Trobe University in Melbourne) '"and Phillip Adams." I was curious why he kept singling me out, most famously when he said the ABC should have a right-wing Phillip Adams, which helped because the ABC couldn't get rid of me then. It spent years trying to fill the slot with Imre Salusinszky and Tim Blair and, more recently, Michael Duffy. So I have to thank John, with his inept statements, for the ABC keeping me on.'

The greatest evidence of Howard's strange attitude to Adams was when his Arts minister, Peter McGauran, came to see him, ostensibly to talk about the film industry. They talked about it for hours but Adams was sure there was another reason why he had come.

'At the time my main problem was a very painful arm,' Adams told me. 'I couldn't even stir a cup of tea without it hurting. As the minister was leaving, he grabbed my bad arm. I nearly passed out with the pain.

'McGauran said, "You've got to stop doing it. You've got to stop saying these things."

'"What are you talking about?" I asked.

'He said, "You've got to stop saying these awful things about the prime minister. You've no idea how much you're upsetting him."'

'I didn't feel the pain in my arm as much after that.'

Adams kept smiling at the memory as he told me, 'John Howard and I have a strange relationship. Perhaps one of these days, when we're much older, we might sit down and talk about it, as I did with BA Santamaria (the Catholic activist) near the end of his life. We had always detested each other. But at the end of things, you sit down and talk things out.'

* * *

Just as with Paul Keating, Adams' first contact with Kevin Rudd was by ear, when he interviewed Rudd, who was in Queensland, for *Late Night Live*. Phillip had never even heard of him at that time but found him fantastic, forensic, intelligent and articulate — 'all the things most Labor Party people are not'.

'I said to the producers, "Let's get him on again."'

Rudd started calling on Adams regularly for a cup of tea and a talk. He was the longest of prime ministerial long-shots for millions of reasons: his physicality, religion, conservatism and bureaucratic background — everything was against Kevin ever becoming a Labor Party leader.

'I tried to talk him into running against Kim Beazley. He didn't have anything like the numbers but he was very bitter that Beazley didn't step aside. His next chance was when Beazley floundered and Mark Latham became parliamentary leader from December 2003 to January 2005.

'Latham said in his Sydney *Daily Telegraph* column there was no place for me in his Labor Party, largely because he wanted a tougher illegal-migrant policy than the Immigration Minister Philip Ruddock's. So for that reason, apart from anything else, I crusaded for Rudd against Latham as Labor leader. I used to say it was a choice between "The Bomber"' (Beazley's nickname) 'and "The Bomb".' This was the nickname Adams had given Latham. 'But Labor caucus leaders became desperate and Latham won the leadership — he was in the earthy, vigorous bullyboy Labor tradition and people thought they saw glimpses of Keating in him. They still couldn't see Rudd, a strange, pristine, nerdy person.'

Adams suggested to Sally Warhaft, then editor of *The Monthly*, that she ask Rudd to write an essay, and talked to Rudd about it. 'He rewrote a speech he'd given about his hero, Dietrich Bonhoeffer (a Lutheran pastor and anti-Nazi resistance fighter) and Warhaft put it on the cover. It caused a storm in the party and confirmed the worst suspicions of some but neutralised Kevin's religion by putting it on the table, like Blanche d'Alpuget did when her biography of Bob Hawke revealed some of his amorous behaviour, but not all of it.

Adams continued, 'Rudd won the leadership, and bloody hell, to everyone's astonishment (including his own), he won the 2007 election because he ran a Howard

Lite campaign. He didn't frighten the Liberal voters, it looked like a painless transition and he wasn't a sort of Hillsong God-botherer but was identified with a martyred Protestant theologian who stood up against Hitler, which I'd argued would kick in over any ethical crisis like refugees.

'Just after the election, Kevin rang me up and asked Patrice and me to dinner at Kirribilli House. It was a nice way to say thank you. We got out of the car at the front door, the door opened and there was Kevin. We laughed and laughed. We laughed in disbelief.'

Chapter Ten: **Hilarious Tales of Politicians and Others**

I decided to tackle Phillip Adams for anecdotes about politicians and phoned him at the usual time, 9 a.m. on a Monday, to arrange a meeting. He answered, 'Yup?'

'Hello, it's Philip Luker. How are you?'

'Okay.'

'Can we have another meeting this week?'

'Okay. Will you come here tomorrow at nine-thirty?'

'See you then.'

That was always the extent of the call. The next day, as arranged, I pressed the security intercom on the front door of his office in Paddington, Sydney.

'Yes?' said a voice.

'It's Philip Luker.'

'Come in, Philip.'

He welcomed me warmly and remarked that, as we were both wearing black shirts, 'People won't be able to tell us apart at the book launch.' Adams went into the small, dark kitchen next to his large office and living room. He made each of us a cup of tea, two teabags each. The phone rang. It was his executive producer at *Late Night Live*. They discussed the interviews Adams would conduct that night. I set up my tape recorder on his desk and prepared to ask him for anecdotes about the dozens of politicians and other personalities he has known.

* * *

'Bob Hawke is Australia's Bill Clinton,' Adams told me. 'He's enormously affable, feeling the electors' pain and shedding the occasional ritualistic tear, but without much substance. Bob relishes the idea of becoming a welcome conciliator in a devastating dispute and used this tactic many times to settle strikes when he was ACTU president. It created a rush of affection for him.

'But it's amazing how little Bob is considered these days. He's almost written out of the narrative.' For such a popular prime minister, Hawke does not have the gravitas within the party or the public of another former PM, Gough Whitlam.

'I much preferred Bob's former wife, Hazel,' said Adams. 'We set up the Children's Television Foundation to make children's TV. Hazel loved that kind of thing. We all expected she would have a long twilight with or without Bob, but it was not to be. It's immensely sad.' He was referring not only to Hazel's divorce from Bob, who had for many years conducted an affair with the writer Blanche d'Alpuget, but also to the fact that that in 2003 Hazel made public the fact that she has Alzheimer's Disease.

* * *

I asked Adams what his anecdotes were about other federal and state politicians. 'The thing about Nick Greiner (premier of New South Wales from 1988 to 1992) 'is that he set up ICAC' (the Independent Commission Against Corruption) 'and if the same principles were applied nationally, it would be hard to find an Australian political figure who would not be removed from office.'

ICAC returned to haunt Greiner when it ruled that his executive job offer to Independent MP Terry Metherell was corrupt. Four independent MPs decided not to support the government and Greiner resigned, although he was later cleared of corruption.

Adams continued, warming to the theme of political anecdotes: 'You know, on the day Nick lost office, no-one came to see him or shake his hand, which shows what a dreadfully tough business politics is — other people can fail quietly, but not politicians.'

'What about Joh Bjelke-Petersen?' (the notorious National Party premier of Queensland from 1968 to 1987).

Adams said that after most premiers decided to have a film corporation like South Australia's, Bjelke-Petersen gave the job of running his to his aide-de-camp and heavy hitter.

'I'd never met the man,' Adams said, 'but one day two federal police called to see me and ask me questions about gifts they said I'd received from this head of the Queensland film body. So I said, "What gifts?" and they read out a list of gifts like gold watches. I said I'd never seen these gifts and that I wouldn't have accepted them anyway. Turns out the film boss had been buying the gifts for himself and recording them as gifts for me.' Adams said with a laugh. 'He was relieved of his gold timekeeper before doing time himself.'

Adams met Joh several times and although he loathed everything the premier did in Queensland, Phillip nevertheless found him delightful, charming and amusing. 'It's annoying meeting people you want to hate and not being able to hate them,' Phillip said. He told me the story of a film producer who went to see Joh to ask whether the Queensland Government would help him make a film in that state. "What's in it for me?" Joh asked him. The producer went through his sales pitch again while he pondered the question and Joh again asked, "What's in it for me?" The producer left without offering the premier the bribe he sought. Joh's government started to fall apart after ABC Television exposed rampant police corruption in Queensland in a *Four Corners* program. Joh died in 2005.

'While you loathe people like him being around,' Adams told me, 'you miss them when they've gone.'

* * *

I asked him about Bob Brown, the openly gay leader of the Australian Greens. Phillip said Bob is one politician with 'total integrity, although as a party the Greens sometimes drive me nuts. People don't realise that Bob started green politics in Australia and what he did with the Franklin River in Tasmania was the first time any green group had really organised themselves politically.' Brown led Australia's biggest conservation battle, in 1982, to save the wild Franklin from being dammed for hydroelectricity.

Adams continued, 'Bob showed that environmental activism could have political expression through a party. He's still there. At a Sydney Town Hall meeting on illegal migrants, he got a standing ovation before his speech. In his strange, amateurish way, he showed he was a person of total integrity. I have great respect and affection for him.'

* * *

What about Carmen Lawrence, the West Australian Labor premier from 1990 to '93? Adams said, 'She's terrific on social justice issues. She should have been a prime minister.'

While a nasty hiccup destroyed Lawrence's political career — a Royal Commission found that she had misled the State Parliament concerning her knowledge of and role in the tabling of a petition — her media presence remains: Phillip often gets her on *Late Night Live*.

'One night I had three women on the program,' Adams said, 'Carmen and two British Labor MPs who had voted against Tony Blair backing George Bush's invasion of Iraq. I found that all three of them were lapsed Catholics. I wouldn't mind joining the Catholic Church briefly so I could become a lapsed Catholic myself.

'It's all too easy to denigrate politicians. People globally have poor regard for MPs. There are good people in all parties.'

* * *

Then I asked him about Joan Kirner, the Labor premier of Victoria from 1990 to '92.

'I once spent an hour with her at a public meeting in Melbourne,' he said, 'and I admired the way she used various strategies to handle people who came up to speak to her. I learned from her tactics, because I have similar problems with people who recognise me. I never know whether they'll punch me or pat me on the back. I find aggression — but preferably without a punch or a knife — easier to handle than affection.'

* * *

Joan Kirner was ousted by the Liberals under Jeff Kennett, who was premier of Victoria until 1999.

'Jeff was somewhat toxic,' said Adams, 'but you had to be gobsmacked by his audacity. He closed local councils, ran a Reagan and Thatcher-style privatisation campaign and transformed Melbourne, which had been slowly dying. Like Keating, Kennett used power while he had it. But he terrified people.'

* * *

Next came Neville Wran, the New South Wales premier from 1976 to '86.

'The first time I met Neville was when I arrived in Kerry Packer's office to talk about film finance and there was Neville, looking embarrassed, being a Labor premier, to be seen with the personification of rampant capitalism.

'Neville was doing a deal with Kerry to sell the state lotteries jointly to him, Rupert Murdoch and the British racehorse owner Robert Sangster. I was horrified about it and after Neville left, I told Kerry, "This is terrible, the worst kind of privatisation. You don't need money from lotteries." Kerry said he wanted to see whether Neville could deliver.'

Adams concluded that Nifty, as Wran was called, was building himself a media buffer zone by selling the lotteries to two media magnates, Kerry Packer and Rupert Murdoch.

Another time, Neville Wran, Kerry Packer and Adams had dinner together. 'Neville is a great raconteur,' said Adams. 'When he's telling a story, he walks around the room; it's a show. When he left, Kerry said, "I'm worried about Neville. He's got no money." I replied, "You mean he's got no money like you've got money." Kerry said, "He's got no fucking money." I was pleased to hear that rumours about Neville accumulating money were untrue.'

Neville Wran once told Adams, 'What you've got to look out for is politicians who go to the races a lot and bet heavily.' He told Adams about shysters and lobbyists who came to his office, high up in a city building, to offer him money and he said to them, 'I'm going to chuck you out the fucking window!' Once, when Neville's wife, Jill Hickson, organised a celebration of Neville's successful term as premier, each of his ministers was required to do a turn.'

* * *

'Bob Carr, who was Neville's minister for planning and the environment, chose to do a song and dance act.

'It was not a pretty sight,' Adams told me. 'Like me, he lacks physical co-ordination. When he was made leader of the NSW Labor Party' (in 1988) 'he came to my studio at 2UE very depressed. He didn't want to be premier; he wanted to be federal foreign affairs minister, because that was his passion, along with American history and politics. He is very intelligent and interesting but I always thought he was a disappointment as New South Wales premier.' Carr reigned from 1995 to 2005.

'Towards the end of his political career,' Adams continued, 'I asked to see him to record five minutes on George W Bush's imminent visit to Australia. Two hours later I'd taped enough for two programs and Bob showed no sign of stopping. What amazed me was that at no time did the phone ring or his chief of staff come in. I suddenly realised that a modern premier is front of house and does photo ops and public occasions, and ten-second grabs for the 6 p.m. news. The real work is done elsewhere. Bob was passionate about the environment and opened a lot of national parks but didn't really get on top of the central issues that would plague New South Wales for years to come.'

* * *

Adams said the most impressive social reformer of all Australian premiers was Don Dunstan, who openly declared himself gay but only towards the end of his career as South Australian premier from 1967 to '68 and 1970 to '79. At Adelaide University he met his first wife Gretel and they married in 1949, four years before he won the Norwood seat he held for the next 26 years. In the late 1960s, he was still energetically heterosexual and in 1974, as premier, he had an affair with one of his staff, a Malaysian, Adele Koh. Gretel and he were divorced and he married Adele two years later after she told him she was pregnant. By that time he was sexually ambiguous and after she died of cancer in 1978, he read in her diary that she had not been pregnant. The next year, he announced his sudden resignation as premier. (Apparently the media attended his home for this televised announcement which he made at home in his pyjamas after collapsing and sleeping for 40 hours.) In 1986, he met Stephen Cheng, they became partners and in 1994 jointly opened a restaurant, Don's Table. Don died of cancer, aged 72, in 1999.

Adams called Don 'the Pierre Trudeau of Australia' although more consequential. Trudeau redefined Canada as its prime minister in the 1970s and '80s. Don Dunstan recognised Aboriginal land rights, decriminalised homosexuality, appointed the state's first female judge, relaxed censorship and drinking laws, overhauled the upper house of parliament, lowered the voting age to 18 and encouraged the arts. With Phillip's help, he established the South Australian Film Commission (see Chapter Four) and nationally he helped abolish the White Australia Policy. Adams told how he was invited to the tenth anniversary of Don's death in February 2009. Everyone who could find one wore a Dunstan-style safari suit. The Premier, Mike Rann, announced the formation of the Australian Centre for Social Innovation, with Phillip as chairman.

* * *

Mike Rann, who was Don Dunstan's press secretary and speech writer, did the same jobs for Don's successors as premier, Des Corcoran and John Bannon, and was elected premier himself in 2002. His Labor Party won again in March 2010, although it lost two seats. Phillip said, 'Mike energetically pursues Don's commitment to social change and justice and likes people to realise this.' Al Gore, the former US vice-president and the world's best-known environmental activist, named the South Australian Government as the one doing the world's best job on climate change. South Australia has little manufacturing industry, an ageing population and is at the dry end of the Murray River.

* * *

Adams praised Rupert Hamer (Victorian Liberal premier from 1972 to '81) because, like Don Dunstan and Mike Rann, he was good on cultural issues. Adams told me, 'When Rupert attended the launch of the Melbourne Film Festival, he got a standing ovation from the largely left-wing audience. Another time, after I convened the Friends of The Age to try to keep *The Age* independent, Rupert phoned me to say he would hold a judicial inquiry into *The Age's* independence — the Norris Inquiry' (see Chapter Seventeen).

* * *

Adams told me some anecdotes from other personalities he has known: He said, 'I was driving over the Golden Gate Bridge in San Francisco with Peter Faiman, the *Crocodile Dundee* director, when Peter gave me a joint. I kept laughing for a week and started to like it. We went to a horror movie and I wandered out of the cinema and couldn't find my way back to *The Bride of Frankenstein*.'

It showed Adams that narcotics are not for him and he thinks Faiman wanted to teach him that. Faiman had given up marijuana and he warned Adams, whose only previous experience of it was when Richard Neville (the *Oz* founder and current futurist) gave him a joint and nothing happened.

Earlier, when Adams was a partner in the ad agency Monahan Dayman Adams in Melbourne, he would go into the Channel Nine studios and watch Peter Faiman as a television director juggle the world, with up to nine cameras recording a program — Faiman directed many Channel Nine shows, often interspersed with commercials Adams had planned. He has always found that other people's skills are mysterious to watch and was astonished by how Faiman organised the programs, made the cameras dance and at the same time was a choreographer and a psychologist to the temperamental performers.

Adams said Faiman was 'appallingly' treated by Paul Hogan and John Cornell over their *Crocodile Dundee* film, which Faiman directed. 'He could have made it a much better film, but they wouldn't let him cut it the way he wanted to.'

Peter Faiman also directed The Nine Network's four-hour *Australia Live*, which from 70 locations around Australia and overseas recorded a day in the life of Australians on January 1, 1988. The first of a multitude of celebrities on camera was Adams, at Uluru. Before the program, Faiman asked Adams to write speeches for about 20 world leaders who would take part, including US President Ronald Reagan. He wrote the speeches in a day for what he believes is still the world's biggest telecast.

* * *

Neither Adams nor Peter Faiman want to be anyone except themselves, but Bob Ellis, the eccentric, audacious, outrageous, quirky but skilled and funny left-wing writer, always wanted to be other people, according to Adams. For a long time, Ellis wanted to be David Williamson, then he wanted to be Adams, but finally he discovered that being Bob Ellis was great.

'He had an extraordinary gift with women but also quite spectacular halitosis,' Adams said. 'Bob took part in one of the annual Australian Film Institute Awards, in Perth. Another person on the program was an American actress called Brenda Vaccaro, who was outraged by the newly-launched vaginal deodorants. I introduced her as the President of the Society for the Promotion of Natural Body Odours and Bob as Australia's playwright with the most halitosis and left them to it. I don't know what the outcome was.

'Another of my memories of Bob Ellis was when I was chairman of the Australian Film Commission and Malcolm Fraser was prime minister. It was a delicate time in negotiations for film funds and Bob hated Fraser but was obviously going to win an award that night. At the hotel before the awards, I told Bob he had to behave himself, gracefully accept his award and not bucket Fraser, in spite of wanting to do so. He promised me he would behave.

'I sat in the audience with Brit Eckland. The awards were made of plastic and were so weak that they disintegrated on the stage. Every time someone was presented with an award, a bit would fall off and the stage was littered with pieces of broken AFI awards. Ellis arrived on stage drunk. Fraser presented him with his award, which started to fall apart in his hands. He forgot his promise to behave, bucketed Fraser and vomited — on national television.

* * *

Long before US President Jack Kennedy's sexual shenanigans became public knowledge, the late British author Malcolm Muggeridge told Adams about them, which upset Adams because he held Kennedy in high regard. Muggeridge said Kennedy was second in sexual low-jinks only to Benito Mussolini, the Italian Fascist leader who used his office largely for sexual purposes but in Milan in April 1945 was hung upside down by Italian partisans — not yet a fate of any Australian politician. No-one published newspaper stories about sexual affairs by Kennedy or Mussolini in those days and it was the same when Junie Morosi had an affair with Jim Cairns, the Australian deputy prime minister.

* * *

Bill Kelty (Secretary of the Australian Council of Trade Unions from 1983 to 2000) is 'The Killer Koala,' according to Adams, because he looks like one. 'He is as tough as old boots but one of the smartest strategists and he should be working for Barack Obama. He and Paul Keating were a great double act.

'Bill and I believe the Australian political system has deep troubles. Not only does the public despise it; the politicians do also. They are bored, irritated and frustrated, particularly by being whipped into line to vote on bills, often against their consciences. The only time politics really comes to life is in conscience votes.

'Bill and I came up with the idea that a party should campaign and seek a mandate on only a handful of issues such as foreign affairs, health and education, and let MPs vote as they and their electors want on all other issues. It would revitalise all parliaments and make politics more interesting to politicians and the public. I played with this idea in a series of *Australian* columns but Bill and I couldn't get Paul Keating to take it seriously. No prime minister or premier likes the idea of losing control. This great and glorious idea has never been taken up by any party.'

* * *

Dr Philip Nitschke is another person who has campaigned long and hard for a basic change in society, and failed. He is the founder and director of the pro-euthanasia group Exit International and he was the first doctor in the world to administer a legal, voluntary, lethal injection (in Darwin, before the Federal Government overruled the law). His successive campaigns have failed to change Australian laws, but Phillip Adams says, 'He's a hoot! He could help people to die laughing — that's not a bad idea! He should introduce the idea of laughing yourself to death. He is one of those odd people — those with passion and talent. They don't fit in, so they stand out.'

* * *

Another person who stood out, but for different reasons, was the late, unlamented Sydney entrepreneur and banned stockbroker Rene Rivkin. Phillip remembers him struggling free of a $400,000 Bentley 'like a maharajah demounting from an elephant's howdah', settling into his favourite possie at the Dee Bee Restaurant in Double Bay, Sydney, fingering his gold worry beads and reciting his variation of the Rosary, in spite of his parents being

Russian Jews. On that day in 'Double Pay' (as it is called), he was happy and expansive, until Adams told him the colour of his Bentley (imperial purple) was 'crook.'

Over the years, Rene Rivkin's fortunes rose and fell like his moods. Adams told me, 'A few months later, I shared a plane with Rene's wife Gayle to Hayman Island, where Rene and I were to speak at a convention. Rene asked me at the hotel, "What are they saying about me?" I told him of rumours about arson, a $50million insurance payout, and murder.' (Rene was implicated in the Offset Alpine printing-plant fire. His former chauffeur, Gordon Wood, was in November 2008 jailed for murdering Wood's former girlfriend, Caroline Byrne.)

'At the convention, Gayle Rivkin told me, "He's living on Prozac." Rene said, "It's all that keeps me going." Gayle said, "But it's changing his personality." I said, "That can only be an improvement."'

It was not Rene's only problem. He was sentenced to nine months' weekend detention for insider trading; he had surgery for a tumour; he collapsed in jail; he was banned for life from stockbroking; Gayle and he divorced; he went broke and sold all his paintings and properties; then he killed himself, aged 61, in 2005.

* * *

More of Adams' anecdotes: He doesn't have a suit, but once he had a sports jacket, which he bought to be presented with his first Order of Australia badge by the Governor General, Sir Ninian Stephen, in 1987. Then he lost the badge. He wrote to the GG at Government House in Canberra, asking whether he could make him another one. He pretended he thought Sir Ninian made the badges at the back of the garage. The GG's secretary wrote back to say he could have a new badge but it would cost him $9.90. Adams told me, 'Some people work for nothing for charities all their lives and get one of these things and it's worth $9.90. That's hilarious!'

Also in the queue at Government House waiting to be presented with an award was Charles Spry, the chief of ASIO. Adams said to him, 'Here's a turn up, you the head spook and me the naughty leftie, both getting a gong.' Adams asked Spry to show him his ASIO file and Spry strenuously denied there was one. But when the National Library asked Adams to give a speech, he agreed to do so if they produced his ASIO file, and they did. 'What shattered me was that several people had reported me to ASIO. Their names had been blacked out but you could guess who they were. The file is still current.'

* * *

One wet day Adams was shivering in a New York City doorway when the actor Stewart Wagstaff slid past on the footpath. Stewart had a toffy West End image for the theatre, although his childhood had been harrowing and he was brought up on a little English farm and Adams had heard him say in a radio interview that a horrible childhood makes it almost impossible to be loved. Adams said to Wagstaff when they met in New York, 'Stewart, how good to see you. Let's have a cup of coffee because I owe you an apology. I always thought of you as an effete, upper-class lad.' They had a cup of coffee and Phillip told

Stewart that damaged-goods children's capacity to love takes a lot of time to work through.

* * *

Adams himself was 'lying at death's door' (his words) in a Sydney hospital after 'massive surgery' when, as he was coming out of the anaesthetic fog, he saw Jim Soorley, a former Catholic priest and from 1991 to 2003 the Labor Party Lord Mayor of Brisbane, sitting at the end of his bed. 'I told him to bugger off because I thought he'd come to give me the last rites.'

Soorley did not bugger off but cheered Adams up. Like Carmen Lawrence, he is a lapsed Catholic — 'they bring with them the great strength of Catholicism, its universality. It is the world's biggest multinational corporation.' Jim Soorley achieved a lot as Lord Mayor of Australia's biggest local government area, from improving the sewerage to starting the Brisbane Festival of Ideas. He is now a management consultant and until recently wrote a column in the Brisbane *Sunday Mail.*

* * *

Another newspaper, another era, another city — *Nation Review*, the 1970s, Sydney and the most colourful character Phillip Adams has ever known, Gordon Barton. Gordon came from Java, got three degrees simultaneously at Sydney University (which then changed the rules), drank with The Push, admired the notorious philosophy professor, John Anderson, who used to recommend free love in the 1950s, built a fortune from the Ipec transport company he formed, expanded into merchant banking in Tjuringa Securities, started the Australia Party, which became the Australian Democrats, became a careless millionaire in the way he spent his money, conducted multiple affairs at the same time, and in 1970 launched *Nation Review*, which was how Phillip knew him.

Adams, together with a string of other left-wing *Nation Review* contributors, poked fun at the establishment with verve and style, which were words that fitted Gordon Barton, the Australian version of F. Scott Fitzgerald's Great Gatsby character.

By 1981, *Nation Review* was costing Gordon too much money and he asked Adams to meet him in his city apartment. Adams told me the story, 'As Gordon's butler filled the open fire with mallee roots that Gordon had freighted from Victoria, he offered me *Nation Review* for not much money at all. I was about to shake on it when he showed me a file of unsettled libel actions and I said, "Thanks, but no thanks."'

Barton closed *Nation Review*, got bored with Australia, set up Ipec in Europe and moved into a medieval castle in Holland, where according to Valerie Lawson in *The Sydney Morning Herald,* he once met a group of bankers dressed in a suit of armour. Within ten years, he had to sell his European Ipec to pay for losses on his Australian companies. It was the start of a sad decline — sad for such a rip-roaring entrepreneur. He became increasingly deaf and started to lose his memory and his reasoning and he died in Spain in April 2005, aged 76.

Chapter Eleven: **The Ideas Adams Gave Two Premiers**

From one idea, others flow: Greg Mackie owned the Adelaide bookshop Imprints and took part in Adelaide Writers' Week ... He listened regularly to Phillip Adams' *Late Night Live* on Radio National and realised it was a festival of ideas ... So he asked Adams to help launch the SA Festival of Ideas in 1999 on alternate years to Writers' Week. Adams has played a large role in developing the ideas festival and chairing many sessions ever since. Often the speakers have already had conversations with Adams on *Late Night Live.* Mike Rann, the South Australian Premier, told me by phone from Adelaide, 'The festival is a wonderful event that attracts thousands of people to sessions ranging from astronomy to feminism and modern Islam to sex.' The 2009 festival theme was 'Pushing the Limits'. The man who originally came up with the idea, Greg Mackie, is now Deputy CEO of the Department of Premier and Cabinet in SA.

But the ideas festival was only the start. Mike Rann wanted the state to benefit more from the brains of people who came to the festival and were prepared to stay in Adelaide for several days or several months, attend Cabinet meetings, give public lectures and talk to local people. So he launched Thinkers in Residence. Four recent Thinkers in Residence have been: Professor Fred

Wegman, managing director of the Holland Institute for Road Safety Research; Fred Hansen, general manager of TriMet, the transport authority of Portland, Oregon; Genevieve Bell, who also came from Portland as a director of Intel Corporation's Digital Home Group; and Laura Lee, Professor of Architecture at Carnegie Mellon University, Pittsburgh, USA.

One of the earliest Thinkers in Residence was Baroness Susan Greenfield, Professor of Neuroscience at Oxford University and Director of the Royal Institution of Science. Ideas keep flowing: As a result of her visit, the institution established its first branch outside London in Adelaide in October 2009, the Royal Institution of Australia. It holds forums where scientists, engineers, students, educators, media, government and industry can discuss the challenges of science in shaping the future. The Australian Science Media Centre, which was set up by the Rann government to give the media information and access to scientists, has been moved into the Royal Institution of Australia's premises.

Another idea that Adams initiated: He interviewed Geoff Mulgen, who was one of Tony Blair's chief advisors on social policy, on *Late Night Live*. Mike Rann told me, 'I brought him to Adelaide as a Thinker in Residence and he gave us the idea of establishing the Australian Centre for Social Innovation. We naturally made Phillip the chairman. Another example of the ideas chain of events was when Phillip interviewed Rosanne Hagerty, a New York expert on homelessness. We invited her here as a Thinker in Residence and the ideas she gave us led to Common Ground being set up to tackle homelessness. It has now gone national. Just as more than 30 years ago

Phillip influenced Australian film policy, the ideas and people he has introduced to us are having a profound effect on national policy in areas such as social innovation, social justice, climate change and science.'

Mike Rann said Don Dunstan used to always tell him, when Rann was his young press secretary and speechwriter, that we must always question our own assumptions and that people who always held the same beliefs show intellectual cowardice. Adams had never been an intellectual coward and had always been prepared to tackle hard issues and to support unpopular causes. That was why he was respected, said Mike. He first met Adams when he was working for Don Dunstan, who told him a lot about Adams.

'Phillip and Don set up the South Australian Film Corporation in 1972 and it was the renaissance of the Australian film industry,' Rann told me. 'Many of the corporation's films, like *Picnic at Hanging Rock, Breaker Morant, Ten Canoes* and *Look Both Ways*, have won Australian Film Industry Awards. Don was the first person in Australia to set up government-funded studios and films. If you look at the film industry today and how rich and varied it is, it came about because Phillip came to see Don Dunstan when he was South Australian premier and told him that if he wanted to get a film industry going, someone had to build facilities for it. It was Phillip who convinced Don to embrace film as an art form as well as an industry and to use film to tell the Australian story, to help define us to the world and to explain Australians to themselves. Almost every other state followed, but the idea came from Phillip,' said Mike Rann.

The ideas link: Mike said Adams' position in society is similar to the late US Senator Ted Kennedy's. During the entire Reagan Presidency, when liberalism was unpopular, Ted Kennedy had held his course and sailed against the wind, which is why he was enormously respected by politicians of both sides. Likewise, Adams had always been prepared to question not only other people's assumptions but also his own, which was critically different to most people. He had always been prepared to say 'Maybe I was wrong.' His deeply-held views had never been influenced by fads or populism. Rann said Adams had earned his enormous respect because he had always been about ideas. He asked difficult questions in the nicest way, which was why he evoked such good responses. Some other interviewers backed you into a corner. 'The great thing about being interviewed by Phillip is that he brings you into the centre of the ring and dances with you,' said Mike.

Mike Rann was born of manual-worker parents at Sidcup in Kent and in 1962 moved with them to New Zealand. He was inspired by the ideas of Don Dunstan when in 1977 he travelled from New Zealand to Adelaide to go to his brother's wedding and, while he was there, found a job in Don's Unit for Industrial Democracy later becoming Don's press secretary and then a Labor MP in 1985. In the late 1990s he married Jenny Russell and they had two children, David and Eleanor. In 2006 he married his second wife, actress and Greens MP Sasha Carruozzo. His Labor government was re-elected in March 2010 but lost two seats, with 26 seats to the Liberals' 21.

What drives Phillip Adams? 'A love of ideas and also a profound view that Australia should be a leader, not a follower,' Rann told me. 'He is deliciously naughty. When he was on the Commission for the Future, he used to chair meetings lying on his back in his lounge room, surrounded by Egyptian mummies. One moment he is serious and encouraging and the next naughty and provocative. He is simultaneously both supportive and provocative.'

* * *

A man of ideas: Anna Bligh, the Queensland Premier, was reading Adams' columns long before she met him, in connection with the Brisbane Ideas Festival. The festival was suggested by Adams and the former Brisbane Lord Mayor Jim Soorley and has been held every two years since 2000, with Adams in the chair. Adams is the Queensland Government's Ideas Advisor and he has helped plan every festival. The 2009 festival from March 25-29 had more than 50 sessions in five streams: Invention and Innovation, Development and Design, Ecology and Ethics, Action and Advocacy and Self and Society.

Anna Bligh was the 30th person I interviewed about Adams and one of the very few who I had to interview by phone, but I could feel her drive. It was in July 2009, the same month as her 49th birthday and Adams' 70th and four months after her Labor government was re-elected and Anna was re-elected Premier. She told me, 'Phillip is a man of ideas, and all political movements need to be driven by ideas. His ideas have not atrophied, which is incredibly valuable in the public life of our country and among politicians. Phillip continues to hold strong views about right and wrong and justice and injustice.'

The challenge of ideas: Anna Bligh said Adams challenges us, particularly the busier you are and the more responsibilities you take on. You had to guard against your ideas becoming stuck in the past, which meant you needed people who will challenge you with a new way of thinking. 'Phillip is a larger than life character, not only intelligent but generous with his time and ideas. He wants to be part of great community activities. For someone who has spent 70 years on the planet, he's still looking for ways to make the world better. That's very attractive to everyone. He is never condescending and does not seek to dominate people, in spite of having so much to contribute. He is just as interested in listening as talking.'

The ideas festival: Anna said Adams has driven the success of every Brisbane Ideas Festival, has used his network to encourage people to take part and broadcast some debates from every festival on *Late Night Live*. Adams himself was a big drawcard and the calibre of the festival's speakers reflected people's confidence in him.

Thriving on ideas: Adams' column in *The Weekend Australian Magazine* is one of the columns Anna Bligh said she turns to regularly because she knows it will contain something to provoke her thinking, even though she would not agree with everything in it. 'It's always intelligent and provocative and exposes me to a way of thinking or an idea that has happened in Australia or the world. I listen to *Late Night Live* now and again if I'm coming home from a function. Phillip has loomed large in the Australian landscape for a long time. He absolutely thrives on ideas and relishes debate.'

Bligh said Adams has had an influence on Labor ideas in Australia and it is hard to think of major public debates that he has not been part of. He had confronted the Labor Party with its own failings, but he did it from such a constructive framework that you were compelled to at least listen to him. He wasn't inside the party having to grapple with getting the numbers.

Anna Bligh grew up on the Gold Coast; her parents separated when she was 13; she considered becoming a nun, but the fact that the Catholic Church would not allow her divorced mother to take Communion estranged both her mother and Anna from the church. She and her husband, Greg Withers, a senior public servant, have two sons, Joe and Oliver. She is the great-great-great-great granddaughter of William Bligh, the fourth NSW Governor and captain of the Bounty, which was overthrown by mutineers in 1789.

I asked Bligh, 'As a woman, what is Phillip Adams' appeal to you? Cautiously, she replied, 'That's a leading question. As a woman, I've always felt Phillip treats me as an equal. He is interested in what I might be doing and the challenges I'm facing just as much as his own ideas. While he has a very healthy ego, it is not one — as with many men — that gets in the way of a great conversation. Ego is not a dirty word; it's a healthy thing. If I have a mind as useful as his when I am 70, I'll have nothing to worry about.'

Chapter Twelve: **Phillip Adams' Seven Women**

Phillip Adams is attractive to intelligent women as a charming, super-brainy softie who does not talk down to them. He has had particularly seven women in his life: His mother Sylvia (their relationship is covered in Chapter Two, on his childhood), his first wife Rosemary, their daughters Rebecca, Meaghan and Saskia, his current partner Patrice Newell and their teenage daughter Aurora. His relationship with each of them is intriguing. For example, Rosemary used to accuse him of having affairs with well-known personalities like Jana Wendt and Patrice has said twice on television that when she first interviewed Phillip, he was flirtatious.

While in Canberra at the National Library reading thousands of letters to Phillip stored there, I bought a transcript of an oral history the library had of two days' verbatim conversations it had recorded with Adams in 1994. He had told me about the recording and given me the necessary permission to access it.

In it Adams said he was eighteen when he met Rosemary, the beautiful sixteen-year-old girl who became his first wife. He said, 'Rosemary came out of the bohemian thread of life. I'd moved into a building in Brighton, Melbourne, where Brian Robinson (his friend) had an apartment. I had an apartment and Brian's artist mates had apartments. So we shared this mouldering pile. Brian told me he was having an affair with a girl called Julie. He hadn't come out then. I knew he was gay but he hadn't told me and he wasn't telling anybody. So often he had "handbags" and Julie was a very decorative handbag and a very amusing lady. Brian said, "Julie's wonderful but you should see her sister. Her sister is the most beautiful girl on earth." That was a bit of a build-up, wasn't it? One day I walked into one of the apartments in the building where a party was taking place and sitting on a beanbag in a corner of the room was this astonishingly beautiful human being. It had to be Julie's sister.

'I looked at her, she looked at me and I was overwhelmed by what I'd seen. I just could not believe that a human being could look so astonishing. She was excruciatingly shy, and I was this terrible young man who was a communist, so I wasn't exactly the sort of young man who respectable middle-class people would want hanging around their young daughter. Even Julie and Brian tried to prevent anything happening between Rosemary and me because I was regarded as just too wild, disreputable and unsavoury. When her parents, who were very distinguished, upmarket Brighton people, found that I was in the offing, they announced that they were going to take her to England to keep her away from me. But nothing, nothing consolidates a relationship like opposition. So Rosemary and I were destined for each other from that moment and when she was nineteen and I was twenty-one, we got married in a church.'

Adams thought the wedding was 'a bit of a hoot' and all he remembered about the ceremony was that a dry-cleaning tag was attached to the vicar's vestments with a safety pin. The reception was at the Windsor Hotel in Melbourne. Adams and Rosemary moved into a funny old two-storey house in Oakley and started an idyllic life together.

Well, as idyllic as it could be. Rosemary was, by Adams' account, excruciatingly shy and threatened by the outside world and by what Adams was doing, because he was becoming 'faintly notorious and even a bit well-known' as a result of his writing. In the oral history he remembers being invited to a house where the Australian author Xavier Herbert *(Poor Fellow My Country)* would be. Adams wanted to go but Rosemary didn't — 'she was terrified of meeting people', he said — but Adams remembers actually dragging her out of the house, shoving her into a car and driving to Mt Eliza, where Herbert 'fell in love with her and they sat and talked all night. But it was always like that. To get Rosemary out into the world required almost physical violence because she just wanted to recede.'

Rosemary had gone to finishing school in Brighton and worked as a dental nurse. She was very intelligent but was threatened by the news in the newspapers. She found people so terrifying that Adams never brought people home for dinner, and Rosemary and he didn't go out much. Some of his friends believed he was keeping beautiful Rosemary out of reach, although the truth was the opposite: he wanted her to come out into the world with him and she resisted.

They moved into a small house in Hawthorn and bought the three houses alongside it. Adams put his rapidly expanding library of books and antiquities into the other houses, knocked down the dividing back fences and built a high fence around the whole compound so the world would be kept away from Rosemary.

They had three daughters, Rebecca, Meaghan and Saskia, and Adams was glad they were daughters because 'girls don't break things and don't go to the football'. He lived quietly with Rosemary and their young family at night, but once he went out their front door on weekday mornings, he worked not only in advertising at Monahan Dayman Adams and writing *Age* columns but also took part in government committees.

He told Margaret Chalker, who interviewed him for the National Library: 'Little by little, tension started to develop because of this. I was a great dad for Rebecca, our first child, an average dad for the second and a hopeless dad for the third. By the time Meaghan and Saskia came along, I was having a public rather than a private life. Although I didn't have a lot of friends, I knew everybody. I was on the Australia Council, running the Film Board, having major shit fights with politicians, and forming alliances with Gough Whitlam (prime minister from 1972 to '75) and Jim Cairns (Whitlam's deputy PM). I was doing what I've always done, rushing around playing with things. Rosemary focused on the girls and withdrew more and more.

'Having been absolutely, scrupulously faithful for all those years, I was being accused by Rosemary of having affairs and I must say she picked some pretty good people for me. She'd always be saying, "You're having an affair with Jana Wendt", or someone else. I wasn't at all. In fact, when anything was on offer and occasionally it was, I would be very prim,' Adams said in his oral history in 1994.

'But then I worked out that if I was always going to be accused of it, I might as well do it, so it became my hobby. I became very active and I had a terrible habit of falling in love at least once a fortnight. I fell in love all the time and this didn't actually help the marriage, as you can imagine, but Rosemary rarely commented on it. She just endured it, but after a while it became untenable and my life, by then, was so public that she hated it.'

I admire Adams' honesty, if not his actions. Even highly intelligent people can fail to have adequate insight into their lives and where they might have gone wrong.

After thirty years of marriage (and after he had met Patrice Newell), Adams and Rosemary ended their marriage. 'Rosemary and I decided it was too painful to have any dealings and so we've had none,' he explained to Margaret Chalker. 'I have not seen her since then.'

Adams said in his oral history that his older daughters, Rebecca and Meaghan, understood it, were not judgmental and thought it was a good decision. They understood that the marriage, which had been great, was now painful for both their parents. But his youngest daughter, Saskia, was 'the meat in the sandwich,' he said. 'She was the one who really felt it and so she became bitter and recessive. She's fine, she's a fire-breathing little radical who's writing novels furiously but she and I have a negligible relationship.'

* * *

Adams told me the very first day I met him and convinced him to talk to me for this biography that Rosemary would certainly not meet or communicate with me and, in deference to their mother, neither would their three daughters, which meant I had to find out about them from him or other sources.

From what he told me, all three of their daughters show evidence of his nature — or nurture — by working in caring or writing occupations or both. Rebecca, who is in her late forties, studied medicine in Melbourne and later worked as an intern for a progressive Jewish magazine called *Tikkun* run by a rabbi and political activist, Michael Lerner, in Berkeley, California. ('Tikkun' is a Hebrew phrase meaning 'repairing the world' or 'perfecting the world'.) Later Rebecca rang her father from California, told him she was converting to Judaism and asked how he felt about it. He admired the magazine and the fact that, as a member of its staff, she would have contact with many progressive American Jewish contributors, such as Woody Allen. But then Rebecca told him that she and Michael were going to get married.

'I was a bit appalled,' Adams told me, 'because Michael was much older than Rebecca. I didn't think the wedding would happen — and it didn't.'

Regardless, Rebecca concluded her conversion to Judaism and phoned her father from New York City to tell him about it, again asking whether he was upset, to which he replied, 'Not as upset as if you'd become a Methodist.' Rebecca continued medical studies, became a duty psychiatrist at Mount Sinai Hospital in Manhattan and then a psychiatrist in a US Vietnam and Korean War veterans' hospital in the Bronx; she kept taking tough jobs because they could increase her chance of gaining a Green Card, which would enable her to work permanently in America. But it never came. In 2000 she returned to Australia, became a psychiatrist in private practice, went to Sweden, married a psychologist from South Africa and now practises in West Perth.

Rebecca wrote a tribute to US President Barack Obama and America in general on Page One of *Tikkun* in January-February 2009, under a photo of Australians celebrating his election: 'Thank you for what you have done for the world already. Thank you for your brave and beautiful words, which have revitalised our formally despairing and paralysed political hearts. Washington and Perth, Australia, are geographically far apart. But every day since I discovered your speeches and books a few years ago, you have been very near, in my psychiatric consulting office, as I'm sure you've been to millions of other non-Americans who love America. We love America for her energy, her creativity, her yet-unrealised possibilities, her contradictions and complexity.' Like many others, Rebecca is possibly disillusioned by President Obama's lack of progress in reform since she wrote those words.

Meaghan, Adams' second daughter, has always been involved in non-government organisations, usually focusing on people with disabilities. In 2009 she was Manager of Community Relations at the Alkira Centre, which is at Box Hill in Melbourne and cares for people with intellectual disabilities, including dementia. Alkira is an Aboriginal word meaning 'a happy place in the sun'. The Alkira website says it 'strives to meet the needs and wishes of people with intellectual difficulties through care and support, to enrich and challenge them to be part of the world community'. It recently completed a ten-year project to create seven 'ordinary homes in ordinary Box Hill streets' to house some of the people it cares for.

Saskia, Adams' youngest daughter with Rosemary, did a Monash University publishing and editing course and now works as an editor at Penguin Books in Melbourne.

Rebecca is Adams' only married daughter. None of his daughters has children.

'They are all fine women,' Adams told me, 'and all do creative, highly ethical work. I see a lot of Rebecca and Meaghan, and Saskia is a very good friend of Rory' — his teenage daughter with Patrice. 'So it's all reasonably okay.'

Adams probably suffers a normal amount of guilt for a hard-working father — guilt for not seeing his children enough when they were small and for his part in the collapse of his marriage to their mother. His children have grown up and made their way in the world; his job as a parent is done. But it's clear that he devotes a lot of thought to them and his relationship with them.

* * *

He said in his Oral History in 1994, 'I packed up and left home and ran away with Patrice Newell, who was compering an SBS public affairs program when we met. I was going to leave anyway, but Patrice was a sort of detonator. She decamped from her marriage and I from mine.' He was forty-seven; she was thirty.

In ABC Television's *Australian Story* on October 4, 2001, Patrice gave her version: 'I met Phillip when I was doing a report for SBS on the film industry. I didn't know that much about him. So I was quite taken aback when I interviewed him and he was pretty pompous and quite patronising to me. He would say things like, "Oh, Patrice, that's a silly question" ... but he was flirtatious as well.

'Phillip and I were both married at the time we met,' she continued. 'The relationship didn't come easily in that way. You had to really believe that it was worth it, to make it happen. I suppose, in the back of my mind somewhere, I knew something had happened.'

In *Australian Story* Adams recalled his first meeting with 'a rather stern young woman in a rather aggressive interview, and these are characteristics of Patrice that survive to this day — she's a stern, hardworking, to some extent humourless and rigorous person. I thought she was great fun. I think we brawled from the first time we met. We argued about everything, and I like that. Patrice is a minimalist and I'm a maximalist. By that I mean she would like to live in a world without clutter; I collect anything and everything. Aurora collects, of all things, skulls. So she and I collect and Patrice is a minimalist, surrounded by ratbags who are accumulators, an area of some tension. Our arrival in the district raised the odd eyebrow. Patrice and I have never accepted invitations to anything. I haven't been to a party for thirty years. We're deeply happy because we love the physical work and we're happy at night because I get a huge fire going. We spend as much time as we possibly can reading and talking.'

Adams continued in *Australian Story*, 'When I met Patrice, she had a little flat in Kings Cross and her only agricultural interest was a ficus plant in a terracotta pot. Within a year or so, she was running a 10,000-acre cattle property. We're both pretty intense. She's very difficult to live with. She says the same of me. I think we might have in fact murdered each other by now if we didn't have fairly long periods of apartness,' when Adams lives in Sydney during the week while Patrice lives permanently on their farm Elmswood, via Gundy, near Scone in the Hunter Valley. It's an arrangement that has worked for twenty years.

Phillip wanted me to meet Patrice at the farm, but she declined. 'She is a very formidable woman,' he explained. 'She doesn't want to have her life examined by others.'

I'm annoyed and challenged — for someone who doesn't want her life examined, she's gone about it a strange way. She has written five books about the farm and the environment; she stood (unsuccessfully) as an independent candidate endorsed by the Climate Change Coalition in the 2007 NSW Legislative Council elections; and she was at the top of the NSW ticket for the same coalition's unsuccessful tilt for the federal Senate in November 2007. The party received 0.89 % of first preferences or 0.0622 of a quota, needing 1.0 to win a seat. She did not stand in the 2010 election.

* * *

Any worthwhile news journalist, when refused information he wants, strives to find the information from other sources, and I did that by talking to several people who know her. Patrice discovered only recently that her mother was a Victorian Aboriginal woman who committed suicide and that she was adopted by the Adelaide couple who she knew as her parents, Felix Newell and Thelma Colechin. In July 2009, Adams and Patrice went to her birth mother's unmarked grave in Fawkner Cemetery in Melbourne and put a plaque on it and also visited her mother's brother in hospital. In Adelaide as a child, she lived with her adopted parents in the humble suburb of Kurralta Park, in a humble brick cottage that was back to front: The front door opened into the kitchen. But her adopted parents worked hard at low-paid jobs and the family was never hungry. Felix was a mail sorter at the General Post Office and Thelma cleaned offices and worked in a shoe factory to help pay for Patrice's schooling at St Aloysius Catholic College in Adelaide. She called them Dad and Mum, she didn't know they were not her real parents, and she always remembered her father's motto, 'Be grateful for what you've got'.

But Patrice dreamed of escaping from suburban Adelaide and planned to train as a nurse in Darwin — until Cyclone Tracy flattened the hospital and her nurse-training job on Christmas Day in 1974. While she waited in Adelaide for the hospital to be rebuilt, she applied for and got modelling work at the John Martin department store in Adelaide and appeared in their catalogues. A modelling agent saw her in a fashion parade and sought her as a client. She moved to Sydney, then, at the age of eighteen, to Melbourne. From there she travelled to Manila, Guam, Chicago, New York and other places, waitressing, modelling, promoting products and conducting interviews with celebrities for magazines. In 1980 at Niagara Falls, she married a composer, Cameron Allan, and they returned to Australia, where they rented a small flat at Kings Cross in Sydney.

Like many intelligent women who make their living from exhibiting their bodies, Patrice wanted more of a challenge than modelling and in 1982, aged twenty-six, she found a job as a Seven Network researcher in Sydney at well under half the income she had earned as a model. Soon she was reporting for Seven. Patrice handled the same problems as most people have in their late twenties. She became frustrated with her life. She wondered what life was all about.

To add to Patrice's problems, her marriage to Cameron Allan was encountering difficulties. She left him, bought her own flat in Sydney and switched from the Seven Network to SBS Television as a newsreader and current affairs host. That was when her life changed direction completely because, when doing SBS interviews for a program on the film industry, she was sent to interview Adams.

Something clicked for both of them at that interview, in spite of Adams being 17 years older than Patrice and the father of three children. Patrice stayed with SBS until 1986, when she became a presenter for the Nine Network's *Today* show.

* * *

Adams told me his own story of how, not long after they met, he and Patrice came to live at Elmswood: 'We went on immensely long drives looking at houses in isolated parts,' he said one morning. 'Neither of us had any interest in farming — that wasn't the exercise. We were driving around near Scone heading towards Belltrees, the great home of the White family, of whom Patrick was the most famous. Patrice remembered being at Belltrees as the handbag of a gay White, who needed a girlfriend for a family function.

'I saw an extraordinary house, two storeys, plonked on a hill, looking like an abandoned paddle-steamer on the Mississippi, completely out of place. I thought it was wonderful and I said, "That's where I'd like to live." So we drove in and found a strange woman planting things in the garden. I asked her whether we could have a look around, so we did, and she gave us a cup of tea. I said, "I'd like to buy your house", and made her an offer she couldn't refuse. She sold it to us for what was regarded locally as a ludicrous price, although I thought it was dirt cheap. It included about 3,000 acres. Over a hundred years it had shrunk, as old properties tend to do. Little by little, it has grown again to 10,000 acres, the title of one of Pat's books about it.' The book is *Ten Thousand Acres — A Love Story*, published by Lantern, a Penguin imprint.

'Pat got a passion for farming,' Adams continued. 'Every weekend we go out on a four-wheel bike, looking for cattle, counting calves or checking dams. We've been doing that for twenty-five years but the farm is so complex and big and full of valleys that we're still discovering new places.'

Watching Adams talk about Elmswood, I can see that the place and the life he lives there make him happy. Patrice once said, on television, that one reason she, Adams and Rory connect so well is that each of them is an only child and so is Rory. So they accept each other's loner personalities.

But they have different attitudes to their cattle and it was shown in the case of Adams' favourite bull, Malcolm X, which used to come to him for a hug across a paddock, like a puppy dog. Malcolm X was so called because he was huge and magnificently black, like the American activist of the same name. Both sadly suffered the same fate: the activist was assassinated when giving a speech in New York City in 1965; the bull was causing havoc and used to collect fences as it strolled across paddocks and was assassinated one week when Phillip was away in Sydney. Adams said it was 'the lowest point of Patrice's and my relationship'.

Despite that, Adams said in *Australian Story* that Patrice is more ethical than almost anyone he's met, a constant inspiration and challenge, determined, full of courage and with an irreverence that 'takes the piss' out of any tendency he has to be pompous, whereas he challenges her with humour.

Patrice sounds self-possessed and self-indulgent in *The Olive Grove* (Penguin, 2000), which probably pleases her readers. Each of her books had sales of between 5,000 and 6,000. She has become very attached to the property; she's proud of what she has done there and becomes emotional when nature damages her crops, especially olives. She goes for long walks alone in the bush on the property and sometimes strips off and has a swim in a dam. Adams and she have wide personality differences. For example, Adams collects things, like pieces of wood, because he likes to surround himself with things rather than people. He also has very simple food tastes, such as biscuits, while Patrice likes to cook creatively, which results in Adams being well fed with good meals when he is at home, whereas he doesn't eat much at all when in Sydney.

Aurora completed her Higher School Certificate in 2009 and in September 2010 Adams and Patrice farewelled her from Sydney Airport on her way to Edinburgh, where she will go to the university for four years. Adams wrote a good column about it in *The Weekend Australian Magazine* on September 25, 2010, a column that would appeal to parents. Obviously sorry to farewell Aurora, he told how eighteen years ago he used to sit on an old couch at the farm — 'the couch is on its last legs and we're both shabbily upholstered' — and toss Aurora as a little girl into the sky and catch her. 'But yesterday she was aloft again. She took off in a big way. Tears all round at Sydney Airport and she was flying high to Edinburgh. Her home for the next four years. Her choice of city and university. Why Edinburgh? Probably osmosis. After all, our nearest towns are Scone and Aberdeen. The homestead was built 120 years ago by Presbyterians fresh from Scotland. Our cattle are mainly Angus, the black-faced sheep would be at home in the highlands and the dogs are Border Collie crosses.

'Emotions had been running high. I took her for a last ride around the place. On a four-wheel bike, the way I have since she was a one-year-old. The place couldn't have looked lovelier. After a decade of drought we splashed through the creek and went up and down hills now lush and plush with grass,' Adams wrote. 'All the animals are having kids. The heifers are calving, the sheep giving birth to black lambs, the kangaroos to joeys. We parked on a ridge and Rory (sorry — Aurora now she's grown up) looked around at the landscape she was born into. It feels as if 18 years have passed in 18 months. Yet Rory is still here. All the Rorys. Like the ever-smaller figures in a Russian doll. The tiny Rory, the big Auroa, and all the others in-between. Little Rory, bouncing around the paddocks on the four-wheeler, laughing with her mum in the kitchen as she learned to cook, which she learned very well indeed. Listening wide-eyed to the ghost stories I made up — all the more plausible in an old house with ghosts galore. Playing with the dogs, collecting the eggs, waiting for the school bus, splashing in the rock pools and the river. Sitting reading book after book. Doing what every child does. Thinking, learning, dreaming, growing.

'And now going. All kids must go. Into an unknown future in a world with unprecedented problems. A young woman full, nevertheless, with confidence and hope. Determined to do something about those problems. Bon voyage, Aurora.'

* * *

I wanted more information about Phillip's partnership with Patrice Newell, and got it from Matt Noffs (Ted Noffs' grandson). Matt, who was thirty-one in 2010, meets Adams regularly and at one meeting, Adams asked him, 'Do you have a strong woman? You need a strong woman.' Matt Noffs told me, 'When I met Patrice, I knew what "strong" meant. Patrice is an incredibly sharp, tough, resourceful and knowledgeable woman who matches Phillip's intelligence. You can tell she's the ruler of the family. I've heard Phillip say that's why they live separately half the week, when Phillip stays in Sydney to broadcast — not so many arguments.

'When I see them together,' Noffs continued, 'they act as if they could kill each other, but they're also loving towards each other. They hold each other and adore each other. Each is trying to get the most out of life, all the time. When they're apart, it's work, and when they're together, it's family. Patrice told me Phillip's a big softie who wants people to think he's tough, which is why he's abrupt on the phone.

'Phillip told me that when Patrice wants something, she just goes for it. He's her number one advisor and she takes his advice very seriously. But it's not as if he runs anything. She runs the home and the farm.'

Chapter Thirteen: **An Edgy Friendship with Packer**

Phillip Adams and Kerry Packer were the most unlikely friends but Adams got to know Packer well enough to fathom him. He witnessed a wide range of explosive confrontations and daring ventures. Packer told Adams he was besotted with Ita Buttrose and he treated her better than some of his other women. He treated his wife Ros appallingly. Idi Amin invited Packer to come hunting elephants in Uganda and Packer wanted to breed them in Northern Australia — until Adams told him they might migrate to Perth and tread on cars in the street.

'I loathed Kerry Packer from afar,' Adams told me, 'disapproved of him utterly, as apparently he disapproved of me. I regarded him as a great lumbering Nazi and he regarded me as a vile sort of communist. But I needed ten thousand dollars to tie up the budget for a film, *The Getting of Wisdom*. I contacted Packer's office in 1977 and asked whether, the next time he was in Melbourne, he would be kind enough to drop into my office in St Kilda Road. He turned up with Harry Chester, who had been his father's bank manager and was now Kerry's mentor. Packer and I looked at each other with great suspicion and open hostility.

'I said, "Look, I need ten thousand dollars for a film you wouldn't like. Got no car chases in it, no-one gets shot but it's going to be a good film."

'He said, "I don't deal in ten thousand dollars. You can have a hundred thousand or nothing."

'We were showing each other our dicks in a ritualistic sense. I said I didn't need a hundred thousand.

'He said, "Everyone needs a hundred thousand dollars."

'I said I suppose we might ... okay.'

So Adams decided to keep going, and that was the beginning of Adams Packer Films, a venture backed by Australia's richest, toughest businessman, a King Kong capitalist, and managed by one-time communist Adams, who at the time was still in advertising but not enjoying it, and leading a hectic life writing columns and making films.

The week after striking the $100,000 deal, Adams went to Packer's office in Sydney to finalise the contract. The Tank Room outside Kerry's office was where Kerry's father, Frank, used to drink with his lieutenants after work, and Kerry continued the tradition, although he had abandoned alcohol for Passiona after surviving a fatal car crash when he was aged eighteen — he had been driving and the three others in the car were killed.

In the Tank Room with Adams and Packer that evening were David McNicoll (former *Daily* and *Sunday Telegraph* editor-in-chief and later a *Bulletin* columnist), Trevor Kennedy (*Bulletin* editor and then Packer's Australian Consolidated Press chief executive), Sam Chisholm (head of the Nine Network) and Ita Buttrose (one of Kerry's former mistresses and *Women's Weekly* editor). In Adams' words in a later article, McNicoll was Colonel Blimp, Chisholm was James Cagney and Buttrose was the Queen of Park Street, the Packer headquarters in Sydney.

Crusty David McNicoll, who had the bearing of a man who believed he was born to rule, told the gathering he'd been to Canberra to sign D-notices on behalf of Australian Consolidated Press — lists of topics that the Australian media agreed not to touch because of 'national security'. Kennedy (more recently the associate of Rene Rivkin and Graham Richardson in the Offset Alpine affair) asked whether the Petrovs, whose deflection to the Soviet Union had been a good publicity stunt for Prime Minister Robert Menzies, were still a D-notice subject. McNicoll said they were and Kennedy remarked that their whereabouts should be a *Bulletin* story.

Packer, who liked to obey the law, exploded. 'You write one word about them, Kennedy, and your arse'll hit the Park Street footpath,' he said, and started monstering almost everyone in the room. The Tank Room regulars were used to Packer explosions, although some turned white as their turn came. Adams, sitting in a corner of the room, watched it all with amazement. After it was all over Packer said to him, 'Come and have some dinner.' He felt at home in cheap Chinese restaurants and they went to one in Kings Cross.

Adams felt confident enough, with a $100,000 Packer cheque in his pocket, to take on the big man over his Tank Room behaviour. He told Kerry, 'That's the ugliest performance I've ever seen from a human being. Your tantrum was hideous. Why the hell do you yell at people?'

Packer stared into space for a long time and then said, 'Because I don't know how to talk to them.' Suddenly Adams realised that Packer was probably afflicted with the same sort of pain from his cruel father as Adams had received from his neglectful parents and violent stepfather. A terrible childhood has nothing to do with class.

They stayed at the Chinese restaurant until 3 a.m. and Packer asked Adams about a whole lot of things, including black holes.

'That's what I've got inside me, a big black hole,' Packer told Adams. The close friendship they ultimately shared revealed to each of them the fact that they had one particular thing in common: their brutalised childhoods. They even discovered that at school they had the same nickname, 'Boofhead'.

As Peter Best, the composer, told me: 'When Packer and Phillip teamed up in Adams Packer Films, Packer was the opposite of everything that Phillip stood for but there was something about Packer that Phillip liked. And, it seems, the reverse was also true.'

* * *

Adams has written a biography of Kerry Packer that has remained unpublished. He emailed me a copy. In it Adams wrote that Packer told him that he had been besotted with Ita Buttrose for a long time but couldn't find the courage to tell her; Adams found this remarkable. Finally Packer found his nerve and sent a dozen roses to her office. When he told him, Adams remarked, 'I bet her high heels made scorch marks in the carpet when she came to thank you.' Packer met his match with young Ita, whose ambition was as great as her talent. She had started off as a fifteen-year-old secretary on the *Women's Weekly*, and as *Cleo* editor had persuaded actor Jack Thompson to pose almost nude for the first issue. Packer told Adams that he didn't like *Cleo* but liked the money it made and was grateful to Ita for that. But after Ita took over editing the *Women's Weekly* and it became the world's most successful magazine for penetrating into almost half Australia's homes, Packer told Adams, 'They say it's Ita's *Women's Weekly*. It isn't. It's my *Women's Weekly*. Ita didn't make the *Women's Weekly*. The *Women's Weekly* made Ita.'

When Richard Walsh was managing director of the book company Angus and Robertson before he had the same role in Packer's magazine empire Australian Consolidated Press, he sent Adams an inflammatory novel by a senior editor fired by Ita. In it, a voluptuous editor had an affair with a powerful tycoon whose potency was not up to scratch. Walsh told Adams it would make a good film; Adams replied that he didn't think Adams Packer wanted to make a film of the novel. It never saw the light of day, but Adams believes that Pat Wheatley, Packer's PA, photocopied it and distributed a few copies around the office.

Years after Packer's affair with Ita ended, Ita rang Adams and said she was about to go into Kerry's office to tell him she was leaving to become the *Daily Mirror* editor and asked him to try to do a deal with Myer, the department store chain, for her to be its front person in television ads — an idea Phillip had put to Myer earlier but which Packer had vetoed. Adams told Ita he could hardly arrange such a deal in the hour between when

Ita quit Packer's company and signed on with Rupert Murdoch.

Adams told me, 'I phoned Packer and asked him to behave with dignity when Ita arrived to quit; later Ita told me that Packer burst into tears. Packer's relationship with Ita had not been a frivolous one for him.' In the unpublished biography, Phillip wrote that he believes that Packer loved her.

Loyalty meant everything to Packer. After Ita had later fallen out with Rupert Murdoch (it didn't take long), she started a magazine called *Ita,* but she told Adams that Packer had done all he could to hamstring its distribution. After six years, it closed.

Adams made fun of Packer, Ita Buttrose, Trevor Kennedy and David McNicoll in columns in *The Age*, *The Bulletin* and *The Australian*, some of them reprinted in his books. He devoted a whole column, called "Thomething thpecial," to Ita's well-known but now less-pronounced lisp: 'Hello. Thith ith Ita Buttrothe, editor of the Authralian Women'th Weekly, thittingb here in the thudio, thmiling at you from the thcreen ...' Many readers wrote to complain about the column and Packer was outraged , but Buttrose told Adams she thought it was hilarious.

Ita was only one of Packer's mistresses, when both were comparatively young. Paul Barry says in his unexpurgated *The Rise and Rise of Kerry Packer* (Bantam/ ABC Books) that Packer had a four-year affair with an African-American model, Carol Lopes, who killed herself in 1991. After the affair ended in the early 1980s, she organised summer bordellos in rented beach houses at Palm Beach in Sydney and arranged for prostitutes from

London, New York and South America to fly to Sydney, where they were paid $10,000 a week to service some of Packer's business and political friends. But Packer cut her off later in the 1980s and she said in a 16-page suicide note found in her apartment, 'Kerry Packer is the only family I know. He has taken care of me for twelve years. I have been denied access to him … I have no alternative but to end my life.' After Packer died, it was revealed that shares in property worth at least $10million were given to his long-time mistress Julie Trethowan, who managed the Hyde Park Club, owned by Australian Consolidated Press. She was close to him until the end of his days.

Adams told me, 'Adams Packer Films was possibly Packer's smallest company but, funnily enough, it was the only one carrying his name. It made not only *The Getting of Wisdom* but also a string of other films which were not to Packer's taste at all. One was an adaption of *Tom: A Child's Life Regained*, in which John Embling, co-founder of the Families in Distress charity I promoted, told how he tried to save a deeply disturbed schoolboy from suicide. Packer writhed during the first screening, from recognition and boredom.'

He didn't like Paul Cox's *Lonely Hearts* either, but roared with laughter when he saw *Kitty and the Bagman*, about the Sydney brothel-keeper Tilly Devine, because his father Frank used to be one of her patrons and sometimes had to escape over a back fence when police raided the premises. Tilly's arch rival in the Sydney brothel business was Kate Leigh and each owned not only a string of brothels but also sly-grog shops when Sydney hotels opened only until 6 p.m. and not at all on Sundays. They created publicity for themselves as their own spin doctors by having public fist-fights and abusing each other in the pages of *Truth* and the *Daily Mirror.* I interviewed Kate Leigh one day when she arrived at *Truth,* where I was a cadet reporter. *Truth* had far more guts than present-day Sunday newspapers and specialised in two ex-detectives exposing quack doctors, the kind of story now covered by commercial television current affairs programs.

Adams told me, 'Packer had genuine affection for Ros' (his wife) 'but he treated her appallingly and not only by having affairs, which Ros was well aware of. One night I was sitting in Packer's study in Bellevue Hill in Sydney when he abused Ros for having the room repainted — in exactly the same colours as it had been for generations.'

Adams also told me that Packer's daughter Gretel was very special to him and that they adored each other. 'She knew of her father's torments. I always thought she could take over running the company from her father. James was a gentle, soft boy with no killer instinct when he was young, although the American Al 'Chainsaw' Dunlap toughened James up when Dunlap ran the Packer empire for a time.'

*   *   *

Adams' friendship with Packer lasted for the next couple of years. They would often spend Monday nights together. Packer's personal assistant, Pat Wheatley, or his mentor, Harry Chester, would phone Adams and plead with him to come to Sydney because Packer was in another black hole or 'impossible'. They would sometimes send a plane for him.

Adams said in his 1994 oral history for the National Library, 'I started to make Packer more user-friendly; I even persuaded him to be interviewed by Michael Parkinson for British and Australian television — he was well known in Britain because of his launch of World Series Cricket. I also persuaded him to agree to be interviewed for Terry Lane's book *The Twig is Bent*. In the interview, Packer typically defended and praised the father who had brutalised him and ruined his childhood.'

Adams told me, 'Like many very rich and powerful people, he was lonely and trusted no-one. When the Seven Network planned to screen a film called *Holocaust*, he told Sam Chisholm, the boss of Nine, to screen a rival documentary about the Holocaust in the same timeslot, not because he cared or knew anything about the Jewish Holocaust — it was just to spoil Seven's film.

'I told Packer, "You don't muck about with the Holocaust. It's not just another program."

'Packer replied, "Son, what's the Holocaust?"

'I told him about it. He hadn't read about it, or if he had, it had not made any impression. He was far more interested in football, gambling, TV dramas and Chinese restaurants. He knew nothing about world affairs except that few Australians cared about them. When Russian soldiers invaded Afghanistan, he told me, "The Russians will clean up those fucking Afghans in ten minutes." As time would tell, the Afghanistan mujahedeen cleaned up the Russians but the war continues today.'

Adams said Packer regarded himself as hideous. He had a particular hate of trade unions. Packer, the adman John Singleton and broadcaster John Laws organised an anti-union petition. Adams told Packer, 'You don't know anything about trade unions', and one night took him to the gloomy Melbourne Trades Hall, where the sight of Packer caused as much astonishment as if Hitler had been spotted in London. They climbed the stone stairs scarred by generations of hobnailed boots and Adams made Packer read a memorial to the battle for an eight-hour day. Then, typically, they went to a Chinese restaurant in Little Bourke Street.

Packer chose the Imperial Peking at The Rocks in Sydney for Trevor Kennedy's fortieth birthday. Bob Hawke and Paul Keating, who were at the time jostling for the Labor Party leadership, were there. Packer said. 'My father would turn in his grave to see me here tonight surrounded by Labor riffraff, but they're more fun than the Liberals.' Adams told the birthday party that he had first met Trevor at Oxford, 'where Kerry Packer was doing his PhD in greed'. Twenty years later, when relationships between Keating and Packer had soured, Keating used the same line.

* * *

When Adams and Patrice bought a farm not far from Packer's huge Ellerston property at Scone in New South Wales, Packer arrived at their place in a helicopter and told them to hire his manager's brother to run it (they did) and to get a cattle dog. Packer even told them a well-worn story of how to choose a cattle dog: 'Get a litter of pups and throw an empty tin at them. They'll run off yelping. The first one that comes back to sniff the tin — that's your dog.'

Adams said, 'Kerry, that must be the way you choose your executives.'

His strongest memory of Packer is the 'black hole' conversation. His regret is that Packer never used his great wealth and power for any great purpose. He made billions from two licensed addictions, television and gambling, but didn't leave behind a foundation or a university. Kerry Packer died aged sixty-eight on Boxing Day 2005 and is buried on his Ellerston property.

One of the most critical points Adams made about Kerry Packer in his unpublished book on him was: 'Australia did a lot for Kerry but in the final analysis, what did Kerry do for Australia? Kerry cracked it for his first billion when he sold the Nine Network (largely his father Frank's creation) to an over-eager Alan Bond. It was a licence to print money.' He was the most skilled and successful television proprietor and programmer in Australia's history. The network started to decline when Packer became terminally ill and has never recovered.

One of the more complimentary points Adams made about Packer in the book was: 'He was like King Kong, but he had a sensitive side. He was insatiably curious about everything, intensely loyal to the handful of people he felt he could trust and determined to be a better father to James and Gretel than Frank had been to him and his brother Clyde.'

The book told where Adams and Kerry used to meet: 'He came to my (previous) home in Melbourne a couple of times and later to our farm in the Upper Hunter, but mostly we'd meet in the gloomy Packer mansion in Bellevue Hill, Sydney, shadowed by giant Morton Bay fig trees and protected by security men and Rottweilers, or in the suite he had inherited from his father at the Australia Hotel in Melbourne, or we'd talk for half the night at one of the secret apartments he had bought around Sydney for R & R.'

They often compared their childhoods: 'Like me, Kerry would try to gain approval from his school class by provoking teachers with smart-alec comments. Where we differed was that Kerry had bounced back from polio to become remarkably good at sport whereas I was absolutely bloody hopeless. Kerry happily conceded that he was academically stupid but used to play everything. At school, he lived for sport.'

'Kerry used to ask me how I defined a friend, and answer it himself: "A friend is someone who stands beside you when you're in the wrong."

'My friendship with Kerry faded after we became neighbours in the Hunter Valley. There was no row, no yelling. It was just that Kerry was high maintenance and I got busier. He'd phone me occasionally, write me a thank you note for something, and became a billionaire. My strongest memory remains his "black hole" conversation all those years ago.'

Adams in his office in Paddington, Sydney, where the author interviewed him for about 40 hours over three years. The office walls are full of portraits, prints, books and antiquities from Adams' collection, Australia's largest private collection of antiquities. The rest of his collection (see Chapter 21) is stored elsewhere, including his home, Elmswood, at Grundy, in the NSW Hunter Valley.

(Photo: Bob Finlayson, News Ltd, 2005.)

NSW Central Coast artist Peter Smeeth's entry for the Archibald Prize showed Adams in his Sydney office. Smeeth was a GP until 2007, when he became a full-time artist. Victorian-born artist Wes Walters won the 1979 Archibald Prize with a portrait of Adams.

(Photo: Waide Maguire, News Ltd.)

Adams, Don Morris (centre) and Brian Monahan announcing the merger of Monahan Dayman Adams with another highly-successful Australian-owned ad agency, Mojo, on July 24, 1986, when Adams was 47. Three years previously, he, Monahan and their partner Lyle Dayman had floated MDA on the stock exchange. Mojo was owned by Don Morris and his brother Alan (the 'Mo' of Mojo) and Allan 'Jo' Johnston. In 1989, Adams and his partners received the lion's share of a $77million takeover from Chiat-Day of Madison Avenue, as outlined in Chapter 3.

(Photo: ACP Magazines. The Southern Cross on the Australian flag is to the right of the picture.)

Cartoonist Alex Stitt (left) drew the cartoons for both the 'Life. Be in it' and 'Slip! Slop! Slap!' community advertising campaigns which were devised by Adams partly to overcome his feeling that he was 'supping with the Devil'. (Chapter 3) Both campaigns became legendary.

(Photo: Swinburne University of Technology.)

Adams gave the author this photo of him with Gough Whitlam. He said, 'When Gough says, "I'm the greatest," it sounds okay, but not when it appears in print. Gough really believes he is the greatest. He ran a shambles of a government, but he's hard not to like. He loves food as fuel — it doesn't matter what the food is.' When Adams wanted to interview Whitlam for Late Night Live, *he took along some 'disgusting' cakes and custard tarts. Whitlam scoffed the cakes while Adams interviewed him. 'It looked like Mount Vesuvius erupting.' (See Chapter 9)*

Kevin Rudd (right) fell out of favour with the Labor Party and some voters but not with Adams, shown here with Robert Macklin at the June 2007 launch of Macklin's Kevin Rudd: The Biography *(Penguin). Adams was the first columnist or broadcaster to promote Rudd as Labor leader and prime minister and secured the first major interview, on* Late Night Live *in August 2010, with Rudd after he was knifed as prime minister.*

(Photo: David Sproule, Herald Sun.)

(5)

SECRET

File No: VPF 11844

15th July, 1965

MINUTE for File

ADAMS, Phillip Andrew A/25/64 [redacted]

The above named is presently employed by Paton Advertising Service, 18 Albert Road, South Melbourne. He is in charge of the Television production department.

[redacted] (A.S.I.O.) had in mind approaching ADAMS [redacted] would first appreciate [redacted] assessment.

3. [redacted] stated that ADAMS was a highly intelligent, extremely egotistical, intellectual left winger who lacked basic stability and could not be trusted to keep a confidence of the nature I had in mind.

He said ADAMS would actually consider any approach by A.S.I.O. a huge joke, would possibly play along with us for awhile, but would eventually be unable to resist discussing the matter with others. He said that ADAMS gave the indication that he failed to treat with proper seriousness those loyalties which we considered normal.

4. [redacted] said that he had no knowledge whether or not ADAMS had Communist sympathies, but as regards asking him to assist us in our work he personally would very strongly recommend in the negative.

[redacted]

S. SECTION

[redacted]

Headquar

(SF

[redacted] ✓

SECRET

F. ...ion and record. [redacted]

PA

REGIONAL DIRECTOR, VICTORIA
16/7/65

This 'secret' ASIO (Australian Security Intelligence Organisation) report in 1965 says Adams, who had then just turned 26, was a 'highly intelligent, extremely egotistical, intellectual left-winger' but would treat any ASIO approach to work for it 'a huge joke.' As usual, ASIO has obliterated all sources of its information. Adams joined the Communist Party aged 14 but quit when Russia invaded Hungary in 1956. Other amusing ASIO reports from the National Archives seen by the author: 1) List Adams as chairman of a Victorian Fellowship of Australian Writers seminar in 1971, with speeches by Bruce Petty, Barry Humphries and Professor Leonie Kramer; 2) List Adams as being on the mailing list of the Congress for International Co-operation and Disarmament in 1970; 3) Said a Mrs Jean McLean had reported that Adams was going to help her with advertising a 'Save Our Sons' (from the Vietnam War) meeting in 1966; 4) Report that Adams was the honorary vice-president of the Humanist Society of Victoria in 1972.

Adams helped instigate both ideas festivals in Adelaide and Brisbane, each of them held every two years. Anna Bligh, the Queensland Premier, told the author, 'Phillip is a man of ideas and all political movements need to be driven by ideas.' He is shown here addressing the Brisbane festival, which he has done every two years since it was started in 2000 after Jim Soorley, as Lord Mayor of Brisbane, asked Adams whether he would help launch a Brisbane festival like the Adelaide one. (Chapter 11) He has chaired every Brisbane festival.
(Photo from the Ideas Festival, Arts Queensland.)

Adams at the 'What Makes a Champion?' event opened by Nelson Mandela in 2000, when Dame Leonie Kramer (centre) was Chancellor of Sydney University. The event was sponsored by the University's Centre for the Mind, launched by Professor Allan Snyder (right), one of Adams' most vocal champions.
(Photo: Centre for the Mind.)

Adams said in his National Library oral history: 'I packed up (in 1986) and left home and ran away with Patrice Newell, who was compering an SBS public affairs program when we met. She decamped from her marriage and I from mine.' He was 47; she was 30. Newell said in a 2001 ABC Television Australian Story about them, 'When I interviewed him, he was pretty pompous and quite patronising to me…But he was flirtatious as well…In the back of my mind somewhere, I knew something had happened.' Adams told the same program, 'She's a stern, hardworking, to some extent humourless and rigorous person. I thought she was great fun.' (Chapter 12)

(Photo: Domino Postiglione, Fairfax.)

The one-time model and television interviewer Newell says the biggest change in her life was being outside. When she met Adams, her only agricultural experience was caring for a ficus plant in a pot at her King's Cross flat. Within a year or so, she was running a 10,000-acre farm. Adams says that if they did not have fairly long periods apart they 'might have murdered each other' because they are so different. (Chapter 12)

(Photo: Quentin Jones, The Sydney Morning Herald.*)*

Patrice Newell and Aurora, her daughter with Adams, and Badger, in 2006 on the veranda of their farm home, Elmswood, at Gundy, near Scone, NSW.
In September 2010, Adams and Newell farewelled Aurora, who will study at Edinburgh University for four years.

Newell with two of their dogs, Bella and Rose, at Elmswood. Some of Adams' best columns have been about their dogs, such as Annie, a Jack Russell that, 'like the little girl who had a curl in the middle of her forehead, was sometimes excruciatingly good, but when she was bad, she was the Hound of the Baskervilles.' (Chapter 19)

(Photos: Dean Osland, Newcastle Herald.*)*

Adams had no interest in collecting artifacts until he was walking down Bond Street in London with Barry Humphries in 1972 and saw, in a shop window, a little blue amulet the size of a fingernail with a card on it saying it was Egyptian, four thousand years old and cost ten pounds. It now sits on a shelf in his office. Since then, he has accumulated Australia's largest private collection of antiquities, totalling 4,100 objects according to this catalogue. (Chapter 21) His favourite is Egyptian art because of its serenity — the eyeline is beyond you and beyond the horizon because the Egyptians looked to eternity.

Chapter Fourteen: **Bob Ellis on the Intellectual Santa Claus**

I am sitting in a coffee shop on the ground floor of a Sydney city building, waiting for Bob Ellis, the legendary literary figure, screenwriter and Labor Party stalwart. It has taken me weeks to get Ellis to agree to meet me about Phillip Adams. I don't think it's because he's reluctant to talk; it's just the way he is. We are meeting at this building because he said he'd be there writing speeches for a Labor Party figure.

When I arrived at the café I called him, as agreed.

'I'll be down soon,' he said and hung up.

Half an hour later, I was still waiting. So I called again.

'I'll be down soon,' he said once more.

My hopes weren't high. But I waited anyway, for another half-hour and reviewed my notes on Ellis.

In June 2004, George Negus, in an ABC Television program *George Negus Tonight,* affectionately described Bob Ellis as 'a wise old romantic fool'. On the program Ellis said, 'I fell in love a great deal at Sydney University and I proposed, I think, to fourteen girls, knowing they'd say no, but liking the thrill.' Bob's wife, the screenwriter and novelist Anne Brooksbank, was one of the many girls who fell for him and she told the program, 'We were both twenty-three at the time and he was very skinny.' (He certainly isn't now.) 'He had a sort of intensity and an intellectual attack and he could make you laugh.' Others who attended Sydney University at the same time as Bob, in the 1960s, were Clive James, Bob Hughes, Germaine Greer, former Justice Michael Kirby and Bruce Beresford. George Negus ended the program by saying, 'Don't stop being Bob Ellis, not that I think there's much chance of that, do you?' Bob replied, 'No chance.' He is a poetic ratbag, although well worth listening to and reading.

Suddenly Ellis is in the coffee shop, all moveable chaos and rumpled shirt, and he motioned me towards a table as far away from the other patrons as possible.

As we sat down, I said, 'I'll hold the tape recorder close to you so the background noise doesn't get in the way.'

Without saying anything, Ellis took the tape recorder from me and held it to his mouth. I didn't even have to ask a question — he just proceeded to talk.

'Phillip Adams is the best in the world, in all of history, at what he does, the best interviewer, brow to brow, of the greatest intellects of our time. He meets, as an equal, Henry Kissinger, Arthur Miller, whoever, and gives them an intellectual run for their money.'

I raised my eyebrows at the superlatives but didn't have a chance to say anything. The Ellis charge continued. This is the easiest interview I've ever done.

'Phillip, who never went to university, runs what I call our spare university, *Late Night Live,* with the most user-friendly Australian voice and accent. He is quite remarkable. And when he vanishes one night from the earth, people will be amazed at what they've lost. They've come to take him for granted as a kind of intellectual Santa Claus.

'There is none like him. He has the combined gifts of Michael Parkinson and Malcolm Muggeridge. He covers both ends of the spectrum. I'm a writer and the hardest thing to achieve as a writer is clarity. The greatest writers have clarity above all and Phillip has that clarity. There is never a doubt as to where he is in his mind and where you are following him. He goes to depths and shadows and ambiguities and heights that you can't imagine can happen on mere radio in a mere conversation with a stranger, often a person he has not grappled with before, and often in another country.'

Even though I suppressed a laugh at Ellis's ability to talk without seeming to draw breath, I was also impressed by his verbal dexterity. While I agreed with the tenor of what he's saying about Adams, he's no slouch himself. And he continued, not knowing my thoughts because I have no chance to express them.

'Phillip rode Howard fatigue, as Julian Burnside called it, over all those eleven years of torture, wrongful imprisonment, invasion and death. It hurt him, as it hurt me. His survival as an ABC broadcaster was narrowly achieved. Howard told the ABC to sack Phillip in 1997 or 1998. Phillip rang me, and over the next thirty-six hours my wife Anne and I rang everyone and asked him or her to ring and write to the ABC. It saved him. Phillip told us we were his campaign managers. Once Phillip survived, it followed that Kerry O'Brien' (the then presenter of *Lateline* on ABC Television, and later presenter of *The 7.30 Report*) 'survived. Two critical people survived in the most critical ingredient in our democracy, the ABC. It was close and scary. Never underestimate Howard's capacity for manipulation. At another time he said,

"What we need is a right-wing Phillip Adams", but what he meant was, "We need Phillip Adams erased from the Australian consciousness". Howard's one purpose in life, and to some extent the Liberal Party's purpose, is to get a result. For example, Kim Beazley got 400,000 more votes than Howard in 1998 and Howard called that a mandate for the GST.'

Ellis was clearly enjoying this chance to talk about Adams — or perhaps he just likes talking. He galloped on.

'*Late Night Live* is an equality of discourse, an assumption that you won't get left behind, that you are as acute an observer as he is. Kevin Rudd spread his phone calls around, before and after he was made federal Labor leader. He spoke to Phillip and he spoke to me. He was a notorious leaker, conniver, conspirator and flatterer. Rudd has the absolute equivalent of an ABC voice. He's like a prefabricated ABC newsreader, with no natural accent.

'When I was pro-Kim Beazley — and I still am — Phillip was pro-Rudd, because he believed Beazley had dropped the ball over Tampa.' Ellis was referring to the incident in 2001 involving Afghan refugees who were picked by a Norwegian freighter, the Tampa, after their boat to Australia became distressed. John Howard's federal government used the issue to inflame anti-immigrant sentiment and make it a key election issue. 'But by campaigning as guilefully as he did, Beazley saved Rudd in his seat.'

* * *

Bob Ellis drew breath and continued, 'Phillip's influence on the Labor Party is less strong now. I put the critical years as 1968 to 1976 or '77. He got the film industry up after befriending John Gorton. He mounted a campaign to dislodge Whitlam and install Jim Cairns and he wrote Cairns' speeches, thereby nettling Whitlam.'

Ellis believes that it will be five years before the Labor Party gets out of the mess it got into over the Tampa. 'It was a shocking matter,' he said. 'Those couple of months turned many Labor voters into Greens supporters.

'Because Phillip was of that camp, he was regarded as unrealistic and unable to count the number of seats we would lose. He said he didn't care how many; we had to save our integrity. It did matter. If we had lost Rudd's seat — which we would have, if we had followed Phillip's advice — we would still be in the Howard era and festering in a squalor of self-contempt and we would maybe not have got out of it.'

Ellis paused to take a sip of water.

'His double act with Barry Jones was wonderful, over films and over ideas. I wish he'd done more film production. He was brilliant at it. He became a film bureaucrat rather than a producer. During his expensive divorce from Rosemary and his acquisition of most of the antiquities of Egypt, plus a great deal of money (from selling his share of Monahan Dayman Adams) and a Rolls-Royce, he lost perspective until he became a full-time ABC broadcaster. There was a gap of six or seven years when he became self-indulgent. He was a womaniser and a quite successful and secretive one for a good few years before he met Patrice. I heard it so constantly that he had affairs towards the end of his first marriage that

I believed it. I first met him in about 1966 and went to the house in Melbourne where he lived with Rosemary. She was not intellectual.' It was a cruel way to dismiss Rosemary.

'Everyone feels intimate with him but no-one really knows him,' said Ellis. 'He doesn't go to parties much, never carouses, never drinks. *Late Night Live* is a gift. But we'll be surprised by the strangers at his funeral because he has so many relationships, conducted by phone, letter and email. In friendships, he skips like a stone over the water. And like many great men, he dominates any conversation he's in. Kenneth Tynan once said about Ernest Hemingway, "Ernest not only closes the subject but sits on the lid", and Phillip is the same. He is driven by a tormented childhood, a hated father, a curious upbringing with his grandparents, and a lack of formal education. What do these people have in common with him: Charles Chaplin, Ingmar Bergman, William Shakespeare, Charles Dickens, Judy Davis, Noel Coward, Tom Stoppard and Alfred Hitchcock? No university education, although each of them seems to have one. People without a university education often have a *Brideshead Revisited* vision of what they've missed. So Phillip is constantly striding through his undergraduate years long after others have left them behind. He's still an undergraduate. It's like an ongoing tutorial that he's in, every night.

'No-one treats interview subjects as well. We're in an age when very shallow women ask you about your sex life, or something, by way of interview. If you're ever unfortunate enough to turn on Channel Nine, you'll see what I mean. Phillip is the majestic exception to the others. He's comfortable in his own skin and confident of his abilities. But he's aware that he's not an artist in the usual sense, although he's perhaps the most-read columnist in our history. He's never done what he threatened to do, go to Sardinia and write a great big bloody novel or something like that. I think he's a little ashamed of his spiflicated attention span in that he doesn't last long in any one place or discipline. His ideal venue is to be out of town chairing an ideas festival and having coffee afterwards with the speakers. He's secretly convivial and doesn't know it. He actually enjoys crowds but he's so infrequently in them that it doesn't occur to him that it's what he most enjoys. He likes to be the life of the party but doesn't go to parties. He's a gregarious recluse. I'm like that, too. I'm never happier than when I'm alone in a Chinese restaurant reading a book review. But if I go to a writers' festival, I'm over the moon with the company.

*   *   *

'Phillip preaches to the converted but every now and then a person he has interviewed changes our thinking. There are fewer fundamentalist Christians around because of him: the people who listen to him talk to their families, and so on. Today I have been re-reading *The God Delusion* by Richard Dawkins. Dawkins came into our consciousness through Phillip. These are subtle influences but they are real. We are immensely a better country because of Phillip. And we're a worse country because of John Howard. The rollback of decency is happening partly because of Phillip and largely because of the extraordinary impact and reach of the ABC which, especially in country towns, has civilised Australia over the past fifty years.

'Phillip once made an interesting concept and it has passed into the language. He said a referendum on capital punishment might be won by the people who want capital punishment, but you had to measure the intensity and the thoroughness of the thought that went into the votes. And the votes from the left would always, by that measure, be greater. The total intensity of belief and intellectual wrestling would always outweigh that of the right, which was always shallow.'

Ellis and Adams were both contributors to *Nation Review*, the weekly newspaper which was founded by the quixotic transport magnate Gordon Barton and from 1970 caught a wave of left-wing, anti-establishment feeling until materialism (and a materialistic shortage of advertisers) killed it in 1981. Other left-wing contributors to *Nation Review* included Mungo MacCallum, Michael Leunig, Germaine Greer and Francis James.

'Phillip and I meet from time to time over the years,' Ellis said. 'He is always over-amusing. He treats our meetings as if he was compering a comedy show. One night I got really drunk and we had a whole hour on *Late Night Live*. I can't remember what was said but Bob Carr, who was not yet the New South Wales premier, rang up and said it was the best night of radio he had ever heard. Clearly we did something right. I've never been as good with Phillip since and I get a little irritated by his man from America' (he means Bruce Shapiro) 'who talks at such length over matters of no great significance. There is a kind of intimacy. Some friends who don't see each other for years on end have an instant intimacy. I see

Germaine Greer maybe once every five years, but the conversation resumes at the same level. There is little diffident politeness at the beginning of our conversation. We just pick up where we left off. Phillip and I are like that.

'Phillip is a year and a half older than me, or something.' In fact, Phillip was born in 1939 and Bob in 1942. 'We're both overweight and aware of our mortality. We're both privately scared of death. I wish I saw more of him, but these days you can catch up just by pressing a button on a computer. I feel unworthy to interrupt whatever he's doing. He's very abrupt. He ends the conversation when he wants to. But consider what he might have done. Imagine he was in the Senate and he was the font of ideas. It's also true of Kerry O'Brien. These broadcasters, who are touched by the best minds, are always the best-informed people. They're not just well read, they've done this brow-to-brow thing, and what a loss they are to politics! In Britain, there are some people who are both broadcasters and politicians.

'But you have to address the question as to whether Phillip is lazy or not. You can be active and also lazy. He's never written a significant book, and I've written twenty.' I smile at this small evidence of hubris. 'He's not a writer in the way you understand writing. He doesn't enjoy words as much as he pretends to do. His *Australian* columns don't have as much impact as *Late Night Live* has, because no-one in his camp reads *The Australian.* If Phillip would still be writing for *The Age* and also for *The Sydney Morning Herald*, it would have improved his attack and his impact. Writing for *The Australian* is like not writing at all, because it's so corrupted by Rupert

Murdoch's will to reduce the western world's intelligence. Phillip gets lost in the wash.'

Bob Ellis abruptly handed back my tape recorder and shuffled off out of the building. I felt a little bit like I'd been mugged, but, like George Negus, I hope Bob Ellis goes on being Bob Ellis. He is a good writer, sometimes a bit hard to take, but he adds a distinctive taste to Australian society.

Chapter Fifteen: **Late Night Intercourse**

Phillip Adams aggressively flatters his highly-qualified *Late Night Live* guests, in spite of what The Wizard of Oz told Dorothy, 'Professors have no more brains than other people, but they have a Diploma, and generals have a Medal.' In 2011, Phillip Adams has been presenting the program for 20 years and the ABC will all the year promote the anniversary on-air and hold functions attended by Adams in all capital cities. Gail Boserio, *LNL*'s acting executive producer, issued a statement late in 2010 outlining celebrations of the 'extraordinary milestone', stressed that the program is 'all about ideas' and added: 'Phillip Adams' experience as a broadcaster, his innate curiosity, his passion for ideas and wicked sense of humour have not only guaranteed compulsive listening but ensured an impressive rapport with people from every walk of life.' *LNL*'s audience of more than 350,000 people is rising. Worldwide it's a unique program. This chapter tells how it's done.

Adams is too nice to his guests and interrupts them too much although no-one is better at making their audience feel the presenter is talking only to them. But the program *works* and the internet is taking it around the world. Adams told me, 'I assume familiarity and try to make people laugh, no matter how serious the subject is. Once people have even chuckled, they're human again.'

There are not many laughs on *Late Night Live*. Certainly there are some chuckles and many smiles and Adams tries (sometimes too hard) to turn them into laughs, thus giving the program a cheeky irreverence, even when discussing topics that are important, as most of them are. He believes being light about serious subjects does not diminish them, but makes them bearable. James Lovelock, a scientist and environmentalist, was once on-air with Adams to discuss potentially millions of people dying from global warming. It was so depressing that Adams started to laugh. Then Lovelock laughed with him.

The best *Late Night Live* sessions are conversations, not interviews, and this has been a big reason for its success, plus Adams' ability, knowledge and devotion to the program (even after twenty years), the wide range of usually provocative subjects and guests chosen by his producers and his ultra-conversational style. Adams tries hard to break down barriers, to himself, to whoever he is talking to and to their audience — as if two people are talking to a third at dinner.

* * *

The third person became known as Gladys one night when Adams said on-air that he had only one listener, Gladys, and they were going around to her place. Some ABC executives chastised him for talking down to the audience, but he made Gladys such a permanent feature that he often introduces programs by saying, 'Hello to all the Gladdies and Poddies.'

'Gladdies' have nothing to do with the 'gladdies' (short for gladioli) which Dame Edna Everage throws to theatre audiences. 'Poddies' are the rapidly-increasing number of *LNL* podcast listeners. Adams once welcomed another listener, a one-year-old baby whose mother told Adams by email that she listens in Hobart while suckling her new son, George. Adams called the new listener category, 'Titties'. In 2010, he added another listener, 'Noddy' after a young boy sent him an email. With Gladys apparently the only listener to what Adams often calls 'our little wireless program', inevitably some people invited to speak ask how many listeners *LNL* has. In 2010, the cumulative audience (the number of people who told Nielsen Research they had listened to the program in the past week) was 98,000 for the night session and 135,000 for the repeat, a total of 233,000, in Sydney, Melbourne, Brisbane, Adelaide and Perth. But Radio National is also broadcast in 220 other cities and towns rarely or never audited such as Canberra, Hobart, Newcastle, Wollongong, Ballarat, Albury-Wodonga, Townsville and Rockhampton. So *LNL*'s total audience would be more than 350,000. Only two Australian daily newspapers, the Melbourne *Herald Sun* and Sydney *Daily Telegraph*, have bigger circulations. *Late Night Live* is the top program on Radio National, with 7.8 per cent of audiences in the five mainland state capitals, and is only third in all ABC Radio programs in spite of ABC Local Radio having a much broader audience than Radio National.

Who are *LNL*'s listeners? It's very interesting. Ninety per cent are aged 40 or more; 55 per cent are female; a massive 65 per cent hold university degrees; 36 per cent have annual household incomes of up to $50,000 while 20 per cent have incomes of $110,000 plus; 40 per cent are in 'AB' (high level) occupations (for example, white collar professionals); and 45 per cent are not in the workforce — they have retired or have home duties but are not unemployed. Melbourne has a slightly bigger audience than Sydney. But the boom in *LNL's* podcast listeners is the big news and has turned it into an international program. In August 2010, the program was downloaded 217,463 times, third among all ABC programs after *New Music* on Triple J and *AM* on both Radio National and Local Radio. Three-quarters of the downloads are in Australia, 6 per cent in the USA and 3 per cent in Britain. The ABC management is impressed.

A podcast listener who had been four months in Hamburg from Sydney emailed *LNL* to say she listens each day at the same time as her father listens in Brisbane and asked Adams to give him a 75th birthday greeting, which he did. One, teaching English in Japan, said he always tunes in 'over coffee and misty eyes'. A listener in Poland said *LNL* helps him to improve his English and this shows how podcast technology makes the world smaller. One in Chile said *LNL* 'remains the most intelligent update on the continuing comedy known as Down Under'; one in the Czech Republic listens on a bus taking him to a school where he teaches English. Another in Kenya chided Adams for not mentioning Poddies in Africa. One listens while working night shifts in an English supermarket. Another email, which Adams mentioned on-air, told how 'Gladys, of Perth' went to hospital to have a baby, her husband forgot to pack birth music, so the nurses brought her a radio, she listened to *LNL* and as the final music came on, gave birth. Her family now calls Adams 'Uncle Phil'.

* * *

Adams' conversation on-air is as casual as it is off-air, spiced with Australian slang and occasional swear words. He likes stirring the possum: he obviously enjoyed having an on-air conversation with the author of a book about US place names such as Squaw Tit, Shithouse Mountain and Whorehouse Meadow. He never uses 'Mr', 'Dr' or 'Professor' but introduces people by their first and last names, then adds their qualifications and continues using their first names. If an academic comes from an overseas university, he asks them who their university was named after and this slows them down and makes them more conversational. He's inquisitive rather than interrogative and this natural curiosity makes for a better experience for his guests.

LNL, like any broadcast program, has to be kept moving but Adams deliberately talks slowly on-air because he's found that radio requires a slower pace so listeners can take in the thoughts and ideas. That's also what he's found when chairing public forums. His main aim is to make the program enjoyable and informative; he wants to go off-air knowing more than when he went on-air and for listeners to do the same. But his relaxed on-air style is not often easy to achieve: most of his on-air conversations are with people in another ABC studio or on the 'dog and bone', as he calls it, and this means he can't read their body language and react accordingly. If they pause during the conversation, he wonders whether they have slipped off their chair.

The main reason *LNL* is viewed as left-wing is Adams' left-wing views, which he never hesitates to give. He often mentions that the former prime minister, John Howard, declined to appear on the program. Why advertise a failure? Appearing humble is part of Adams' style. But he is one of the very few left-wing Australian media commentators or writers.

He is a conversationalist, not an interrogator: he doesn't grill people but prefers to let their views stand, even if he disagrees. His program presents ideological subjects with him as a moderator, not a player. He has never told his producers he doesn't want a certain person on the program. Some people he's had spats with have come back on, although there is a fairly long list of people who won't appear.

Chris Bullock, who was the program's executive producer until he was switched to another program in 2010, told me Adams is easy-going and easy to work with. 'He's not demanding. After all, he's been around for a long time and doesn't have to prove anything. He knows *LNL* back to front. He's comfortable with what he does, likes doing it and has developed a warm relationship with listeners, with the program and with many guest speakers, some of whom return years later and find that Phillip remembers their last conversation. Even if the guests disagree with his views, they want to have on-air discussions with him because he doesn't try to impose his views on them and also because of his large audience. Many guests, for example, have just published books and jump at the chance. The conversational *LNL* format is what attracts many listeners. It is relaxed compared with current-affairs programs, at times of the evening (10.05 p.m.) and afternoon (the 4.05 p.m. rebroadcast next day) when listeners are starting to slow down. No other program in Australia, the United States or Britain is as personable.'

Bruce Shapiro, who has been the program's US correspondent for the past 12 years, told me on a visit to Sydney that *LNL* is unique in the English-speaking world: 'Phillip is far more subtle that US broadcasters. I can't think of any broadcaster in America or Britain who brings such a combination of intellectual subtlety, craft and connections to the listener. Phillip is one of the greatest interviewers of English-language radio. The way listeners are invited into the program makes it different from any other. It's a powerful program and I always encourage Americans invited to take part, to do so. The guests are shown respect, and the intimacy Phillip has between him and his guests and his listeners is remarkable. But we mustn't neglect his producers' hard work and dedication to getting the right guests and the right background.'

Each week, Shapiro sends the producers an email saying where he'll be for his usual Tuesday night slot and suggests topics he could talk about. The producers also suggest topics. But Adams likes to make a game of it and sometimes asks Shapiro something not on the radar. Adams is good at creating a dramatic structure so the listener is taken by the hand at the start and walked through the program. It's expertly crafted. The story-telling craft of having an underlying argument is the big secret challenge of doing good radio. It's rare and invisible to the listener. Few broadcasters master structured conversations on-air. Shapiro writes a column in *The Nation* in the US and is executive director of the Dart Center for Journalism and Trauma, a resource think-tank for journalists covering violence and tragedy.

* * *

The most common criticism of *LNL* is that Adams interrupts his guests too much. He also sometimes talks too much before introducing them. He has a lot to say on many subjects; he has a good memory of a rich life and brings some of those experiences into on-air conversations, often while his guest is talking. His producers talk to him about this habit of interrupting guests and give him the emails complaining about it, but to no avail. Other listeners complain about his left-wing views; some say they don't agree with his views but like hearing his guests. The listeners who complain most strongly claim he has sold out to the right wing. Others accuse him of making fun of serious subjects. As an example of the many ratbag complaints, The 9/11 Truth Movement attacks him because he doesn't believe its claim that 9/11 was a conspiracy.

Sometimes Adams' producers wonder why he spends more time talking to one person and less on another, or takes the program in a particular direction. They discuss these matters with him but ultimately see it as his program and believe he knows what listeners want to hear. It is up to Adams to decide which questions to ask; his producers suggest questions and he may ask them, or he may take the conversation in another direction.

Adams, not his producers, carries the program and they will not tell him what to say.

LNL's presentation style and content have not changed over the years except that, while the standard program still has three stories, there are more one-hour conversations on a single subject with one, two or three guests, usually in three different locations around Australia or the world. The only people *LNL* avoids having on-air are the celebrities who fill popular magazines, and it has few politicians, as they are current-affairs fare. Not only John Howard but also Kim Beazley won't talk to Adams. He has fallen out with Bob Hawke. But the ex-Attorney-General Philip Ruddock and ex-Foreign Minister Alexander Downer, both strong Howard supporters, have appeared. *LNL* policy is to have guests who are actually doing something rather than reporting it, but this is often harder to achieve. The program is necessarily locked into the English language and Adams admits it doesn't do a good job with the rest of the world because it is often hard to find Eastern European, Asian, African or Latin American decision-makers who can speak reasonably fluent English. Even among English speakers, many people who are good at writing are not good at speaking. So *LNL* often has to use commentators rather than decision-makers. Rarely, Adams turns down a conversation with someone whose views or personality he detests. But many of the people who won't go on-air with him, or who he doesn't want to talk to, are pro-establishment or right-wing. He sees no point in having hostile people on air with him in a conversational program, although many people he does have on-air disagree with him or he with them. But in four years of listening almost every night I have never heard voices raised.

* * *

The funniest *LNL* story Adams tells concerns David Hill when he was the ABC managing director in the 1990s: 'I used to attack him in newspaper columns, although it was a golden age compared with one later under Jonathan Shier. David was intensely disappointed with me and *LNL* but heard we had booked a conversation with Henry Kissinger, who had written a wonderful book on diplomacy. David was particularly interested because he had visions of becoming secretary-general of the UN, as did Bob Hawke and Gareth Evans, in spite of the fact that no-one with English as their first language has ever had the job. I was not entirely convinced that Henry would turn up in our New York studio to have a talk with me in Sydney. I had one ear on the studio and the other on the rest of the program, which I was stretching in case Henry spat the dummy. I heard that David had flown to New York to meet Henry. To my delight I heard David welcoming Henry in our studio. Henry sounded as if he was in a foul mood as he sat in a chair to be interviewed by someone he had never heard of in far-away Australia. So I quickly wound-up the other conversation I was having on-air and tried flattery on Henry. It always works. I said it was a tradition in the US that anyone could go from log cabin to White House but the log cabin can't be in Poland, which had prevented my next guest from getting to the White House — he had always worked for someone else there. Henry purred.

After the interview I could hear him telling David it was the best interview he had ever had and who was I? David replied that I was a very good friend of his!'

LNL has hour-long and shorter conversations in reserve in case it can't make contact with people. Sometimes Adams stretches the rest of the program and tries to work out what is happening on the other side of the sheet of glass between him and the producer. If they can't locate the first person to come on, they often start with the second or third. Often it's a chat between Adams and three others in different parts of the world and if one or two can't be found at the crucial time, Adams starts with the others and hopes the two lost ones are found before the segment ends. If not, he apologises to the audience, which proves it's a live program, although some ABC people regard an apology as bad form.

Adams' interviewing technique is carefully crafted and practised. He uses the well-worn device of praising guests on-air, slightly exaggerating their influence and often downplaying his own, to get the guests and listeners onside. He briefly outlines the guest's career before easing the conversation into the first topic and then steers it the way he wants it to go. He aims to make the conversation a subtle, sophisticated dance, although sometimes it goes off in other directions.

He leads the conversation and keeps it going. The *LNL* producers give him a written introduction to the speaker and the subject, but often he does his own introduction because he believes that too much on Radio National is read, which results in a loss of spontaneity. He has never found a subject that is simple — there is always something to say on either side. Much thought goes into the questions. Some guests would have been answering the same kind of questions for 30 years and Adams could leave the studio to make a cup of tea. Each program is planned days or weeks in advance. The producers might start by phoning a potential guest on the basis of researching a subject, to see if they are articulate and if their ideas would fit in with others' to make a good program. Not everyone wants to take part anyway.

Although Adams sometimes interrupts his guests, he doesn't argue with them. Confrontation doesn't work on radio because, when people who would lustily argue with each other in print face each other in a studio or over the air, they're irritatingly nice to each other. But chatty conversations do work on air. Speakers tend to relax when they can't see their audience. If Adams is not reasonably nice to establishment guests, they won't return. Some nights, he comes off-air furious with himself, a guest, the technology or the producers for mistakes in the brief, although he always admits mistakes on-air and cops the flak for monumental clangers.

* * *

Adams has never had a cross word with an executive producer, but he believes cross words would improve other Radio National programs because some presenters depend too much on their producers. Other Radio National programs are jealous of *LNL* having a staff of six: Adams, acting executive producer Gail Boserio, the other producers and the technical director. Some producers have good contact books; others have good subject knowledge — and these individuals have to be prevented from bending the program their way.

Often Adams' age (he turned 71 in July 2010) and 56 years experience as a journalist collecting information on many subjects gives him an advantage over a young producer. If he doesn't know much about a subject and cares less, he sticks to the brief. Otherwise, he speaks off the cuff to get into the subject, introduces his one or more speakers and it's off and running. He told me that sometimes his producers don't even listen to what he's saying on-air: he can see them through the glass wall, chatting. They regard their job as preparing briefs, not babysitting their host. They have even been known to type suggested questions on the computer, only to have him reply on the intercom, 'I asked that five minutes ago.' He often suggests subjects and speakers that are eventually taken up by his producers, although in the end it's their decision. That said, they're constantly looking for new topics and speakers. The media is incestuous and many subject ideas and speakers' names come from other people in the industry. Regular topics are: the Pacific Islands (particularly the Solomon Islands, East Timor and Papua-New Guinea), Aboriginal affairs, philosophy, political ideas, science, the environment, Africa, Asia, Europe, and the Middle East, justice, freedom, the Iraq war and the US and British governments. Australian politics are covered regularly only in one third of a program a week.

Former executive producer Chris Bullock told me *LNL*'s aim is to present cutting-edge discussions on public debates; Adams said its prime duty is to alert people to ideas and issues that have not yet reached the other Australian media. Usually, few of the program's guests are in Sydney. The 10 p.m. timeslot makes it easy for Adams to have conversations with people at breakfast time on the US East Coast, lunchtime in Europe and early evening in Asia but not with people in the early morning on the US West Coast or the Pacific Islands, when stories are often pre-recorded. Each of the four producers does one night shift a week. In the ABC's head office at Ultimo, they sit at work stations and talk a lot about possible subjects and guests and no doubt about how Adams handled the previous night's program.

Bullock outlined a typical run-around to find a speaker who had been lined-up: 'I phoned her home before the program. She was not there and I spoke to her daughter, who didn't know where she was. She gave me her mother's mobile number. I rang it and left a message and rang her daughter back. She said she would try her father's phone. I phoned her daughter back again. She said to ring her mother's mobile now. I did but it didn't answer because she was driving home. I finally got her when she arrived there and she joined in after the other speakers had started. There had been a mix-up over times.'

Some Jewish people think anything Adams says about Israel is anti-Semitic. Comments on the violent US culture, going right back into its history, cause complaints and also anything about Northern Ireland or the former Yugoslavia. Some people complain when he splits an infinitive, misuses a participle or mispronounces an obscure overseas politician's name. Adams' defence is that he doesn't know what a participle is. He likes the way Australians are — like himself — irreverent about the establishment, particularly politicians. He can tell from the letters and emails he and the ABC receive that his *LNL* listeners and *Weekend Australian Magazine* readers are the same type of people. The program is classified as opinion, not current affairs, so listeners tolerate opinions more. The producers answer as many emails and letters as possible.

Bruce Shapiro is the best US correspondent *LNL* has ever had. Adams thought from the sound of his voice that he would be soft, pale and round; he is small, thin and dark, angry and tight. Christian Kerr, who also reports politics for *The Australian*, is one of *LNL*'s Canberra reporters and is upright, carefully prepares what he says and doesn't adlib. He reports on alternate Mondays to Laura Tingle, who is chief political correspondent of the *Financial Review* and wife of *The Sydney Morning Herald's* former acerbic left-wing writer Alan Ramsey. She is bright and a good writer but is sometimes taken aback by comments Adams throws at her. Bea Campbell, who reports from England, is sharp, tough and a hard-line left-winger. Adams has tried to lighten-up conversations with her by calling her 'Queen Bea.' Her accent from Newcastle in North England is delightful.

When Adams arrived at Radio National he was shocked by the lack of comradeship among the staff. They concentrate on their own programs but do not interact much with other staff. Few people spoke to him, especially because he arrived at the nearly-deserted studio late at night after having phone and email contact with the *LNL* producers during the day. He used to hypothesise that some ABC Radio executives don't exist. Soon after he was appointed, the then head of radio took him to lunch but he's had only a few conversations with people in that position in the 20 years since.

Adams told me ABC Radio presenters rarely talk to each other and they are not rated highly by the organisation, unlike those in ABC Television. Radio is production-based and the most influential people in ABC Radio are executive producers. Adams has watched new presenters come and often their executive producers try to tame them, limit them and overproduce them from their first program. 'I always tell new presenters there will be a tussle between them and their EPs, so they will end up reading their briefs on-air rather than saying what they want to say. That way lies death. It's been sorted out at *LNL,* so now we get along wonderfully.' Adams believes the standard of Australian political reporting could be greatly improved by irreverence, which is not only a very Australian attitude but something that would also break down politicians' interview tricks. 'Most public-affairs programs are incredibly pompous and humourless. I like something that takes the piss out of the program. Some presenters have no sense of humour and try to give the impression they run a very important show.'

Patrice Newell, at their biodynamic farm, can't get Radio National and doesn't have an iPod, so she knows very little of what Adams says on air. At their first-ever joint presentation, at the 2006 Sydney Writers' Festival, about her book, *Ten Thousand Acres: A Love Story,* she got exasperated with Adams on stage and they staged little arguments, causing laughter. Adams uses humour where possible but told the audience his partner has no sense of humour at all. Ideally he would like to work from a studio at the farm but can usually spend only a long weekend there every week, driving the three hours there after the week's final live program at 11p.m. on Thursdays and returning to his pad in Paddington on Sundays or Mondays. The Friday night program is from the archives and reveals how Adams' voice has aged over the years.

Adams told me he stopped worrying about death threats years ago. Someone recognising him on the street is always dangerous because they might accost him, so he avoids eye contact because some people see it as an invitation to talk. He finds strangers' over-affection harder to handle than criticism, so he has developed tactics for enclosed areas such as airports. He has no social contact with the *LNL* staff except perhaps taking them to a restaurant before Christmas, and has no personal friends in the ABC. In truth, he knows many people but has few friends. He seems less-relaxed off-air than on-air, partly because he cultivates a relaxed program although the stress is still under the serene surface. His life is now more relaxed than when he was chairing government bodies. He told me, '*LNL* is my hobby as well as my job. It changes all the time and its great success with podcasts has reinvented it. I have no other ideas about what to do with my time. If I didn't do *LNL,* I'd be bored and irritating. I particularly like doing one-hour conversations. It takes about an hour to begin to know someone.' Adams' long conversations with left-wing friends are unbeatable radio. Some of them have been shortly before the guest has died.

The ABC board won't sack Adams because it knows there would be an uproar from his fans. He has *LNL* for as long as his body can deliver it because his body is more likely to quit before his mind will. Then his successor might conduct a one-hour conversation with him, preferably a long time before he finds out whether there is, in fact, a Heaven.

Chapter Sixteen: **Letters to Adams — Bashings and Body Odours**

'I am in the local Anglican Church choir and one lady to the left of me farts regularly', wrote Mary of Gilgandra, New South Wales, to Phillip Adams. I held her letter and read this extract in the Manuscript Room of the National Library of Australia. Mary must be the first person to write about anti-social behaviour in an Anglican Church choir.

Over three weeks I looked through many thousands of letters in this archive — there are about 500 large boxes of them, here at the library's behest. It asked Adams to forward them. He had given me permission to read them.

I picked up another, from Matthew, of East Malvern in Melbourne: 'The highlight of a book launch I attended came when an oh-so-young man groped my wife. Naturally I asked him to stop and he explained his behaviour by saying he thought she was my daughter.'

There seemed to be a theme developing: people write to Adams to complain, but few of them complain about anything he has done or said. They complain about other people. Adams the father confessor of the Monahan Dayman Adams office has turned into Adams the confessor of the nation. The letters are full of pertinent, funny, sad and shocking quotes from Adams' listeners and readers, about what concerns them. That's the crux.

'As a 14-year-old Christian,' wrote Abby, 'I was infuriated to read your article, "A Matter of Disbelief" in *The Weekend Australian*. I have never been patient with ignorant people.'

'Ignorant' is the last thing you could accuse Phillip Adams of being. And, as I can see from these letters, it is clear that a great many of his readers and listeners believe him to be empathetic.

Adams has created such a personal relationship with his listeners and readers that those who send him letters and emails reveal a lot about their private lives, feelings and beliefs. When readers' and listeners' letters and emails express views, they are mostly strong, either for or — almost as often — against what Adams has said or written. The most strident attacks, sometimes abusive, come from Christians, like Abby, angered by his professed atheism. Some plead for his 'salvation'. Paradoxically, a few ministers of religion write to praise him for being forthright.

Some letter writers seek his help in personal matters such as their love lives, or how to get social services. The ABC has found through research that *Late Night Live* listeners are usually graduates, but most letters and emails to Phillip Adams are decidedly unacademic.

Some letters beg for money. More often, they ask Adams to open their functions or attend their meetings or to come to their homes for dinner.

Overall, the letters and emails reveal the issues that concern Adams' listeners and readers, either about their own lives or about what he says or writes. Many people enclose their poems, books, movies or play manuscripts. Obviously, Adams rarely has the time or inclination to even scan them, but the fact that people send them shows how much help and support they need.

The letters and emails are full of Australian expressions, like Adams' columns and broadcasts. Some people write every day for long periods, but he opens few of these letters. Lonely letter-writers obviously have no-one else to turn to. Or maybe they just like Adams.

Many letters enclose donations to charities Adams founded or promoted, or suggest topics for columns or broadcasts, or include Bible passages. Any time Adams says he is going to hospital, or has been ill, there is a flood of 'Get Well' cards. A few letters are abusive or threatening, or enclose crude sexual drawings. Some have up to ten tightly-written pages. Quite a few of the letters are just plain bizarre.

A retired colonel, of Greenacres, South Australia, wrote: 'A leading citizeness invited me to leave a party, get into her car and go to her home because her leading professional, aged husband was in hospital. Later I was offered $10,000 to marry a publican's daughter, spots, myopic eyes, dribbling dialogue and all.'

Bully for him.

Loneliness sticks out of most letters like a bandaged thumb. Ann wrote, 'I will be 85 on Thursday, the loneliest 85-year-old this side of the black stump.'

Nancy, of Townsville, wrote: 'I was feeling shit, as if the whole world was against me because of my breakdown and Bob seeming to hate me, when I picked up Bob's *Weekend Australian* and read "Our Crumbling Pillars", by you. I got the joke,' continued Nancy. 'The whole bloody world feels shit and everyone's throwing tantrums when they don't get things their way. Your article stopped me dead in my tracks and I'm grateful. Even if Bob's a bit of a control freak, he's not the only one. I am, too, and we both love our baby. The truth is Bob is sexually abusing me. I hate him but I forgive him because he's insane.'

And this from a social worker for abused children: 'Yesterday I saw a ten-year-old girl. Her bottom was covered with dark welts. Her mother had belted her 20 times on her bare skin with a large strap.'

From despair to humour. I pulled out this missive from Ben, of Surry Hills in Sydney: 'I am running short of a quid, so any ideas would be appreciated.'

Frances, of Footscray in Melbourne, wrote: 'Thanks for your letter. I haven't laughed so much since my father nearly choked on a Christmas pudding charm back in '52.' She then described how she met 'a most beautiful Indian' who took her to a curry restaurant in Carlton: 'The curry was so god-awful hot that my eyes started to water and one of my micro lenses popped out and landed in the curry. I had three choices: to wash it in the wine, to suck it, or as a very last resort, to eat it. I ate delicately around it as it stared up malignantly at me from the plate. The pile of curry got smaller. The thought of walking around with only one good eye for the next three months until I saved up enough for another lens was so horrific that I started to cry. My Indian was alarmed but when I pointed to my lens glistening on the last bit of curry, he was quite magnificent. He snapped his fingers at a passing waiter. "Here, boy," he said. "A glass of water for the lady." The "lady" washed the lens and replaced it.'

The next letter I read closely was from a far-flung fan: Larry, of Maison d'Arret, Bethune, France, who wrote:

'*The Weekend Australian* reaches me rather late, usually two months after publication. The Australian Embassy in Paris gathers up the old copies from the waiting room and sends them to Australians, like myself, who languish in French prisons. So it was only yesterday that I had the pleasure of reading your very fine article, "Taming the Dinosaurs". It was of particular interest to me because I am being detained in France as a suspected terrorist.'

I began to wonder exactly how many letters and emails Adams reads and what his own impressions of these correspondents are. I know that his audience is broad — and, thanks to the readily-available podcasts of *LNL*, it is now international — but this is something else. I have never read anything quite like these letters. Margaret, of Malvern in Melbourne, sent a drawing she had made of her room and wrote, 'It has blue walls, blue lino and blue curtains and a room facing west. Can you imagine the gloom when I wake up? On Fridays, the head shrink brings me my pills. For a moment, I go along with the medication. But it is numbing my body and mind.'

Then this from Bill of Neutral Bay in Sydney: 'I really do enjoy your program, except that my batteries are a bit flat. Do you think you could talk a bit louder until I can afford some new batteries?' Either Bill has a strange idea of how radio works, or he has a good sense of humour.

* * *

'Dearest Old Bean,' wrote Annie, of Mosman in Sydney, 'I am 90 and six months old but I don't look old and I don't feel old. My hair has gone grey and I have a few wrinkles and warts. I heard myself referred to as, "Old

Annie, is she still alive? If she was on fire, I wouldn't piss on her to put her out." I am so lonely without Len, Phillip. I would walk over hell barefoot to spend another hour with him.'

What I am looking through is a sort of social history of Australia. All the cares and delights one might imagine are here. All these people wanted to tell Adams about themselves.

Helen, of Fitzroy in Melbourne, wrote, 'I am not soaring into fantasy land, just lying on my bed going quite bananas. I have the traditional hymn "Praise to the Lord" running through my head and I am talking in my mind with this person and that person and I'm scared of the night ahead of me. What do I do? Jesus Christ says it's okay to write to you. P-l-e-a-s-e send me a reply if you feel like it. Rang Mum early a.m. and when she discovered it was me ringing, she hung up on me. Dad visits me a lot.'

Joe, of Kew, wrote: 'Apologies for bombarding you with irrelevancies but I've had a lot of fun and you've been invariably courteous and good humoured in your replies. However, from this letter, this nuisance will cease. My ex-prostrate has acted up and now I have bone cancer. I shall be in bliss in about two months. Thanks, mate, you've given me a lot of entertainment.'

But Fred, of Burleigh Heads, wrote: 'I've written to you before. You were ungracious in your reply. You are unfair to pitch your ingrained biases with public money on ABC Radio. Your unrelenting libertarianism could be over-compensation for maggots eating your spirit.'

This is in sharp contract to an email from Pam, 'May your bed never be empty of pretty young girls.'

* * *

From the flippant to the definitely serious. Jack, of Mt Eliza, wrote: 'I read your article in *The Weekend Australian*. Three times. I thought it was amazing, wonderful, that anyone should speak the truth, the truth that has been covered up for so long. Religious intolerance was what it was called. A licence to commit every evil known to man. To enslave millions mentally is so much easier and more effective than the physical slavery they exercised in past ages in their so-called Roman Empire.'

Bob, of Torquay, wrote, 'The most endearing characteristic of your column is that it is not comment in the usual journalistic sense but a weekly introspective ramble, seemingly prompted by whatever bounced off your head in the preceding seven days. The intimacy generated, at least to this reader, creates a familiarity.'

Anthony emailed, 'Heard you on the radio the other night. Good show. I've got all those intimate sexual problems I want you to help me with. My main problem is the number of women who don't want me to make love because I'm not famous.'

Everything Adams does and has done — creating memorable advertisements, making movies, writing columns, answering letters and emails, hosting *LNL* — comes back to people. As much as he keeps his private life to himself, not attending parties, spending hours in his office alone or in his car driving to his Hunter Valley farm, he clearly seeks connection with people.

Josephine, of Lismore, wrote to him, 'A man I know raped me in the mental health clinic but I wasn't well and let it happen. I shared a bed with the Devil himself. Do you know what this bastard did? My wonderful

18-year-old daughter woke up one morning to find him standing over her, naked. She called out, "Mum, Jason's being disgusting." I put her on a bus back to her father's.'

* * *

Gerald, of Broken Hill, New South Wales, wrote, 'The fact that Australians are racists is very obvious. I have been to posh parties with people who have turned out to be bigoted twits. After thirty-six years in Australia, I still have a strong Yorkshire accent and have learnt to avoid Australians in most of the towns in this country. I will generally not drink with them and certainly avoid country pubs. I will never go to Queensland or Tasmania because of my experiences there. Still I love Australia and I know some decent ordinary people and I love them, and they love me.'

Valerie, of Pascoe Vale in Melbourne, wrote, 'After spending many years in Western countries, I believe the capacity for compassionate feelings becomes atrophied with civilisation. The more "socialised" people become, the more "breeding" they receive, the more they camouflage impulses, feelings and passions until there is nothing left but society marionettes doing the "right" things. If you ever mixed in Eastern European circles (particularly Slav), you might have noticed the greater spontaneity but also less palatable aspects, in a Western sense, such as hatred, unlimited capacity for intrigue, rudeness and cruelty.'

Then this from Jeff, in an email, 'My brother calls you the conscience of a nation and while I don't agree with him, I have come to the conclusion that anyone who likes both Voltaire and *The Simpsons* can't be all that bad.'

The adoration continues, 'My name is Anne and I'd like to thank you for hours and hours of stimulating reading. You seem to be a lone, sane, unrelenting voice against a mob of dickheads.'

I laughed at this letter from Tom, of Victor Harbour, South Australia, 'I have complained to the ABC about the way you use *Late Night Live* to push your own views and ram down the listeners' throats your prejudices on religion, politics, homosexuality, etc. The reply I received was that it's extremely difficult for producers to handle people like you and we have to accept the good with the bad.'

Marjorie, of Monbulk in Victoria, wrote, 'I am 92 years of age. Although a non-believer in some ways, I do believe in the benefits of starting each day with an optimistic approach. I lost my husband nine years ago and it left a big hole in my life. It is good to hear your voice in the wilderness of pessimism, speaking up loud and clear for optimism.'

And from Molly in Elizabeth, South Australia, 'You are fortunate in that you do not need the prop of a belief in God and Jesus but there are many people who have such a need.'

But Michael, of Hebersham in New South Wales, said he is a retired minister of religion and told Adams, 'You are my favourite agnostic. I enjoy the way you so gently take the mickey out of some of my religious friends. Our world needs such insightful and thoughtful people like you to help people like me keep our feet on the ground.'

Michael and all Adams' tens of thousands of other letter-writers pour their hearts out to a person they will never meet but who they feel will understand their fears, hopes, heights and despairs, loves and hates. He has that kind of relationship with his listeners and readers.

* * *

Graham, of Charters Towers, wrote: 'The older I become, Phillip, the more I am aware that I know almost nothing about anything that amounts to anything. Holding that belief about myself is, I believe, the pathway to true wisdom.'

Andrew, of Toowoomba, Queensland, wrote: 'I have found Gladys. She is a Pom and works as an announcer on 4DDB Toowoomba. If you get to hear one of her programs, it is a listening experience you will not forget.'

Leonie, of Seymour, Victoria, wrote: 'Here is a photo of one of your listeners, not Gladys but Gabrielle. Gabrielle, my mum, will be 86 next Sunday and is avidly interested in life and is still learning. We both want you to keep up the good fight.'

Adam, of Ashfield, Sydney, wrote supporting Adams' campaign to retain Australianisms and listed these recent conversions to Americanisms (in brackets): 'Bullshit! (No way!); biscuits (cookies); galah (jerk); bastard (arsehole); g'day! (yo!); pram (stroller); dummy (pacifier); chips (fries); bloke (guy).'

Ron, of Eaglehawk, Victoria, wrote: 'Michael has freaked out and is upset, crying and suicidal since his bout on the grog and so on. Max has taken him to the mental health centre this arvo, trying to get help. The other day they declared that Michael wasn't schizophrenic at all but has a mild personality disorder.'

Alan, of Narrikup, Western Australia, wrote: 'Average Australia, you know, quite likes Pauline Hanson, not because of what she stands for so much that she has the cheek, in these days of correctness, to enunciate the concerns that many feel about the fundamental changes they see around them, which they are downright frightened to talk about in case they are called racist.'

Peter, of Chirnside Park, Victoria, asked Adams, 'Have you a secret cache of my unanswered letters? I was talking to a retired cleric yesterday and he told me he has written 2,767 letters to God and still awaits a reply.'

Valerie, of Mooroolbark, Victoria, wrote: 'The Jews, Christians and Muslims have got it all wrong. There are only two types of people in the world, those who have brains and no religion and those who have a religion and no brains.'

Sylvia emailed: 'I used to teach psychology and my students often asked me (as do others) what causes homosexuality. My inevitable reply is that I will tell them if they can tell me what causes heterosexuality. It fair stops them in their tracks.'

* * *

John, of Chatsworth, NSW, wrote: 'I've worked in abattoirs, mines and picking vegetables and fruit up and down the east coast. I married when I was 41 and I'm still married. My wife Margaret and I are good friends. I drank as well as worked my way around Australia. I'm 47 now and have not had a beer for eight months or so, thanks to my friends at Alcoholics Anonymous.

I've never officially studied anything since I left my formal schooling after half-completing the Intermediate Certificate at Marist Brothers College, Bendigo. However, I have become aware of the fact that I am no lesser or better person than anyone. My mission in life is to believe in myself and to help others know that they have minds as capable as any academic's and could do all that clever, famous people can do if they train and believe in themselves.'

Lois, of Braidwood, NSW, wrote chastising Adams, 'I am not a Gladys, a term I find a little patronising (shades of Barry Humphries' gladioli) and suggestive of an uncritical species of female fan who is a bit in love with your undoubtedly attractive voice and charming what-the-hell personality. I can't help thinking that you need better intellectual resources to deal with the charges of bias and that you are to some extent hoist on the petard of your own commitment to objectivism.'

Even a parrot likes Adams' voice: Val, of Mt Hutton, NSW, wrote, 'When you talk, my parrot, Billy, sits on top of his cage and whistles so loudly that I can hardly hear you. I'm sure he learns heaps from your programs.'

Joseph, of Darlinghurst, Sydney, wrote, 'Remember the three murderers of Christ: the Government (rule by propaganda and fear), the Church (rule by superstition, power and confusion), and the Mob (rule by ignorance). Before mankind can live together in harmony and understanding, the Mob's ignorance must be transmitted into wisdom, the Church's superstition transmitted into illuminated faith and the state's fear into love.'

* * *

Some letters are very perceptive: Harold, of Deception Bay, Queensland, wrote, 'Someone once remembered that, for Westerners, the aim of life is to do and for Easterners it is to be — to be one with entire life, which embraces nature, to be one with the cosmos. This is what has priority in old Chinese thinking.'

Joc, of Casino, NSW, wrote: 'You have done a fair job of beautifying Gough Whitlam. My favourite joke about the great man runs like this: Gough and Margaret had retired for the night and Margaret threw herself on the bed said, 'God, I'm tired!' Gough patiently remonstrated with her, saying, 'Margaret, when we are alone, do you think you could call me Gough?'

Peter, of Mt Lawley, Western Australia, wrote: 'Cheer up, old boy. You are not completely to blame for your putrid manners, boofhead appearance and complete lack of any decent behaviour. Your ancestors, if they are identifiable, must share some of the responsibility. Please try harder.'

Lucy, of Cascades in Tasmania, wrote: 'Your talk on eugenics reminded me of how, a few years ago, a teacher friend of mine was asked by a pupil the meaning of the word. The teacher replied it meant not leaving human reproduction to anything as random as love but instead choosing a partner by what is in his or her genes. As this sounded like "jeans", you can imagine the hilarity it caused.'

* * *

Even as a schoolboy, Adams admired women: Marie, of Hawthorn, Melbourne, was a young teacher at Eltham

High when Adams was there as a student and wrote, 'I remember you so well, always on the edge of any shenanigans, enjoying to the full but not participating — an admirable but safe position. You made my day on one occasion after a female teachers' beauty contest at an Open Day or some such event. You said I had the best legs. If it was so then, I wish it were still so!'

Rosemary, of Queanbeyan, NSW, wrote in support of Adams' campaign over the Stolen Generation. She said she remembers in Alice Springs in 1950, when she was visiting a friend near Heavy Tree Gap, she saw a small group of people walking down the road. Suddenly, a utility appeared. It stopped and two white men jumped out and snatched a small child from the group and drove off again.

Lucy, of Hawthorn, Melbourne, wrote: 'I wish you would stop suggesting that the net isolates people. I have made contact with three members of my extended family who I had completely lost contact with, thanks to the net.'

Robert, of Charlestown, NSW, wrote: 'In spite of all your diatribes against God for so many years, about 80 per cent of people still believe in God. How many people have you made happy by destroying their belief in God?'

Norman, of Castlemaine in Victoria, wrote: 'Lesley's here, staying for the weekend. Gives her a break from her boyfriend Greg in Bendigo and her ex, Laurie, who boards with her. Apparently Greg has acquired a brain injury and is friends with the bikies that drink at the Victoria Hotel, Bendigo, and even threatened to kill Lesley and Laurie over something. They even blackmailed Greg into getting Lesley stoned for the first time about a month back. Lesley brought me a Christmas present, *The Phillip Adams and Patrice Joke Book*. Second-hand but okay. I think the last owner (due to the penciled stuff in it) was a name I recognised as a psycho patient.'

Martin, of St Leonards, Sydney, wrote: 'When I was picking up the kids from school on Tuesday, the usual coven of mums was sheltering under a tree talking about you and *LNL*. They all knew you had been unwell. They said that you always sound as if you are confiding in just them and ask the questions they would ask. You sound the nearest in Oz to a public moral conscience.'

* * *

R J R, of Adelaide, wrote: 'I'm disappointed to find you so thin-skinned. You dish it out on a weekly basis, but a minor wrap from *Media Watch* and you behave like a big girl's blouse.'

Millie, 'a worried Gladys', emailed, 'Re: $9billion spending on defence. Please tell me why we spend so much on defence when we are not at war with any country that might invade us, nor might any other country threaten us. Please tell me how this amount compares with the budgets for education, health or community services.'

Rosemary, of Jimboomba in Queensland, wrote, 'The awful subject of child abuse continues to rear its ugly head, but the very worst aspect is the painful spiritual abuse that so many children experience at the hands of a father figure. Mothers can be father figures also. The experience turns children into the agnostics, atheists and god-haters who proliferate in our world. To search for God, Phillip, is the one important thing you will ever do in your life.'

Tony, of Bowden, South Australia, wrote, 'I have just returned from three months in the UK and Ireland. Daily I have read *The Guardian, Independent, Scotsman, Irish Independent,* even the *Daily Telegraph*, and I have watched the BBC, ITV, Channel Four and Five. When I returned to Australia, never have I read so much crap and watched so much shit, especially in *The Australian, The Advertiser, The Sydney Morning Herald* and *The Age* and on ABCTV and SBS. You are a media analyst. Why is there so much childish crap in Australian media? And why, oh why can't people speak English? Even *The South Wales Evening Post* is better than *The Australian*, although it's gone downhill since Dylan left.'

Pam emailed, 'You seem to have a finely-tuned bullshit detector. Very handy, as there is a lot of it around.'

* * *

Many letters to Adams talk of tragedy: Jason, of Nakara in the Northern Territory, wrote to him, 'This note is to tell you that your article in *The Weekend Australian* on love is helping me a lot as I try to cope with the loss of my beloved and loving wife to cancer at the age of 53. My life went into reverse a month ago. The pain was indescribable. You are probably right: "Love is the triumphant response to life's inevitable tragedy." Love is the only thing that makes life worth living.'

Judith emailed, 'A wealthy friend of mine seduced doctors, barristers, even a judge and was well paid by them. My husband said to me recently, "She must have had something." I told him, "She talked her men into thinking they were supermen, then she fucked them. They did not fuck her. What extraordinary children you men are on that note."'

Tony, of Chirnside Park, Melbourne, wrote, 'As your listener, I have been faithful for many years. So often I have left my couch to let your dulcet tones gently violate my eardrums. Is this oral sex?'

Julie, of 'The University from Hell', University of Melbourne, wrote, 'The university has flung me as from the end of the year. I am not sure what I will do for the rest of my life. The only job in *The Age* classifieds that appeals to me so far is as a barge attendant in Nauru ... Someone on one of your programs reminded me of the lady who, when asked how many husbands she had had, replied, "Including my own?"'

Jock emailed, 'Dear Phil. Do you want to come to my birthday party? I've got a new cook and there will be lots of pink gin, beer, cakes and all sorts of splendid amusements.'

Susan emailed hopefully, 'I do not know the name of the father of my little girl. She was conceived at a party where I had unprotected sex with a man I met that night. I do remember the sex was so good that I fainted. If you manage to track down the father, can you send me his phone number?'

Alastair, of Lower Templestowe, Melbourne, wrote, 'Hello, my name is Adam. I am 26 and currently studying in Melbourne and I enjoy your program very much. In fact, it is one of the very few shows in the whole broadcasting world worth listening to. I look forward very much to the day we meet, perhaps in London, as my folks are very much part of the West End scene and we might bump into each other one sunny day.'

* * *

Many letters criticise Adams: Graham, of Yarralumla, ACT, wrote, 'I have had less and less enthusiasm for *LNL*, partly because of the dreary topics covered but mainly because of the way you allow some characters to waffle on without seriously challenging them. You don't declare yourself as standing for anything (except Egyptian mummies) and seem content to demonstrate your brand of warm, moist empathy as if that's a substitute for real content. The ABC reeks of it.'

Anne, of Devonport in Tasmania, wrote, 'I am writing to thank you for my best English teacher. I am 13 years old and in Grade 8. My first eager task every weekend for many years has been to turn to *The Weekend Australian* and read your column. No-one else I know uses language as you do. I sometimes wet my pants laughing.'

Most letters to Adams are full of slices of life: Kristian, of Junee, NSW, wrote, 'Genes do play a major part. I have the crankiest sadist as a husband, the living image of his dead sadistic mother, and she could give the Marquis de Sade points. I am told our eldest daughter, who is as sweet as a nut and kindness personified, has this ugly jealousy, too.'

Edward, of Whyalla, South Australia, wrote, 'I am writing in reply to your letter. So you regard my letter and opinions as disgusting. You got upset, you poor little thing. A large part of the Australian community supports the detention of asylum-seekers. Likewise with

Aborigines. I would round them all up, build a large camp capable of holding all 400,000 of them, surround it with 20ft-high cement walls, top it with 2000-volt electric wire and let them cope. If they want food, let them eat each other.'

Leonie emailed, 'I am a struggling artist. At first I struggled with who I was, then with those around me, who I love. Art at present in Australia seems to be heavily influenced by old-fashioned emus. Surely the Archibald Prize should be more at the cutting edge of art than it is. Or is art such a puzzle that even the judges don't know what it is about?'

Adams told me nothing causes more angry letters than the Israel-Palestine conflict: John emailed, 'Israel and Pakistan need to be urgently squashed to death like the cockroaches they are. You are over-influenced — even scared — by the Jewish holocaust. The Jews are the Nazis of today. The holocaust is in Palestine and the jackboots are on Jewish soldiers.'

* * *

Religion causes anger in many letters to Adams: Michael, of Burswood in Perth, wrote, 'You border on being blasphemous with your remarks about the Lord Jesus Christ. Demons come in many shapes and sizes and forms. Some of them are huge and some are so small that you breathe them in and sneeze them out when they want to change house. If you want to see a real live demon, go to the following address on a Saturday morning ... The demon goes to town on a Friday night and when it returns in the morning, its wings make a sound like a helicopter. Then it does a U-turn and stops at the corner of the house, lets out a loud squawk and disappears.'

Andrew emailed: 'There is no doubt that religion is the worst thing that ever happened to God. Doctrines, dogmas and the Bible ask people to park their brains at the door of the church. They have left God with a congregation of scared, weird and little people.'

Horst, of Molendinar, Queensland, wrote, 'Phillip, you are truly in a mess of your own doing. You have become an emotional wreck. You have capitulated to demon forces who are playing on you and laughing at you for being so vulnerable.'

Steve, of Bellingen, NSW, wrote, 'I think the Australian media is partly responsible for the people's sports obsession. The commercial media tend to make more money out of the projection of sport than out of any intellectual forum.'

Letters and emails contained many home truths: Gunnar emailed, 'I had a discussion recently with a retired major general, who has fought in four wars (World War 11, Korea, Malaysia and Vietnam) and he said war is rarely justified and never achieves anything except mass misery.'

Michael, of Queanbeyan, wrote, 'It's time! It's time you did it again, Phillip — get the Oz film industry re-started. You did it before, almost single-handed. Why not another effort? I've just met friends in the film industry and, I tell you, they are worried.'

* * *

Andrew said he was from Perth in Tasmania and emailed, 'Thank you for your accurate, brutally honest and courageous attack on us, the public, in *The Weekend Australian Magazine*, "Ignorance is no defence." Once again, you have hit it (us) right on the head. A dear friend and I are constantly pulling our hair out at the "She'll be right, mate" attitude of friends, work colleagues, acquaintances and strangers we encounter in our daily lives.'

Alex emailed, 'I am 20 years' old and began reading your articles three years ago. Thank you for opening my eyes, Mr Adams. I appreciate your relentless ability to not accept the world as it is and to strive instead to make others aware. You are a beacon of light.'

Josie, of Camp Hill, Queensland, wrote, 'Last night I picked up a woman and brought her to my house for a visit. My friend was visibly upset telling me that in the past few weeks she had found out that her two daughters (now 25 and 29, then four and eight) were sexually molested by the man she lived with after her husband left. The widespread repercussions of the terrible things that people perpetuate on one another are complex and far-flung.'

Hazel, of Golden Square, Victoria, wrote: "You have really gone too far. This week you again took the Mickey out of all those good people who believe in the supernatural. You degrade a most worthy group, who deserve your sympathy. You refer to pigs' 'trotters'. Really, Mr Adams, sheep have trotters, pigs have feet, as any butcher could tell you.'

Simon, of Dunnstown, Victoria, wrote, 'As a believer in God, I have read widely and made some fascinating discoveries in the past few years. The Bible does not forbid God's ministers to marry but encourages marriage. Celibacy is the Catholic Church's idea.'

Barbara emailed, 'The greatest weapon of mass destruction is religion. There is but one god, so why do we belt each other on his or her behalf?'

Finally, this gem from Alexis, of Tully, Queensland, 'My dad is an intelligent, compassionate atheist. Mum is a kind, devoted Catholic. Dad reckons the Pope needs five kids, a wife and a cow to sort himself out. Mum agrees.'

Chapter Seventeen:
Adams and Other Media Grumpies

Phillip Adams moved from the communist *Guardian* to *The Bulletin*, to *The Australian* before Rupert Murdoch sacked him, to *Nation Review*, back to *The Australian*, to *The Age* and back to *The Australian.* Along the way he tried to stop *The Age* becoming a takeover target, edited nine joke books and indulged in hate wars and petty squabbles with rival media grumpies.

He told me his generation of commentators and public intellectuals are still calling the shots and occupying the front ranks in their sixties and seventies while people in their twenties, thirties and forties are "pissed off" waiting for a chance. But will he surrender *Late Night Live?* In Australia, once you're on the totem pole, you stay there, whereas you don't in the United States or Britain, because others push you off, the competition is so fierce. In Australia, most film makers, for example, are in their sixties and seventies; also newspaper columnists and radio commentators. It's the same in public life — much of the public agenda is still controlled by ageing baby boomers. Many talented young people communicate via the internet, but that doesn't yet create public recognition like the old media does for people like Alan Jones, Neil Mitchell, Clive James, Robert Hughes, Germaine Greer and Adams himself — The Media Grumpies. They and many others have benefited from boom newspaper years, now declining as newspapers close down or shrink in size in the face of the internet boom and the 2007-09 world financial slump. Adams would no doubt be killed in the rush if he offered his *Weekend Australian Magazine* half-page to a younger columnist.

Why do The Grumpies stay on their totem poles longer in Australia? 'I don't know,' Adams said in one of our regular fruity sessions, at about 9.30 a.m. with Phillip grumpier than he had sounded on-air at 11 p.m. the previous night. He fortified himself with tea (two teabags), rolled the first of several cigarettes, left his shoes off and leaned back in his office chair under the eyes of an ancient Egyptian head. 'The new generation of commentators is blogging, not going into the old media. So the doddering old master class is unchallenged but in a newspaper medium that is declining. It's not healthy. And it wasn't always the case that most media commentators are right-wing while many other media people are left-wing. At *The Age*, the opposite was true and the commentators' left or liberal attitude was quite marked. I remember telling Graham Perkin, the editor (1966-75), that *The Age* really needed some conservative commentators. Graham said he would appoint one if he could find one with a sense of humour. This became a huge obstacle.'

But for the past 15 years, lefties have been rare except for cartoonists. It's hard to think of any Australian cartoonists who are not left-wing. The grumpy old columnists have grown grumpier and have been joined by new, younger conservative columnists like Miranda Devine. If Adams or I were running a newspaper today, we would look for younger, fresher, progressive voices to balance the conservatives.

Adams has caustic views about some fellow grumpies: "Piers Akerman (Sydney *Daily* and *Sunday Telegraph*) is a performing seal. There he is with simulated rage, like Miranda Devine (formerly Fairfax and now News Ltd tabloids). Andrew Bolt (Melbourne *Herald Sun*) is unreadable. They get everything wrong and never apologise. They're now even angrier than ever. So whatever they're on, I want some."

On a slow news day, columnists and commentators get stuck into each other. Adams wrote in *The Australian* that John Laws will become morose and melancholic now that he has retired from 2UE and Laws wrote back that Adams twenty years earlier had been 'without a doubt the greatest failure ever to open a microphone there because he couldn't deal with talkback people'. Laws returned to radio (2SM) in 2011, aged 75.

But no columnist upsets Adams as much as Gerard Henderson, executive director of the conservative think tank The Sydney Institute. Adams told me, 'Gerard and I are old enemies. He is a bizarre form of stand-up comic. I don't take much notice of him' (incorrect) 'as he's utterly predictable.' Both Adams and Henderson did take enough notice of each other to engage in a typical spat via emails and newspapers in May and June 2009. On May 17, Phillip wrote in his *Weekend Australian Magazine* column: 'Many columnists are content to proffer the same column ad nauseum. Gerard Henderson is the classic case. In *The Sydney Morning Herald*, he regularly erects the same column in the space provided, attacking either Robert Manne (Professor of Politics at

La Trobe University in Melbourne), the ABC or me, or all three at once. Readers know it off by heart.' Henderson replied in an email to Adams, headed 'Phillip Adams' wilful distortion': 'This statement is entirely false. The fact is that I have never devoted a *Sydney Morning Herald* column to attacking you or Robert Manne. Not one. You, however, have used your column in *The Weekend Australian Magazine* to attack me previously, for example in February 2007'. On June 5, 2009, Adams emailed Gerard: 'Would it be possible for you to stop, just for a moment or two, being such a humourless bore? Silly question. The average house brick is more amusing, the most pigeon shit-splattered bronze statue of some long-forgotten 19th century personage propped up in a park is less pompous than Gerard, who spends so much time and effort trying to keep himself on his pedestal. Big hug, Phillip.'

Henderson said in his *Media Watch Dog* newsletter on June 23, 2009, 'Nancy (who I suspect is Henderson in drag) was thrilled to receive an email this week from *Late Night Live* presenter Phillip Adams. The good news is that Phillip is an enthusiastic reader of *Media Watch Dog*. So enthusiastic, in fact, that he believes he was short-changed in the gongs area last week, as the following documentation demonstrates:' Then followed Adams' email to Henderson: 'As well as two Orders of Australia, I've got not one but FOUR hon. doctorates. And you'll have to add FAHA (Fellow of the Australian Academy of the Humanities) to the honorifics. Let's gloss over my being (along with Don Bradman and John Howard) an official National Treasure, a Walkley, the Human Rights Medal, a pile of AFI Awards, the Longford, Humanist of the Year and even an ancient Logie … etc. etc. Don't forget to take your pills.' Henderson replied the same day to say he had in his *Media Watch Dog* a few days earlier referred to Adams as: Phillip Adams AO (1992), AM (1987), Hon Duniv (Griffith), Hon Dlitt (ECU), Hon DUniv (SA), FRSA.'

I have chosen a few examples of these rather silly spats between Adams and Henderson to help reveal their personalities. But they should avoid boring their readers and insulting each other in print and either choose genuinely funny jokes or (better still) worthwhile subjects.

Local shock jocks are pale imitations of American ones and on his worst day, Alan Jones is about ten per cent as fierce as Rush Limbaugh, who has 13.5 million listeners in the US. Adams told me American right-wing radio commentators are raving monsters and Rush is said to be now more or less running the Republican Party. In *The Weekend Australian* on May 26, 2007, Adams wrote: 'I loathe shock jocks and I detest the way locals mimic and plagiarise the bigotries and production tricks of Rush Limbaugh — the US source of such John Laws phrases as "femi-nazis" and the "keeping the dream alive" twaddle.'

Adams has been back and forth to and from *The Australian* three times and is now its longest contributor. After being a teenage freelance on the Victorian Communist Party's *Guardian,* he began writing part-time for the old pink-cover *Bulletin*, sometimes under established writers' bylines when they were too sick, or too drunk, to write. *The Bulletin*, which had a rip-roaring, legendary background with J F Archibald as owner-editor and Henry Lawson and Banjo Paterson as contributors, was well past its prime when in 1961 its owner, Samuel Prior, sold it to Frank Packer (Kerry's father) and its new editor, Donald Horne, turned it into a glossy newsmagazine modelling it on *Time*. Kerry Packer kept it going despite losing circulation and money until the financiers who took control of his company after he died closed it in January 2008.

The cartoonist Bruce Petty persuaded Adrian Deamer, *The Australian's* editor from 1966 to '71, to hire Adams as a television critic, and as *The Australian* had no television investments, Adams could write as he pleased, which he did, usually not about television at all. The staff journalists had a whip-around to buy him a TV set and it was a standing joke around the office that he never saw television but wrote about it. He also wrote an *Adams Rib* column in *The Weekend Australian* and recalled to me: 'I experimented with mumblings about things previously the province of novelists, poets or academic essayists, juxtaposing them with political satire. The response to my self-educated, indulgent outpourings was surprising — we got sugarbags full of letters, often in response to such non-newspaper topics as death, dying and the deity.' He began the trend towards irreverence, which was widely imitated both in *The Australian* and in *Age* columns like *Pinkney's Place*. *Adams Rib* lent weight to the rebelliousness of the era, satirising institutions such as schools, religion and censorship. Adams later equated the spirit of censorship with 'the great hush up' and Western taboo about death. Former High Court Judge Michael Kirby, in *Murdoch's Flagship* by Denis Cryle (Melbourne University Press), subsequently characterised Adams' distinctive journalism as a 'jumble of history, philosophy and whimsy, humorous anecdotes about his past and musings on popular culture, a combination of self-confession and nostalgia, more burlesque than macabre.'

But the first blow struck Adams' career after Rupert Murdoch, *The Australian's* owner, bombed in a 1969 British television interview with another satirist, David Frost. Murdoch had published, in his muck-raking *News of the World*, the memoirs of Christine Keeler, the call girl who six years earlier was at the centre of Britain's biggest postwar sex scandal, the Profumo Affair. Frost's show had been running for only three weeks when it caught fire over the way he poured scorn and dislike over Murdoch. Murdoch himself had only recently arrived as a London publisher but in Frost's interview defiantly defended the story in spite of the fact that the disgraced ex-Cabinet minister John Profumo had devoted his post-scandal life to charitable works and the story had already been thrashed to death. Murdoch arrived in Australia, asked Adrian Deamer whether he had any satirists on his staff and told him to sack them. Adams switched to Gordon Barton's *Nation Review* but was reinstated by *The Australian* when Deamer pointed out to Murdoch and Adams himself that *The Australian* received more letters about Adams' columns than about the Vietnam War, although for almost 12 months Adams' column was buried in *The Australian's* marketing section before returning to the weekend issue.

Adams had another row with *The Australian* and accepted *Age* editor Graham Perkin's invitation to join it with two columns a week after Perkin arranged for the column to be syndicated also to *The Sydney Morning*

Herald, the Brisbane *Courier Mail*, the Adelaide *Advertiser* and the Launceston *Examiner*. He didn't last long in *The Advertiser* or *The Examiner* and the *Courier Mail* and *Sydney Morning Herald* worried about what he wrote and censored some of it. But he stayed with *The Age* until the fierce battle over Fairfax control of it. This was described by the author and journalist Les Carlyon in *Paper Chase: The Press Under Examination* (Herald & Weekly Times) as the most important battle in Australian media history.

Carlyon's description of Adams' character and his part in that battle are pertinent. Under the will of David Syme, *The Age's* original owner, control was to pass to the family's third generation when his last son Oswald died. The family, management, staff and supporters were worried that the third generation would cash in their shares to get their hands on the money. Already, the Herald & Weekly Times, which Rupert Murdoch much desired but had not yet bought, and Sir Frank Packer (Kerry's father) had shown interest in buying *The Age*. The board arranged a marriage with Fairfax under which *The Age* became a 53 per cent Fairfax subsidiary but the Syme family retained editorial control. Les Carlyon said in his book: 'The marriage to Fairfax was consummated amid bizarre diversions. While the documents were being finalised on the fifth floor of *The Age*, an emissary from Rupert Murdoch was wandering around with a piece of paper which amounted to a counter offer. Sir Frank Packer of Consolidated Press sent a counter offer over the reporters' room telex.' Adams, perhaps Australia's best-known columnist, film maker, advertising man and wit convened the Friends of The Age and arranged a public meeting for December 17, 1979.

Adams told the meeting his column had been 'torn to shreds' by Fairfax and eventually disappeared from *The Sydney Morning Herald*. He ended what was a typical Adams production — lively, witty, highly personal and a touch exaggerated — with the rhetorical: 'God, we've already lost David Williamson and Graham Kennedy to Sydney. I'd hate us to lose the paper as well.'

In 1981 the Victorian Government set up the Norris inquiry by Sir John Norris QC into the ownership and control of newspapers in Victoria. It revealed that between 1923 and 1981 Australian capital city and national daily newspaper companies fell from 21 to three. Les Carlyon's book described Adams, then in his early forties, as 'something of a cult figure. To some, he is a hero in what they see as a world of journalistic sameness. To others, he is a deep pool of contradictions. He is a frantic worker: he used to write his *Age* columns as a sort of Sunday purgatory. For years he has worn black skivvies, which presumably save him the bother of shirts and ties; equally, the beard saves the bother of the razor. What no-one denies are Adams' gifts. He is a rare person: someone who writes the way he speaks. In conversation, as in print, he is witty, inventive, fluent and gently mocking. His voice is modulated and his speech, like his writing, is a mixture of whimsy and the best, the freshest, of Australian idiom. He was never an ambulance-chasing cadet reporter. He is rarely in *The Age* building and doesn't waste his time drinking with journalists.

'His columns are usually free of conventional journalistic ploys and forms that can become boring. They are free-ranging in style, anything from dialogue to question and answer, plays, essays, ribaldry, send-ups, pieces from the heart and jabs into other people's viscera. Adams strides eagerly into areas like religion, death and sexuality, which often seem to threaten more conventional columnists. And he takes as his agenda not necessarily the headlines of the week, which so many columnists do, but what interests him. For Adams loves ideas and the more outlandish the better. He loves to offend and he hates to bore. His writing is relaxed, witty, mordant and above all conversational. He writes with pathos about childhood and death, obviously subjects that attract and trouble him. He writes with bitterness, almost like a defrauded customer, about orthodox religion. His satire can be savage, yet many of his victims seem grateful. There are many reasons why Adams has become a cult figure but one is obvious: he is a sparklingly good writer who refuses to be dull or to take himself too seriously.'

A key to the Friends of The Age members' concern lay in Adams' statement to the inquiry: 'An organisation like ours is essentially a naïve one and an idealistic one. All that we could see was that the Fairfaxes might wish to relinquish their ownership of *The Age*.' As it happened, the inquiry found that Victorian newspaper ownership was concentrated; so far there had been no noticeable side effects, partly because of the proprietors' goodwill; but there was a potential danger if they acted without it. In any event, Fairfax steadily bought more and more of *The Age*; and in 1987 Murdoch succeeded in buying its only rival, the Herald & Weekly Times, reducing metropolitan and national newspaper companies in the Australian eastern states to two: News Ltd and Fairfax.

Like many government inquiries, the Norris Inquiry achieved nothing except acres of words.

The only way to prevent increasing media concentration in Australia is by legislation. But bodies like the Australian Competition and Consumer Commission and the Foreign Investment Review Board listen far more to business lobbyists and merchant bankers intent on gaining huge takeover fees than to the idea that the public benefits from maintaining as much competition as possible.

Adams claims his nine Penguin joke books with Patrice Newell have sold more than a million copies since the first, *The Penguin Book of Australian Jokes*, was launched in 1994. This would be a phenomenal, hardly-believable average of more than 100,000 copies per book, well over ten times average Australian book sales. They were a magnificent money-spinner for Adams, Patrice Newell and Penguin. Adams likes cracking jokes on his programs and in person but says the books were Penguin's idea, not his. He had to find the jokes and rewrite thousands of them into a house style. He thinks they found almost every joke in history. He said in his National Library oral history: 'It was an appalling experience and deeply depressing. But that's what jokes are. Jokes are little acts of exorcism where people deal with things they dislike or fear, whether it's sexual intercourse, impotence, nuns or politicians. So to fill a book which is a record of what people are laughing at — an oral history really — is crazy. Penguin panicked and took out some of the more lurid jokes, a wonderful one about the Queen which I really miss, and some of the more objectionable jokes about Aborigines which would not shock the Aborigines. Censorship in any form is dangerous.'

Adams also discovered that there are few genuine Australian jokes because almost every one has been recycled from overseas. His favourite joke is, however, genuinely Australian, about a couple of bushies who'd been making fences back o' Bourke. One asks the other, 'What are ya gunna do when ya got ya money, mate?' The other replies, 'I dunno. I might go down to S'nee.' The first bushie says, 'Yeah. S'nee's a pretty good place. And what route are ya taking?' The other bushie replies, 'Ah, I think I might take the wife. She's stuck with me through the drought!' The series included *The Penguin Book of More Australian Jokes, The Penguin Book of Jokes from Cyberspace, The Penguin Book of Schoolyard Jokes, The Penguin Book of World Jokes, The Penguin Book of All-New Australian Jokes, Pocket Jokes, More Pocket Jokes* and *What a Gag!More Kids' Jokes from the Net.*

How does Phillip plan his *Weekend Australian Magazine* columns? Not much at all, really. Usually he thinks up a topic but doesn't know where it will go; anything from a dog that has died on his farm to an idea the government should keep alive, like combating climate change. He writes up to four weekly columns in a weekend on the farm and the magazine editor and he decide by email which ones will be run in which weeks. He admits his columns are written quickly and intuitively rather than logically and thoughtfully. Often, this is obvious. Usually, the columns involve no research except through his extraordinary mind and memory.

Adams' columns and broadcasts have one thing in common: he tries to introduce people to ideas. In politics and public affairs, he sees his job as putting a counter view to what is being debated because usually the community is ill-informed, either through shortcomings in the media or in people's minds or because people don't want to be informed. He told me that in the Pauline Hanson era, when people were being brutal to refugees, they chose not to know that the refugees were completely within their legal rights to ask for asylum. To admit to this would have been too disturbing to Australian's sense of being tolerant. Many people did not want to know the truth. They'd rather go shopping.

Adams follows up very few of his *Late Night Live* conversations with highly intelligent and articulate people around the world by writing about the same people or ideas in *The Weekend Australian Magazine*. Obviously he couldn't just repeat his broadcasts, but he could follow-up ideas or concepts in some broadcasts by doing more research and writing about it in his column. Some of his listeners and readers would be the same people. However, my own conversations with 30 of Phillip's fans and non-fans revealed that almost all either listen often to the broadcasts but rarely read the columns, or the reverse.

My favourite Adams *Late Night Live* conversation was with Arthur Miller on February 6, 2001, repeated a few days after Arthur died in February 2005, and followed up in his *Weekend Australian Magazine* column on June 14, 2008. Adams told how he had asked his producers to assure Miller he would not mention Marilyn Monroe but Miller kept talking about her 'as if still awestruck by their improbable and ultimately sad relationship'. (I declare a special interest, as when I was a young freelance journalist hitchhiking around the world in 1956, I read in *The Los Angeles Examiner* that Marilyn was planning that day to fly to New York City to marry Arthur. I got a bus to the airport and tagged along behind a batch of Hollywood reporters. Marilyn sat in the doorway of her limo with her legs well displayed. I asked her as many questions as I could think of while she held my hand.)

Finally in his conversation with Arthur Miller, Adams got him to talk about *Death of a Salesman,* which had its opening night in 1949 but is still being played around the world. Adams wrote in *The Weekend Australian Magazine*, 'In the final scene, Willy Loman's old friend Charley gives one of the greatest speeches ever written for American theatre — about the inevitable end of a salesman's sustaining dream. Willy's wife kneels by the grave of the man she loved, for all his faults, and says, "I made the last payment on the house, Willy, but there'll be nobody home."' Adams said: 'Miller remembered standing at the back of the theatre on the opening night as the curtain fell. Total silence. Behind the curtain the actors were frozen with bewilderment. The silence went on for several minutes. Then they started to clap and they've been clapping ever since. It's no exaggeration to say the play changed my life every bit as much as it changed theatre.'

What interview or column subjects does Adams avoid? He does not talk about business and leaves his partnership in Monahan Dayman Adams out of any CV because 'I always see it as an accidental detour. But to be honest, it gave me money and with money (lots of it) I could bargain with prospective media employers because I was never desperate. I'm not terribly interested in business or economics. I get my weekly economics lecture from Paul Keating when he rings. I've never been numerate so I'm not good at economics.' Adams has, however, often had *Late Night Live* conversations with financial people since the world crash and its aftermath made finance a hot topic. Sport? Not a subject. 'It's not that I despise it or anything. It's wonderful for people who are good at it. But I do not like the mass-marketing of sport — or anything.' One sports interview he had on-air was with Aboriginal Australian Football League hero Kevin Sheedy, about his work with Aboriginal children. Typically, Adams spent the first ten minutes joking with him about their common low-income upbringing in Melbourne suburbs.

Adams tells how once he saved Keating from public embarrassment when Keating's clash with Bob Hawke was hot news. Keating bowled unannounced into Adams' office while a *Sydney Morning Herald* journalist was interviewing him about the arts, and started mouthing obscenities about Hawke. The *Herald* reporter thought Christmas had arrived. Adams said, "Paul, Paul, this is a journalist from *The Sydney Morning Herald*". But he wouldn't stop. After Keating left, Phillip appealed to the reporter not to report the outburst because she had been his guest at the time. She did not report it.

Chapter Eighteen: **Outspoken Views — He Stirs the Possum**

In conversations with me and in his *Weekend Australian Magazine* columns, Phillip Adams tells how to elect an Australian president; why voters have become more conservative; why they join community groups and not political parties; why solar power is an answer to the biggest community concern of climate change; why the world has so much information but little wisdom; why there are some reasons to be happy; what John and Heather did to save families; how drugs killed a politician's son; how the real pornography is violence not sex; how companies indulge in paedophilia; where Melbourne is different from Sydney; how high executive salaries are obscene; how radio talkback taught him a lesson; how he has searched for a solution to Aboriginal problems; and how Western society censors death.

* * *

How to elect a president: If the Australian Government asked the people whether they wanted the government or the people to choose a president, they would want to do it themselves, but Adams has no confidence in that model. The 1999 republic referendum failed because the question was poorly phrased. Asked whether voters wanted to alter the constitution to replace the Queen and the governor-general with a president chosen by a two-thirds majority of federal MPs, only 45.13 per cent of voters (and a minority in all states) said yes. Adams told me: 'People don't realise that they don't elect the prime minister. The Labor Party or Liberal MPs do. And if the voters elected a president, this figure would have a bigger mandate that the prime minister, which would put a big strain on the system. The kind of people I would like to see as president would never put up their hands for a popular vote. You would never get someone like Sir William Deane (governor-general from 1996 to 2001) to run for president although he would have been terrific in the job. Perhaps the best way would be a halfway house: Parliament prepares a short list and the voters choose the person they want from that.'

* * *

Why electorate is conservative: Adams pointed out to me that, as the pace of change accelerates, people become frightened and discomforted. So they turn back and look for simpler answers or they become angry and can then be attracted to groups such as One Nation.

Some become Islamic fundamentalists. In a world where everything changes by the hour, they look for people with simple answers. And because they become angry about the pace of change, they listen to shock jocks who yell, and they buy strident tabloids.

* * *

Community groups grow: Many pent-up progressive attitudes are being expressed not by political parties but by community groups. Australians act together and decisively in a crisis such as the 2004 Asian tsunami or the 2009 Victorian bushfires. (Also the floods in January 2011 — author.) Adams said in *The Weekend Australian Magazine* on February 28, 2009: 'The worst brings out the best. The bushfires were beyond belief, beyond description, beyond bearing. Yet a sense of community was created even as communities were being destroyed. That's the great paradox of such havoc. Suddenly, sometimes too late, people know and care about their neighbours. The Victorian fires were Australia's 9/11.

'Australians have always worried about national identity. We quarrel over it, we fret about it. The bushfires ended the argument. But will it last? When the smoke has cleared, when the ashes are cold, will the sense of identity, of community, endure? The communal energies released by the fires, and the sense of mutual responsibility they intensified, came at a time when we need to rethink just about everything — from capitalism to the climate.'

Adams has his doubts about a rising tide of community spirit although the social researcher Hugh Mackay says there has been a profound change. Adams told me, 'Hugh talks about a future when forty per cent of Australians live alone because they choose not to get married or not to have children, causing a new real-estate phenomenon. They live in alienating cities but they join up and form alliances. They don't join political parties because they are bitter about party politics but they throng to non-government organisations and community and pressure groups. More people are engaged in politics outside the parties than probably ever before.'

* * *

The biggest concern: 'The ongoing crisis of climate change is the biggest community concern,' Adams told me. 'Everything is over-heated — the planet, the economy, the population and industry. The world has to turn temperatures down, to stop over-using resources and having so many babies, and the only hope that this will happen is through community pressure.' In The Weekend Australian Magazine on March 24, 2007, Adams wrote: 'While we squander trillions in wars — wars in Iraq and Afghanistan, wars on drugs and terror — the most important war, on carbon dioxide, gets small change, tokenism and political grandstanding. Yet this is our first truly world war. The last time I counted the dead from decades of terrorism, it was about thirty thousand and most were victims of internal conflict in places like Sri Lanka, not of the transnational bin Laden brand. Yet climate change is affecting all of us and it won't stop after a few years. Already it is too late to stop it; the best we can hope is to take the foot off the accelerator and it will linger. Or failing an effective response, it will intensify for centuries.

'This is the biggest war in human history,' Adams continued, warming to one of his favourite campaigns. 'The weather threatens to impact on health, security and food, with even the optimists agreeing that millions will be fighting for food and water — or for land to stand on. Those disposed from Bangladesh to the Pacific islands will create wave after wave of boat people, many of whom will head our way. Yet it seems that the greatest concern of NSW and federal politicians is voter volatility in mining areas.' There are 1,600 applications to open or extend coal mines in NSW and no coal application in the state has ever been rejected. The Commission for the Future began agitating about climate change from its formation in 1985. (Adams was its foundation chairman; its aim was social and economic research but its federal government budget was progressively reduced and it was closed in 1998.) It had the climate-change data, the information and the knowledge but the wisdom to deal with it was in short supply.

* * *

The climate change fiasco: After Adams was made the first chairman of the Commission for the Future in 1985, it met with Australia's top scientists and decided to make climate change (then called the less-palatable global warming) its top priority. Barry Jones, as Prime Minister Bob Hawke's minister for science, had come up with the idea of the commission so the government could look beyond the election cycle to see what long-term problems should be tackled. He particularly wanted to get a dialogue going between the public and scientists who talked in their own language. The commission, with Adams as chairman, arranged for climate-change scientists to address public meetings in town halls all over Australia by satellite, the first time this had been done.

Adams told me that the more the scientists predicted a catastrophe, the more the audiences seemed to like it. 'It was a religious event,' he said. 'People were not concerned about greenhouse gases coming from rice paddies or cattle; they wanted to hear about the evil automobile and the evil power factory. It was the start of a new religion. The scientific basis of climate change is rock solid. Idiots still deny it. It is a scientific fact but has been made a political issue. The world has to act on it or the world will be uninhabitable and we will die.'

So it is now 25 years since the commission and a whole range of scientists started agitating for action on climate-change — and successive Australian governments have done little about it except talk and worry about losing votes in industrial and mining seats.

* * *

The answer is solar: John Gorton had just retired as prime minister in 1971 when Adams sat at a dinner next to the scientist Sir Macfarlane Burnet and his wife, who was dying of leukemia. The scientist attacked Gorton's idea of a nuclear Australia not just because of the threat of leukemia but also because nuclear power stations are an invitation to terrorists. And you can't get rid of the n-waste. Adams told me the simple answer was solar power. Australia should make solar energy its next Snowy Mountains Scheme. He claimed that if Australia built a solar reflector 165km by 160km in the middle of the Nullabor Plain, it could create enough power for the whole world. That was in the 1970s. Nothing much has happened with solar power in Australia since then. And the coal industry had continued to make fortunes by digging more coal, exporting it and using it to fire power stations that fill the atmosphere with greenhouse gases.

* * *

The system is broken: Phillip Adams told me: 'My concern is that the last time we had a severe recession, it led to Hitler, World War 11 and 55 million people being killed. So if you add climate change and population pressure, no-one — least of all me — can predict what will happen. The system is broken. You can't fiddle with bits of it. The whole situation has to be dealt with, because as the Indians and Chinese buy cars and live like us, the planet will boil. You and I are sitting here today,' Adams told me. 'It looks like an ordinary day. The sun is shining; there is milk in the fridge and petrol in the car. But we don't know what will happen. All we know is that the world is a total mess. Everything needs to change, personal behaviour, communal behaviour and all tiers of government have to be brought into play if we are to get through this crisis. We have the data, the information and the knowledge, but where is the wisdom? We have taken centuries to get where we are and we've mucked it up. And we didn't have the brains to head-off AIDS, which is caused by poverty intensified by over-population.'

* * *

Rome and the condom: On no subject is Adams more aggressive than Rome's prohibition of artificial contraception. In The Australian on July 15, 2008, he wrote:

'Vast numbers of people have died, are dying and will die because of this insane and utterly reprehensible prohibition. The Vatican's prohibition of the condom is on the short list of the cruellest, most appalling pieces of public policy in human history. It is a death sentence passed on to millions, including millions as yet unborn. The two greatest crises on earth are both condom-related: AIDS and over-population. Climate change will continue to accelerate while we continue to crowd the planet with ever-more climate-changers, seven billion and counting. With Catholicism fast losing ground to the fast-faith franchises, the future of the Catholic religion lies in Africa. There, at least, its market share is booming. The condemnation of the condom guarantees life to millions of surplus human beings while condemning millions to death. The fact that this cheap, simple and ancient device can prevent HIV as well as pregnancy will not be admitted by Rome.'

* * *

Cheer yourself up again: Never in human history, wrote Adams in The Weekend Australian Magazine on June 20, 2009, have so many people lived in what might be described as freedom, actual or comparative. The religious and political monoliths have been crumbling. If you're not in a war zone or dying from malnutrition or a pandemic, there's a good chance that your life expectancy has vastly increased. Previously fatal diseases can be cured and it doesn't hurt so much to go to the dentist. Education and literacy, once the province of the aristocracy and their priesthoods, are now, like travel, democratised. And we know thousands of times more than our ancestors did.'

* * *

Saving families in distress: In The Weekend Australian Magazine on June 21, 2007, Adams wrote: 'A 13-year-old girl dies in wretched motel where her teenage pimp has forced her to service one more of many clients, a man in his fifties. She dies in agony after injecting herself with heroin laced with battery acid. A few miles away a 14-year-old girl is hanging out with her friends. To deal with their anger and boredom, they start "bashing a derro". Screaming in terror, he falls to the ground, where she joins in kicking him. Until she recognises his face. It's her father. These scenes did not take place in remote Aboriginal communities but in inner Melbourne suburbs. This column has reported many similar stories concerning kids known to John Embling and Heather Pilcher in the Families in Distress Foundation, which was funded by readers for decades. Horrors like these, plus worsening health, forced my heroic friends to retire. Like the thousands of children they helped, John and Heather were old beyond their years.' Adams told me that although the foundation has been closed, he still receives letters and emails asking how John and Heather are and wanting to donate.

* * *

Cruel and stupid drug laws: Adams clearly remembers when, 28 years ago, Barry Jones phoned to say John Button's son David had been found dead from a drug overdose. Earlier, Adams had briefly seen Button (minister for industry and commerce in the Hawke and Keating governments) at Sydney Airport and Button had told him, 'David's a junkie. You've got kids.' Adams had thought his own children were safe from drugs, but if David Button was addicted, the intelligent son of gifted and privileged parents, anyone's children were at risk. Just after Button himself died, aged 74, from pancreatic cancer in April 2008, Adams wrote in The Weekend Australian Magazine: 'John argued against our cruel and stupid drug laws.' Adams says addictive drugs should be legalised.

* * *

'The pornography of violence': This is a phrase Adams remembers using in the censorship wars of the late 1960s. The church and state were determined to maintain sexual taboos but were turning blind eyes to films of people killing each other. In The Weekend Australian Magazine on May 17, 2008, Adams wrote: 'These days, actors are shot, knifed, minced and torn apart with much more skill. Prosthetic wounds and burns are much more convincing and digital destruction blows the mind as well as the heads off the extras. Yet the churches are still obsessed with sex. Though the pornographic violence in video games encourages our kids to butcher human beings on a Rwandan scale, religious leaders sit beneath their phallic spires and mammiferous domes bleating about bonking. Censorship is dead. Everyone's got a camera or a phone with a prying eye and do-it-yourself porn is a bigger hobby than stamp collecting. For generations movies have taught us what to eat, wear and drive. As sure as Microsoft programs our computers, Hollywood programs our minds. Porn has profoundly changed teenage sexual behaviour. Anal, oral and other sexual variations are now as familiar as Tupperware — and it's not just porn downloads that are responsible. What kids are seeing on free television, from Big Brother turkey slaps to the blow-by-blow depictions of blowjobs on Underbelly, are even more educational. Hence my incredulity when researchers tell me that the pornography of violence doesn't make crims more violent or our kids more predisposed. We live in a culture of what A Clockwork Orange called "ultraviolence".'

* * *

Corporate paedophilia: This was a term Adams coined in 1995 to describe the abuse of children not by priests or scoutmasters but by companies wanting to turn children into customers, into economic units: a new form of child labour. Children in Victorian England were sent down coalmines or up chimneys but our children are sent into shopping malls to influence what their parents buy or to buy junk themselves. And Adams would know about this as he was an advertising agency partner for 35 years. In The Weekend Australian Magazine on November 18, 2006, he attacked the way fashion houses use barely pubescent models, bombard the very young with sex and violence and mass-market to children. 'Bras for eight-year-olds? Guns for their little brothers? Accelerating adulthood long before the teenage years and pressure on parents from children who themselves are subject to peer pressure in school playgrounds orchestrated by executives who recognise no age of consent. We don't see what's happening all around us because it has become utterly familiar.'

* * *

The Sydney-Melbourne divide: When Adams moved from Melbourne to Sydney in the late 1980s, he realised Sydney didn't 'give a stuff' about Melbourne and never even thought about it. Melbourne was where the thinking tended to be done and Sydney was the place for marketing and sales strategy. Melbourne invented the film industry in 1896, when the first Australian film was made; but Sydney has the studios. Melbourne has more writers; Sydney has the publishers. Melbourne is sober, Sydney is entrepreneurial. Sydney had creatures like John Singleton and Kerry Packer, who you could never imagine living in Melbourne. Sydney has never had an Alan Jones; it has Derryn Hinch, 'but he's a completely different kind of ratbag,' said Adams. Sydney has the shock jocks, the racy Daily Telegraph and the energy Melbourne lacks. The Australian Opera, the Australia Council and the newspaper and magazine head offices are all in Sydney. But the balance started to change when Jeff Kennett, who might have been born in Sydney, was Victorian premier from 1992 to '99. The Sydney-Melbourne differences have more recently balanced out a lot.

* * *

Obscene salaries: Adams saw Allan Moss, Macquarie Bank's ex-chief executive, at the federal government's 2020 Summit in February 2008 — the man who was paid $33,480,000 in 2006-07 and got an $80million golden handshake when he left in May 2008. Everything Moss touched was reputed to turn to gold, like the urinal when Adams followed him into the Summit toilet. Adams was worried about Moss' successor, Nicholas Moore, being paid a few million less — such humiliation! 'To make matters worse,' Adams wrote in The Weekend Australian Magazine on June 21, 2008, 'Nicholas doesn't seem quite as nice as Allan, who flashed his gold teeth at us at the Summit as though faintly embarrassed by the obscenity of his income. Even with his reduced income, Nick will be paid more than all 226 members of federal parliament together and nearly a hundred times more than the prime minister. In 1992, the income of a typical chief executive in Australia's top fifty companies was 27 times the average wage; by 2002, it was 98 times the average. To hell with wage restraint!'

* * *

Talkback teaches Adams a lesson: Driving to 2UE before broadcasting one evening in the late 1980s, Adams was shocked, then appalled, then infuriated listening to the broadcaster who preceded him that evening, Stan Zemanek. Zemanek was directing a stream of bigotry at 'those bloody Abos'. When Adams arrived at 2UE, he physically removed Zemanek from the studio they shared and next day complained to the station management about his rabid racism. Adams wrote in The Weekend

Australian Magazine on September 1, 2007, six weeks after Zemanek died of a brain tumor: 'The management's response taught me a lesson about commercial talk radio: it thrives on bigotry. It makes much of its money out of fear and ignorance, so it wants its personalities to pour petrol rather than oil on troubled waters. Social division pays dividends, so stations turn a deaf ear to slanders of Aborigines, Asians, homosexuals, do-gooders, feminists, unionists and Muslims while laughing at broadcasting's ridiculous, sniveling regulators.' Once, when the Australian of the Year was the painter Arthur Boyd, Zemanek said on-air, 'Who the hell's this Boyd bloke? Who's ever heard of him? What's he ever done for Australia?' Boyd had, in fact, just donated his property on the Shoalhaven River and paintings worth millions of dollars to Australia. He died in 1999.

* * *

Searching for a cancer cure: Adams admits he used to have the same view of Aborigines as John Gorton, who as prime minister stood on the Old Parliament House steps, looked at a demonstration by Aborigines below and commented to Adams, 'Inoperable cancer.' Since soon after that, Adams has moved into and out of Aboriginal affairs but has never worked out what should be done, largely because Aboriginal leaders are opposed to each other. He does not accept for a moment that the abuse of women and children is any worse in Aboriginal communities than in white ones. 'Visit your local court on so-called 'Ladies' Day' and see a stream of white women seeking apprehended violence orders against abusive husbands,' he told me during one of our sessions in Paddington. 'Late Night Live has done dozens of programs on Aborigines and I just don't buy the idea that they are any worse in the treatment of women and children than white people,' he claimed, although the evidence is very much against him. 'I've gone to many Aboriginal communities and seen the problems, the glue-sniffing, the petrol-sniffing and the tragedy of children literally beating their brains out on walls. My campaign has been to intensify discussion. That's why we take the program to Aboriginal communities most years. A huge amount of the money poured into the Aboriginal situation has gone to white government servants, whose corruption is breathtaking. Drunken Aboriginal leaders are manipulated by calculating white bureaucrats. Captain James Cook arriving in Botany Bay in 1770 would be like a huge mothership from outer space landing in Centennial Park in Sydney or the Treasury Gardens in Melbourne. Glittering creatures with far superior technology would overwhelm us with their power, education and sophistication. The encounter would so psychologically shatter us that we would despair and turn to grog. I have no answers to the Aboriginal situation. Every time white people try to find answers, they muck it up. The only people who can find answers are Aboriginal people themselves,' said Adams. For a start, their leaders could spend most of their time in remote Aboriginal communities telling parents how important it is for their children to go to school every day.

* * *

Deciding to die: Most people won't face the fact that they will die. We don't have death insurance; we have life insurance. We don't die; we rest in peace or pass away. Adams believes we should use the awareness of mortality as an aphrodisiac for living. Death is censored in Western society. Many adults go to their graves without ever having seen a body. 'Years ago, I was asked to do a program for See It My Way on ABC Television. I wanted to do it on death with a real corpse in the background, not an actor holding his breath. So I asked the props people to find me a stiff but it was vetoed by the management, who thought it would be in poor taste. No other generation has lived under such a cluster of Damoclean swords. We have cancer, we have nuclear war, we have ecological doom, but people don't like discussing death. Parents discuss sex with their children but few tell their children that they, and the children, will ultimately die. Until we know we are going to die and can discuss it, I don't think we can really live. But something else about agnosticism and atheism: if you know you are going to die, and if you believe that will be it, you will be the last person on earth to want to kill someone else. The great butchers of human history have been people who really believe that life is a temporary resting place on the way to heaven and that you are almost doing a pagan a favour by bashing his baby's brains out.'

Chapter Nineteen: **Best Columns — Songs of Satire and Dogs**

Phillip Adams' *Age* and *Bulletin* columns from 1977 to 1983 were among his best ever. Lord Byron (1788-1824) wrote, 'Fools are my theme, let satire be my song.' Adams' satire in those early columns certainly sang, as is shown in these extracts from his *Age* and *Bulletin* columns, reproduced in Penguin books. The columns reveal his remarkable insight and humour about humour itself, about loving, growing-up and the Royals. Some of Adams' best writing is about animals on his farm and also in this chapter he brings to life Two-Up (an orphaned kangaroo joey who adopted Adams as her mother), silly Willy (a Jack Russell with a death wish), Annie the butch bitch, and Molly, whose problem was tyres. Adams writes with considerable insight born of constant study that dogs have got humans bluffed.

*   *   *

In 'On Laughing' in *Uncensored Adams* (1981, reproduced with permission by Penguin Group Australia), Adams wrote: 'With all due respect to the appeals mounted on behalf of the heart, the kidneys and the Salvos, please ignore them for the next ten minutes. The venture which I am officially launching this morning, my Joke Appeal, must take precedence. Humour is, believe it or not, the Latin word for wetness, which only emphasises our current drought conditions.

'The Old Testament made just 29 references to laughter, of which 13 have to do with scorn and derision, while only two are born of joy. Aristotle said laughter was related to ugliness and debasement, Cicero linked it to deformity and Descartes stressed its links to hate. When compiling the top 40 subjects that could be relied upon to produce a chuckle, Francis Bacon put cripples at the top of the list. According to a study of the Bushmen of the Kalahari, regarded as among the most primitive people on earth (second only to the Young Liberals), ancient humour erupted when they were watching the death of a speared animal, the jitterbugging choreography of its final spasms. As late as 1961, a group of American researchers found that children between the ages of 8 and 15 laughed loudest at the mortification, discomfort and hoaxing of their fellows, while turning deaf lungs to witty remarks.

'Scientists looked at humour from a mechanistic, behaviourist viewpoint, so that if you asked them, 'Why did the chicken cross the road?', they'd say, 'To produce a reflex involving the co-ordination contraction of 15 muscles in a stereotype pattern and accompanied by altered breathing.' Asked why firemen wear red braces, they'd reply, 'So as to release an electrical stimulus acting on the main lifting muscles of the upper lip and the xygomatic major with currents of varying intensity producing everything from the faint smile to the contortions typical of explosive laughter.' And if you asked a biologist about the travelling salesman and the farmer's daughter, he'd look decidedly thin-lipped. For his calling regards laughter with suspicion in that it has no biological purpose. Indeed, biologists have called laughter 'luxury reflex'.

'The underlying reality of humour is, undoubtedly, absurdity. Absurdity, otherwise known as death, is the central fact of our existence. For 20 years, I've been writing about this subject above all others — it's an awareness of death that both curses and dignifies humanity, that defines us as a species. Life is brief, ephemeral, mortal. Yet our aspirations stretch into eternity. As Woody Allen has observed, death is the inspiration of every comedian, every artist. Without death, we'd be trapped in the boring, eternal vistas of paradise where, as Mark Twain suggested, laughter would be most unlikely. It's because of death that some people laugh at deformity, that intimation of doom. We laugh when a pompous man slips on a banana. That's a metaphoric comment on the nature of humanity. We're all pompous, all vain, all self-important. Yet we're all destined to slip on the banana of death. Three cheers for laughter.'

* * *

From 'On Loving' in *Uncensored Adams*: 'Unless readers have very strong stomachs, they should skip this page. The contents will, I'm afraid, disgust you. But at Australia's leading newsmagazine (*The Bulletin*), we have a responsibility, a duty, to bring you the facts, to expose the soft underbelly of Australian society. A few weeks ago, the press was full of the most excruciating Valentine's Day messages. One read them with growing disbelief and rising nausea. They were so cute, so cloying, so yecch as to threaten the reader with brain damage. Things got underway innocently with endless variations of the 'Roses are red, violets are blue' variety. They began a rapid deterioration. Consider the following message to Casanova from Spunk Bubble:

"The matinee's great on Mondays
With black fellows and bundies
But keep a straight face
As you leap around the place,
In your inside-out undies."

'A few inches further on, we had a ménage a trois Valentine: "Bumbola. To the spunkiest wiggles in the world, happy Valentine's Day. Bulk love, Borrie and Horrie."

'And what of this poignant message from what was, clearly, a wronged woman:

"Alan. If you love her, set her free.
If she comes back, she's yours.
If she doesn't, she never was.
Happy Valentine's Day.
With love. Your wife."

'And what about this, from a Casanova of the electric tram? "All girls. Thank you for being passengers on my tram. Thanks for sharing your East Preston-City journey with me. Thanks for being you. Tram Conductor 2903."'

* * *

'On Growing Up': In the same book of his columns, Phillip, then 42, talked of his 'advancing years': 'When I was a child, I thought as a child. Trouble is I still do. As with a significant percentage of my fellow adults, growing up has eluded me. Having looked forward to maturity for damn near 40 years, it continues to elude me, receding like the rainbow. And discussing the problem with others of advancing years, it emerges that a majority still feel far, far younger than their dilapidated externals suggest. Well, where have we gone wrong? Why didn't we gain the appropriate dignity? Why has the wisdom of our age eluded us? Why are we bogged in a never never land with so many psychic Peter Pans simply pretending to be adults? Always afraid that others, especially our kids, will find us out. In the beginning, I thought that one matured or grew up fairly dramatically, at one or another of life's punctuation marks.

'The odd thing is that while your outsides changed, while you puckered, creased, lost your hair and gained responsibility (and weight), the essential you didn't change at all. So one's situation is perilous. If people woke up to the deception, if they realised that you suffered from this curious form of retardation, they wouldn't let you ride in a lift on your own or vote at elections. And if your children were a wake-up, your already beleaguered authority would diminish completely, anarchy prevailing. Where I'd heard, of course, of second childhood, I'm now inclined to disbelieve it. How can you have a second when you can't escape the gravitation pull of the first? Perhaps the second childhood is merely the moment when you stop pretending, when you just lie back and enjoy it. For all that, it's depressing to see the way your own kids ache for adulthood, trying to force the pace.'

* * *

'On Yarralumla' (*Uncensored Adams*): '*The Bulletin* has, as you know, a proud tradition of anti-monarchism. There was a time when the *Bully's* Republican rhetoric was so savage that Queen Victoria must have considered sending a gunboat to blast editor Archibald out of his quayside pub. So I cannot understand why my gentle gibes at the Windsors have provoked such an apoplectic mail. I am, after all, perfectly willing to let our Royals linger on as a Tussaud-like tourist attraction. For no matter what you say, Her Majesty and the Duke of Edinburgh are remarkably lifelike, albeit in a rather waxen way. So let the Queen be 'heads' to our democratic tails. Let ageing knights wear their decorations on proud bosoms, just as Twinings flash their 'Royal Appointment' crest on their tea chests.

'The Royal Family deserves the same consideration as other beleaguered species, such as the Crest-Fallen Kingaroy Cockatoo and the Splay-Toed Aardvark. Royal breeding stock is at an all-time low and, of course, haemophilia could break out at any moment. You may remember my recent complaint that people of leftish political persuasions rarely receive a gilt-edged invitation to Yarralumla. Well, to my astonishment, one of the crisp, elegantly-embossed cards arrived. Gilt-edged, it suggested that if I presented myself and the child bride at the front door, in dinner jacket and long dress respectively, we'd be given some nosh. Anxious to bury the hatchet, to negotiate a truce, to build a little bridge of understanding, I decided to accept — on condition that I was given special dispensation from the dinner jacket and permitted to front up in my skivvy. This, the aide-de-camp suggested, would be fine.

'Once inside, while I did a quick calculation on the value of the McCubbins and Nolans, the wives piled their pelts on a table in the hall and the husbands were given their marching orders. That is, we each received a little card showing Who Sat Where and Whose Wife we'd be taking into dinner. I cracked it for the beaut Mrs Brissendon, who's wedded to old RF, the chairman of the Literature Board. Later I learned that a Mr Baillieu had won my missus in the raffle. But first, we formed ourselves into two-by-twos so we could be Announced, whereupon I found myself grinning sheepishly at His and Her Excellencies, the very charming Cohens. Sir Zelman, you might have noticed, closely resembles the late Sir Charles Chaplin. The same piano-key smile below the same scrunched-up eyes.

'Having run the Vice-Regal gauntlet, we had a glass of sherry by the fire. Then we promenaded into the dining room, an intimate little chamber for 40 guests and, it seemed, almost as many servants. I found myself between the resplendent wife of a Rear Admiral (a beaut lady with a naughty sense of humour) and an absolutely enormous bloke who turned out to be the token trade unionist.

'"I could have danced all night," Mrs A sang in the back of the cab on our way home, looking curiously dishevelled. She'd also collected a bag full of business cards, two American Expresses and one Diners, not to mention two medals, an Order of Australia and a Royal Darby saucer. As for me, I paid dearly for a good feed — I have sacrificed my last shred of credibility with the left.'

* * *

Gough Whitlam said in the introduction to *Uncensored Adams*: 'It is a fortunate coincidence that Australia's leading comic writer is also her most perceptive social critic. In no-one else do we find that irrepressible and conquering blend of wit and seriousness that mark Phillip Adams' writings: a worried amusement at the eccentricities of our society, allied to an unerring instinct for the absurd and a Nabokovian fondness for verbal ingenuity.'

* * *

In *The Inflamable Adams* (1983, reproduced with permission by Penguin Group Australia), Adams wrote: 'As an ardent monarchist, my heart goes out to Her Royal Maj. I think it's awful the way we've been allowed to invade her privacy, to read the innermost details of her private life. Why can't the poor Queen be left in peace to have a squalid love affair, if that's what she wants? And why not? After all, it's a palace tradition. Ever since that princess had it off with a frog, your royals have been drawn to the virility of the lower orders. In Henry V111, Shakespeare makes mention of the king's promiscuity with 'a little touch of Harry in the night' while a few coronations later we had Charles 11 lusting after Nell Gwyn. There was Louis X1V and Madame Pompadour, Edward V11 and Lilly Langtree, Hamlet and Ophelia, the Prince of Wales and Mrs Fitzherbert — even Prince Charming and Cinderella. You'll recall the nursery rhyme about the king in his counting house counting out his money while the poor queen was in the parlour, consoling herself with bread and honey.

'No-one complains when Prince Andrew, known far and wide as Randy Andy, goes slumming in the least salubrious of night spots. No-one objected when Prince Charles went out on the tiles. Even Princess Margaret was allowed to marry a member of the paparazzi, Tony 'Flash Bulb' Snowdon. If anyone deserves the solace of romance, it's Elizabeth 11. Yet the only declaration of love she's had in the past 20 years was that "I did but see her passing by" line from an old age pensioner who happened to be prime minister of Australia.'

* * *

Former High Court Judge Michael Kirby said in a Foreword to *The Inflammable Adams:* 'Temperence, restraint and decorum are not the strong points of our author. Indeed, I doubt that these sterling but boring qualities are to be found in these pages at all. The infuriating thing is that Adams offers the most telling commentary on our country, our world and our times, almost without our noticing it. So complete is Adams' command of the language that he can instruct us with humour, apparently irrelevant facts and an assortment of ideas. And the whole powerful mixture is utterly painless as it does its devilish work.'

* * *

'Two-Up' was the story of a kangaroo joey which chose Adams as its new mother in *Adam's Ark* (Viking, 2004, reproduced with permission by Penguin Group Australia). Adams wrote: 'At Elmswood, most animals make a lot of noise, which is why we're woken around dawn by the crow of roosters, the braying of donkeys, the barking of dogs, the whinnying of horses and the bellowing of cattle. Almost every animal, wild or domestic, has its characteristic sound, if not a variety of them. Except for the kangaroo. As the world knows from Skippy, kangaroos are immensely talented animals that can not only box but can also defeat evildoers and play the piano. But they have no identifying cry, no mating call, no vocal signal of danger or distress. All you hear from kangaroos, and you have to be very close, is that little Skippy-style chirrup. Even when kangaroos are being culled, they're silent.

'Finding that some paddock gates had been left open by uninvited shooters, I went off on the four-wheel bike to check others and found a female kangaroo dying from a rifle bullet. She made no noise at all but her eyes were huge and reproachful. I hurried back to the homestead, returned with a rifle and gave the poor animal a coup de grâce. At which point I heard a noise, the angry chirrup of a joey. It slowly approached and, as I stepped back a few yards, wriggled into its dead mother's pouch.

'Once again I went back to the homestead and this time returned with an old black skivvy. I knotted the arms and closed the neck with some bailing wire and then eased the joey from the pouch. The chirruping became much louder, yet it didn't put up much of a fight when I popped it into the skivvy. Back at the homestead I dangled the substitute pouch from a doorknob in the laundry. Patrice rang a local vet, who said yes, he had some suitable powdered milk and an appropriate teat that we could stick on an empty Coke bottle, so I made a mercy dash into Scone. We mixed up the milk, popped on the teat and to my astonishment, the joey took the teat instantly, hungrily, and lay curled up in my lap while it drank a good half-bottle. And that was it. Joey decided I was Mum. And from that moment we were inseparable. Everywhere I walked, it would hop behind me. And if I crouched and unbuttoned my shirt, it would stick its head and front paws inside and do a complete roll until it was lying quite happily against my bare chest, its hind legs sticking out near my collar. When I went to the bathroom, it hopped in, too. If I had a shower, it would hop into the shower. Extraordinarily, it would also jump into the swimming pool with me.

'An examination of its ambiguous genitalia hinted that it was a female but, to be on the safe side, we gave it an ambidextrous name: Two-Up. Two-Up and I began a whole series of adventures. At night, she would roll happily into the skivvy and I'd dangle it from the door. While still devoted to her rubber nipple, Two-Up was starting to pick at grass and grow very quickly. She became too heavy for skivvies and increasingly curious about the world around her. Sometimes she'd disappear for ten minutes or an hour. Just when I was getting worried, I would see her hopping back from an inspection of the chicken coops or the hay shed. Two-Up was entirely feminine. She had lustrous eyes, long eyelashes and delicate hands that were almost human in their dexterity. She remained entirely friendly and utterly charming.

'Nonetheless she went AWOL more and more. Soon she was disappearing for a day or a night or a couple of days. Nature was calling; Two-Up was responding to the pangs of puberty. So, sadly, I accepted the inevitable. Two-Up would leave home. And she did.'

* * *

In 'Dogs Are Weird' in *Adam's Ark,* Adams showed his astute understanding of animals of all breeds, particularly dogs: 'The dog is busy. Very, very busy. It is a particularly busy little dog. It has, in rapid succession, gone yelping after a rabbit, had a pee in the garden and followed its nose over a zigzag course across the lawn, as if propelled by its energetic sniffing. It has returned to have a long scratch, sniffed the battered boots lined up against the wall, snapped at a number of blowies orbiting its muzzle and managed to swallow one. It has gnawed at one of the osso buco bones from its considerable collection, run and barked at a passing cattle truck and growled at a couple of brown chooks free-ranging their way through a garden bed. It has run to the kitchen door wagging its tail in the hope of conjuring a pat, a snack, and a walk. It has chased a blue-tongue lizard off the path. It has gnawed the ear of an entirely unbusy, drowsing border collie, desisting when it provoked an angry growl. And it has rolled, cringing, on to its back at my approach, its body language saying something along the lines of "Have mercy upon me, oh mighty one."

'Contrasting with its frenetic behaviour are long periods when it simply switches itself off. It stops scurrying, burrowing, scratching, sniffing, chasing, barking, everything, and it sits, sphinx-like. Or sleeps. Which reminds you that dogs live in an eternal now, their consciousness shining in front of their muzzles like a hand-held torch. They have an area of brilliant illumination, and everything else is obscured, unseen, unconsidered. Dogs aren't into abstract ideas or intellectualising and, consequently, are safe from boredom. And from time itself. Our dogs welcome us back as rapturously after an hour away as they do if we've been gone a month. Instantly alert, instantly gratified, instantly blank of mind, that's a dog.

'A long line of dogs have lived and died at Elmswood. Willy, the greatest boot-rooter of all time, died in a kamikaze attack on a passing truck. Willy, silly Willy. Then there was Annie, half Willy's weight, delicate and deft, but still unmistakably a Jack Russell. No, not a Jill Russell, imbued with the feminine but a little butch bitch who, for all her ladylike appearance, liked to eat cow poo when she wasn't rolling in it. Annie, who liked to chase rabbits down burrows risking permanent entombment in the middle of a honeycombed hillside, only to emerge as dusty as a four-wheel drive, often with a gob full of fur. Often she'd appear at the door muddier than a gumboot following an altercation with a ram in the shearing yards. Annie recalled the poem about the little girl who had a little curl in the middle of her forehead. When Annie was good, which was infrequent, she was excruciatingly good, mincingly good, Lady Fauntleroy good. But when she was bad, she was the Hound of the Baskervilles, a canine crim who you couldn't train to do anything, not even respond obediently to such reasonable requests as, "Come here, you rotten little bastard, or I'll drop-kick you halfway across the bloody paddock."

'Now there's Molly, who is almost exactly the same as Annie, though, as far as we know, they're not related. Same size, same colouring, same temperament. Her tail is highly articulate and can communicate urgent desires for bones, rides in the car or a long yelping run up to the letterbox at the main road. The same tail can also sink to the road in a gesture symbolising the most abject apology.

Will Molly last the summer? So far the problem isn't snakes but tyres. I spend a lot of time charging around the place on an ATV, one of those motorised trikes with four wheels. Molly hates my ATV and attacks it as soon as I press the starter button. She doesn't bark so much as shriek, emitting a series of high-frequency percussions that set the nerves on edge to exactly the same degree as dentistry without anaesthesia. I scream at her, she shrieks at the ATV and, not content with that, does her best to disappear beneath its large balloon tyres. If Molly does survive the vehicles, she's a dead cert to fall victim to venom, because she's drawn to places where snakes hide in the same self-sacrificial way as a Fred Nile is drawn to the habitat of sin. Piles of rocks cleared from the paddocks; stacks of old timber and firewood; the final pile of bales in an emptying hayshed. She's drawn to those snake motels like Imelda Marcos was to shoe stores.

'She digs like the Western Mining Company. Sometimes she'll sit beside us at the gravelly edge of the river and if we start digging in the sand with just one finger, she'll immediately take over, chucking sand around like an erupting volcano without the foggiest idea of why she's digging, or for what. If we dig a few centimetres, she'll dig a metre until, finally, we have to rescue her from the inevitable cave-in. It's even worse when she's near where a snake could conceivably be coiled. Dogs are the traitors of the animal kingdom. They have betrayed all the other species to hunt with man, to herd for man to drive other animals into our clutches, our pens, our bellies. All they ask for in return? That we feed them, protect them and love them. It's a measure of the stupidity of domestic herds that word hasn't passed among them from cattle to sheep to goats to all other victims of canine duplicity — that it's time to trample dogs to death. Overwhelmingly, the dogs have got the other animals bluffed, and they've got us bluffed as well.' The best Adams column I have ever read.

Chapter Twenty: **Ten Bonzer LNL Episodes**

In these ten vibrant edited episodes of *Late Night Live*, Bob Ellis typically bares his soul but thankfully not his body; Hazel Hawke reveals her life before and after Bob; a wombat fancier digs to find their secret life; Phillip Adams burrows into the soul of Jim Cairns; Miriam Margolyes tells how the cruel adulterer Charles Dickens saved fallen women; listeners experience the Romanovs' last days; we hear why Winston Churchill stopped the spy Noel Coward from getting a knighthood; acerbic reporter Alan Ramsey finds grit and grime in 43 Canberra years; incest was probably the reason Lord Byron's prim wife left him after only 54 weeks; and how Bobby Kennedy, the president who never was, inspired America.

* * *

The terrible years of Bob Ellis: Author, playwright, film and speechwriter Bob Ellis had an amusing conversation with Phillip Adams on *LNL* on May 7, 2009 about his memoir from June 2007 to November 2008, *And So It Went: Night Thoughts in a Year of Change* (Penguin).

Adams said: 'There's no holding you back, Bob. You start the book with a good way to end it, at 7 a.m. on Sunday November 25, 2007 (the day after Labor finally beat the

Howard Government). You talk about John Howard's last walk from Kirribilli House. You talk about his courage and audacity at expressing himself in this way.'

Ellis: 'He outran me. I was puffing about a quarter of a mile behind. I saw him below in the park under the Sydney Harbour Bridge pylons, dwindling, getting smaller and smaller and being snapped by the paparazzi as he continued resolutely to walk. It was astonishing. Him in denial. Him in courage, carrying on as if nothing had happened; a remarkable mediocre man.'

Adams: 'It's a measure of your book's quality and impeccable Labor connections that Bob Carr, the ex-NSW premier, compared it with *War and Peace* and *The Iliad*. Surely even you blush at that, Bob. You love writing more than anyone else I know. Prose pours from you. Did you always love it?'

Ellis: 'I've never been near the crime and the lice, such as at a meeting between a property developer and a Labor minister. I concentrate on sex and death.'

Adams: 'Do you think Kevin Rudd will be a heart-breaker?'

Ellis: 'It's likely. There is an element of coldness, tenacity, Puritanism and slave-driving in him that will eventually undo him. I fear for his survival because of the valve in his heart and his sleeplessness. He has no friends that I know of, and fewer allies. He's brilliant but changeable and Napoleonic. He should sleep now and then, and take advice from someone over 30.'

Ellis' predictions and the reasons for them proved to be spot on.

* * *

Humble Hazel Hawke at her peak: The *Late Night Live* interview Adams had with Hazel Hawke in April 1998, three years after she and Bob Hawke were divorced, showed her strength of character and determination to go on contributing to society. Three years later, she was diagnosed with Alzheimer's disease. Adams said when the ABC repeated their conversation on February 24, 2006, Hazel Hawke was 'as bright as a button' when he talked with her in 1998 about: Her romance with Bob; her support for him as he achieved a Rhodes Scholarship; his mother Ellie's determination that he would become a leading politician; her lonely life in suburban Melbourne while he ran the Australian Council of Trade Unions and in Canberra from 1983 to 1991 while he ran Australia; his string of affairs; their divorce and his marriage to Blanche d'Alpuget. It was a poignant conversation particularly because of her eventual Alzheimer's.

Hawke: 'I'm a pretty average girl and I've experienced many things that affect middle-aged and ageing people. I take opportunities the media sometimes gives me to speak out about topics that affect others.'

Adams: 'That's why people love you, Hazel. What was it like to wake up in The Lodge and realise that you were the most scrutinised woman in Australia?'

Hawke: 'I don't think I had such an experience. When Bob became prime minister, I felt a very strong sense of responsibility and opportunity. I was attracted to women's and community issues, and to children's television.'

Adams: 'How old were you when you met Bob?'

Hawke: 'Eighteen or nineteen. He was six months younger than I was. He went to Oxford University for his Rhodes Scholarship and I followed a few months later.

All that was exciting because I had no tertiary education and started work at 14. During our courtship, his uncle, Albert, was the West Australian premier (1953-59). Bob and I were married in 1956. His family was very ALP-orientated and there was a stated expectation in the family that he would become a Labor politician.'

Adams: 'A prime minister?'

Hawke: 'It was talked about in the family.'

Adams: 'Did you urge him, or did you urge caution?'

Hawke: 'I'm not an urger either way. Basically I agreed with the moves he made. We lost a baby boy (Robert Junior) at the time Bob ran (unsuccessfully) for the federal seat of Corio, which made it hard.'

Adams: 'How's life for you now, post the Bob years?'

Hawke: 'Very good, very busy and full of interest. I do things I like doing, such as community work. I have one family in Sydney, one in Canberra and one in Perth. That's how I like to see our children, Susan, Stephen and Roslyn.

(Hazel and Bob lived in Melbourne from 1958 until 1983 while he was ACTU President, but in 1970 he met Blanche d'Alpuget and in 1976 they met again and started one of the most publicised affairs in Australian history.)

Hawke continued in her conversation with Adams in 1998: 'I've got another go at life. I'm not the slightest bit lonely. I've got a lot of friends and a good neighborhood where I live in Sydney. Life moves on. I wasn't raised with books but now I've become more aware of the treasure trove they are. I've got friends who lend me books and round and round they go. Friends and family get you through. Women's friendship is a great resource.

In Melbourne, I was out in the suburbs with not much money and really on my own. I had no family there and had not yet made friends in the local community. You find each other, for example at the local kindergarten. Many of those people I got to know in Melbourne, where I was for 25 years, were from somewhere else and we were looking for each other.

'Melbourne is more organised. Melbourne families have their churches and schools. Totally different to Sydney, not snobby but not so welcoming as Sydney, where it's "How're you going, mate?" Sydney has a different personality altogether. Melbourne has its social structures, and I admire them. For newcomers it takes time, but once you make your connection and your friends, it's a wonderful city, resourceful and with a great community spirit. If an appeal is well organised, Melbourne people give to it. Sydney has a different mentality. It's not mean but it's different in the way it approaches community.'

Adams: 'You must realise you have millions of friends. Is that a good feeling?'

Hazel: 'It's lovely, yes. I do feel a sense of friendship and belonging.

(Three years after the *LNL* conversation, Hazel Hawke was diagnosed with Alzheimer's disease; two years later she agreed to take part in an ABC Television *Australian Story* about living with Alzheimer's; in 2004, she and her family launched the Hazel Hawke Dementia and Care Fund; in 2009 she was placed in high-level care.)

* * *

Wombats' secret underground life: James Woodford, *Sydney Morning Herald* environment writer and author of *The Secret Life of Wombats* (Text Publishing), said in a *Late Night Live* conversation with Adams on July 30, 2001: 'Wombats are mysterious creatures and Europeans know little about them after living in Australia for more than 200 years. Forty years ago, a schoolboy called Peter Nicholson used at night to sneak out of his dormitory at Timbertop, a Victorian country branch of Geelong Grammar School, crawl down wombat burrows, get to know the wombats and learn to make the noises they make. It's a sort of "humpff" and there is another noise, like a loud "shhh" when they want to scare other animals.'

Adams: 'I'll try that when someone is unhappy about being interviewed. I've always been fond of wombats. They are about a metre long and a third of a metre high, like a barrel on legs; they keep themselves to themselves when they're not being skittled by cars, and they do most of their business underground.'

Woodford: 'I had my first wombat encounter when I was 17 and went camping in the mountains behind Nowra after finishing the Higher School Certificate. My uncle left the three of us with a case of beer and we stupidly drank the lot. When I woke up in the morning, a big wombat was three feet away.'

Adams: 'Did you say "humpff' to it?'

Woodford: 'I should have. I've been fascinated by them ever since. They are smarter than kangaroos or other marsupials.'

Adams: 'I've always said that on the Australian coat of arms are a kangaroo and an emu, which have the biggest bums and the smallest brains. I think that's deeply symbolic of our culture.'

Woodford: 'Some scientists say wombats are the smartest marsupials in the world. Their lives are surprisingly complex. People I've spoken to have been sleeping in a tent across a wombat's path and the wombat will just go straight through the tent. They have more personality than a kangaroo and they're much smarter than a koala. A woman made the mistake of building her house on a wombat trail and one day she opened her front door and found a wombat there. It walked straight through her house.'

* * *

The enigma of Jim Cairns: Adams called Jim Cairns, who has a unique place in the Australian Labor movement, 'one of the most valiant and vulnerable people I have ever met'. Adams had a warm and revealing conversation with him on October 28, 1996 and it was repeated on October 19, 2007, four years after Cairns died at the age of 89. Cairns was the minister for overseas trade and the minister for secondary industry in the first Whitlam Government, then deputy prime minister and treasurer but was sacked by Whitlam for his involvement in catastrophic foreign government loans and for misleading Federal Parliament. His career was also ruined by his affair with his sex-charged personal assistant Junie Morosi.

Adams: 'No-one in the Labor movement has attracted more flak than you. Why?'

Cairns: 'The determining forces in society are out to keep you in step, in politics and everywhere else. If you are an employee, you get on in the same way, by pleasing the boss. When Rupert Murdoch comes into the room, everyone knows what he should do. The most important day of my life was May 8, 1970, when I took a leading part in the anti-Vietnam War moratorium march of 100,000 people in Collins Street, Melbourne. It was completely peaceful and completely ineffective. The people had a human energy that could be felt. I've never had that experience before or since. It demonstrated what democracy really is. Parliament is a stage play, like something on television. If democracy is to mean anything, it has to be collective action by the people over something important. The moratorium was the clearest possible example of precisely that.'

Adams: 'Hasn't it been a sad story ever since? That was the mountain. The valleys seem to have got deeper and deeper.'

Cairns: 'No Australian parliament, federal or state, has any values other than money values.' Adams: 'And that is true of all Western democracies.'

Cairns: 'It's true in England and Europe. It's very disappointing and very serious. The alternative to concentrating entirely on economic growth is to concentrate on full employment. To reduce unemployment depends on a high level of government spending. And we can't have that because the ownership of Australia's economic structure has moved into foreign hands. Those companies pay their taxes overseas and foreign companies contribute only about ten per cent of total Australian taxation.'

Adams: 'You didn't run away over Junie Morosi. You copped it. No-one in public life had ever done that. Do you feel, as others have said, that you are one of the tragedies of politics and you blew your opportunities?'

Cairns: 'I presume that refers to 1975.'

Adams: ''You were dismissed before the Dismissal.'

Cairns: 'But to say I blew the opportunities is completely invalid. By the beginning of 1975, the Whitlam Government was finished. Whitlam had sacked three ministers and the speaker in six months. Kerr (the governor general) was looking for an opportunity to sack Whitlam. All this I knew, and I told Whitlam about it. The only thing Whitlam could have done was to recommend to the Queen that Kerr be replaced. But Whitlam was incapable of making a decision of that kind. I didn't blow the opportunity. I went out with it.'

* * *

Revelations about Charles Dickens' women: Adams said on *Late Night Live* on September 10, 2007: 'My friends have warned me about Miriam Margolyes. Miriam is an acclaimed British thespian and now an Australian citizen. She's taking her show, *Dickens' Women*, across Australia.'

Margolyes: 'Dickens was a bit of a shit, a very bad husband, an adulterer, cruel, and he bore grudges, but he wrote like a god. He had a bad time with women and felt betrayed by them. He was not gay, but he was effeminate. His mother and his first love both let him down. He couldn't stand humiliation. His women were scary but funny. He had a relationship with his mistress, Ellen Ternan, for 12 years, and founded a home for fallen women in Shepherd's Bush in London. They must have loved having this nice man come and question them for hours. Dickens was a social reformer and was fascinated by people on the underbelly of life. I think all men are a bit titillated about talking to prostitutes.'

Adams: 'One of the great things about Dickens was his recognition of the relationship between melancholia and happiness. They mingle and blend and enrich each other. That's what is wrong with many television shows — people have only one emotion. It's a comedy, a thriller or a series.' Margolyes: 'Everything's become so bland, one colour. I require highs and lows and that's why my shows are so jolly good. They make you laugh and cry, often at the same time. I do 22 women and two men, and I expose what a cad Dickens was to his wife, Catherine.'

Adams: 'What would Dickens make of your show?'

Margolyes: 'He would be furious! He would have regarded it as an infringement and an impertinence and would have tried to close it down.'

Adams: 'You have been doing this show for 20 years.'

Margolyes: 'I'm 66. I hang on to every year.'

Adams: 'How does the show translate across cultures?'

Margolyes: 'India loved it. But I went back only once to Jerusalem. I'm proudly Jewish but also pro-Palestine, a very uncomfortable position to hold because Jewish people feel I am betraying them. I'm not.'

Adams: 'What did the Queen say to you when you were awarded the Order of the British Empire?' Margolyes: 'I got it from Prince Charles, who I like very much. The Queen, when I met her at Buckingham Palace, told me to shut up! I spoke when I should not have spoken, not according to protocol.'

* * *

The Romanovs' tense last days: Ekaterinburg, the Russian city in the Urals where the Bolsheviks imprisoned and killed the royal Romanovs after the 1917 Russian Revolution, was a city on the brink of chaos and seething with soldiers and spies; the counter-revolutionary Whites were advancing on it, the British author Helen Rappaport told *Late Night Live* on July 30, 2008. She wrote *Ekaterinburg: The Last Days of the Romanovs* (Hutchinson) about the last Tsar (Nicholas 11), his wife Tsarina Alexandra, their daughters Olga, Tatiana, Maria, Anastasia and son Alexei, all of whom the Bolsheviks shot dead on July 17, 1918, after 18 months' captivity.

Rappaport: 'I walked the streets of Ekaterinburg in July 2007 and stood in an all-night vigil with thousands of people commemorating the Romanovs' deaths. It was an experience I will never forget and it connected me with the story. Boris Yeltsin had the house where they were held pulled down because the government was worried about the pilgrims. The Bolsheviks put a 15ft fence around the house, imprisoned the family on the top floor and painted out all the windows. On July 4, there had been rumours of monarch groups planning to get them out and their guards began to sympathise with them. Moscow tightened the security.'

Adams: 'Was there a welcome mat anywhere in Europe for them?'

Rappaport: 'No European royal family volunteered to take them. It was too much a political hot potato. Alexandra was hard to like — she had embraced Russianness to marry the Tsar but her spikey, unsmiling personality did not endear her to people. Once her son was born and found to be a haemophiliac, her world imploded and her life was spent willing him to survive. Nicholas was devoted to her but was dreadfully henpecked and weak, dominated by a very clever woman, a shrew who nagged him but who was a sick, hysterical woman. The government planned how to kill them as the White Russians advanced towards Ekaterinburg. Alexandra and Nicholas had a passionate physical relationship and an assortment of condoms was found in their room after they were murdered.'

Adams: 'Heavens above! The Pope's just been to Sydney. You shouldn't say that. Wash your mouth out! We can't ignore Rasputin in all this.'

Rappaport: 'I'm a bit bored by Rasputin because he's had such a lurid press. He wasn't as influential in state affairs as people make out.'

Adams: 'Did they realise they were about to die?'

Rappaport: 'That's the $64,000 question. Nicholas must have known he was doomed. But what parent would for one moment think that their children would also be slaughtered? There is no way the Bolsheviks would have taken the final step without Lenin's say-so.'

Adams: 'How much of the Romanovs resonates in Russia today?'

Rappaport: 'This is the key. They represented nationhood to the people, a link to the past, to Mother Russia. With the Romanovs being canonised (their bodies are now buried in St Petersburg Cathedral), they are being turned into plaster saints. Even though all their bodies have now been found and identified, false claims by "descendants" will never die down.'

* * *

Noel Coward, the entertaining spy: Barry Day, Trustee of the Noel Coward Foundation, told Adams on *Late Night Live* on January 31, 2008 about his book, *The Letters of Noel Coward*: 'Noel was spying for the Foreign Office from 1937 and this is revealed in his letters to and from them. Everything he wrote had an ironic touch.'

Adams: 'He was the son of a piano tuner and created his own persona, educated himself and learned rather than was taught. Things would come at him and he would absorb them and express them.'

Day: 'He said his good fortune was to have a bright, inquisitive nature but not an intellectual mind. He had to get out there and earn his own living.'

Adams: 'He was only 24 when he started to make good. Did he fall into the celebrity trap of believing his own hyperbole? He was intent on shaping Noel Coward, behind whom he could hide, which he certainly did. Being Noel Coward was his best disguise as a spy.'

Adams read from a letter in Day's book: 'I love smoking, drinking, moderate sexual intercourse on a diminishing scale, reading and writing, not arithmetic and I have a selfless absorption in the wellbeing and achievements of Noel Coward.' He addressed a letter to his mother, 'Dear darling old Mummysnooks, I know you don't love Daddy nearly as much as me.'

Day: 'He was certainly a mummy's boy and quite proud of it.'

Adams: 'There is a vast correspondence with celebrities. Are we talking of genuine friendships, or networking?'

Day: 'You're talking networking. As a young man, he would list the people he knew. But he had some genuine friendships, Gertrude Lawrence for sure, and Lawrence Olivier, although that soured.'

Adams: 'There is ambiguity in a letter to Virginia Woolf in 1928: "I am hot and glowing, and completely at your feet. Will you agree to become one of my top 500 best chums?"'

Day: 'They were friends for a while and then she told someone else that Noel was too clever by half. Most people, when they first came across Noel, felt obliged to be critical because others were so pro.'

Adams: 'Let's deal with sexuality and his long-term partner Graham Payn. Noel wrote the song, "Mad About the Boy."'

Day: 'There are many things you can take either way. One thing that concerns me is that some people want to turn him into a gay icon. There was an impeccable dignity in his sexual life, reticent but untainted by pretense.'

Adams: 'He handled that part of his life with enormous style. Lawrence of Arabia used to preface his letters with his military serial number, 338171, and Coward replied, "Dear 338171. May I call you 338?"'

Day: 'They became correspondents and saw each other from time to time. Whether they had an affair we will never know.'

Adams: 'Why did Churchill stop Noel's knighthood in 1942 after the King had approved it?'

Day: 'There was a definite mixture of feelings. Each admired the other but there was an edge, and I think it was because of two huge egos. Churchill was an actor also, and wanted to be centre stage. Personal jealousy had a lot to do with it. They made it up over the years, to a degree. In fact, Coward hosted the celebration of Winston's 90th birthday. The technicalities of why Winston refused Coward a knighthood were simple. The British Government sent Noel in the early years of the war to America, which was then neutral, to report back on attitudes. He got to know Roosevelt. When he returned to England, those who didn't like him picked on the fact that he had spent his own money to do it and this was a technical crime because finances had been frozen at the outbreak of war. He was taken to court and fined. So Churchill told the King that to give Noel a knighthood would look as if the government was ignoring the offence or rewarding it. Noel didn't get it for another 30 years.'

* * *

The first Australian combat troops to go to Vietnam left Sydney in secret late one night in May 1965 with no band and no cheering crowds. One of the five journalists on board was Alan Ramsey, who retired from journalism in December 2008 after reporting Canberra for *The Australian* from 1966 and then writing an acerbic, notorious half-page in the Saturday *Sydney Morning Herald* for 22 years. When he went to Vietnam he was 27, and he told Adams on *Late Night Live* on October 29, 2009:

'We had no idea where we were going and most of the ten days at sea we were given lectures on VD. I was given a jeep, painted purple so it could not be mistaken for a military vehicle. You could buy anything you wanted from the US Army stores on the Saigon black market and a lot of Americans became hugely wealthy selling American goods to the Vietnamese.

'Each of the three prime ministers after Robert Menzies, Harold Holt, John Gorton and Billy McMahon, is remembered for all the wrong reasons, not for good government. As soon as body bags started coming back from Vietnam containing 20-year-old conscripts, people started turning against the Coalition. Vietnam made Harold Holt's prime ministership and then destroyed it, and the next two. Then came the Whitlam Government, but three elections later, it was thrown out on its ear, after ministers had been waiting for 20 years to get into office. Malcolm Fraser became prime minister and his people were determined not to make the same mistakes.'

Adams: 'Paul Keating was first made a minister in the last three weeks of the Whitlam Government and was desperate to get back into government. He returned as Bob Hawke's treasurer.'

Ramsey: '1983 to '87 was the best period of government in the past 60 years. Fraser was a presidential figure and everyone was scared of him but Hawke was a consensus prime minister, although he was not good in Parliament. I never really understood his relationship with the Australian people but he made it work.'

Adams: 'You were John Howard's most trenchant critic. Why?'

Ramsey: 'Iraq. All politicians manipulate the truth from time to time but Howard was a serial liar. He was a toad. He debauched the goodwill he had when he came into office and after 9/11 he made himself a creature of the Bush Administration.' Allen & Unwin published Alan Ramsey's collection of columns, *A Matter of Opinion*, in October 2009.

* * *

The unmentionable scandals of Lord Byron: Ashley Hay, a Sydney journalist and author, started planning a book about Lord Byron's women and found he had so many of them — in one year in Venice, she said, he slept with a hundred — that she would have to write nine books to cover them. So she wrote *The Secret* (Duffy and Snellgrove) about his marriage to the prim heiress Annabella Millbanke and tried to find out why she left him after only 54 weeks taking their baby daughter Ada with her, would never tell anyone why and never saw him again. The story is full of rumours of Byron's incest, sodomy and affairs. Ashley Hay told Phillip Adams on *Late Night Live* on August 3, 2000, rebroadcast on March 7, 2008: 'Annabella spent the rest of her life justifying her decision to leave Byron and persecuting his reputation. He was incredibly charismatic and women swooned when they saw him and queued around the block to marry him. But Annabella was very different. She was earnest, and serious about her religion. They had a candid and intellectual correspondence in the 18 months after she rejected his first marriage proposal. He needed to get married; he needed a wife and he needed the money.'

Adams: 'Did he know what the secret was?'

Hay: 'He sent letters to her saying neither her lawyers nor her father would tell him why she left him. The year of their marriage was his worst financially. All the people he owed money to pressed him for payment. Annabella was pregnant in the third month of their marriage. Originally when she left him, she said he was mad. She took pride in being unflappable and he took pride in getting people to lose their cool. She saw her duty in being there and bearing the extremities of life and he tried to get her to show him human responses.'

Adams: 'Now that no-one is listening, what about Byron having an incestuous relationship with his half-sister, Augusta Leigh?'

Hay: 'There was a rumour about it in 1814, before the marriage. Annabella seized it and ran with it for 40 years.'

Adams: 'He threw the idea of incestuous love around at a dinner party. He liked to throw hand grenades into conversations.'

Hay: 'He wanted to play to the audience. If he could make someone splutter in their soup, so much the better. People were interested in how the other half lived. Incestuous relationships cropped up among the romantic poets.'

Adams: 'Perhaps incest could account for all the British aristocracy's inbreeding problems. Byron's status as a celebrity seemed to collapse in on itself.'

Hay: 'When London started to turn against him and take his wife's part, the mob that had created him was getting ready to cut him down. He left the scene, thereby opening the opportunities for more and more rumours.

Augusta admitted to having an affair with Byron before his marriage. Annabella said he had admitted it. She started taking memos of meetings and there are 450 boxes of these.' Adams: 'Vampires come into the story.' Hay: 'Byron is someone you can say anything about, and there was a novel published by one of his mistresses, Caroline Lamb, which had a vampire sub-plot. There was also a novel by his physician called The Vampire that leans strongly on Byron as its lead character. There was a rumour that he killed one of his mistresses and had a cup made out of her skull, so no wonder the rumour arises that he drank the blood of his murder victims.'

* * *

How Bobby Kennedy inspired America: Barack Obama's 2008 US Presidential campaign echoed one 40 years earlier, when Bobby Kennedy gave America a message of hope and promises to end the Vietnam War. Americans were beginning to doubt they were the noble, courageous people they believed they were, after city riots in 1965, '66 and '67 and television films showing marines setting fire to Vietnamese villages. On *Late Night Live* on June 11, 2008, Adams read from a book, *The Last Campaign: Robert F Kennedy and the 82 Days That Inspired America* by Thurston Clarke (Henry Holt): 'Bobby's determination to end the war was based on a belief that it was immoral. The only sin, the author said, was America's pride.'

Thurston Clarke said by phone from the US: 'Bobby was torn as to whether he should get into the race for the Democratic Presidential nomination. He had painted himself into a moral corner. He condemned the war as immoral but people asked how could he say that and not campaign for President against Lyndon Johnson, who was escalating it? There was no good answer. Bobby was saying, "How can I support Johnson over the war, but people will be just as angry with me if I do not support him?" Jackie Kennedy said the same thing would happen to Bobby as happened to her assassinated husband, President Jack Kennedy, because some people hated Bobby more than Jack.'

Adams: 'You describe Ethel as "recklessly frank, guarded, canny, guileless, brash and sensitive, a devout Catholic who threw wild parties."'

Clarke: 'She was one of the reasons the reporters described the campaign as a joyous adventure. They all had premonitions. There was black humour among the photographers, "Are you going to miss it?" Bobby was no saint. He had been a ruthless political enforcer for his brother. But after his brother was killed, things changed and he changed. The 82 days of his campaign was when he was at his best. He was absolutely hopeless at small talk and often stumble-tongued as an orator, certainly less charismatic than Jack but more passionate and hence more convincing. His shyness, vulnerability, the way his arms and legs shook when he talked, the way he stuttered, all these were very appealing to audiences. People saw him as so alone and so frail that they wanted to throw their arms around him. No-one wanted to throw their arms around Jack Kennedy because he was reserved. When Bobby spoke, it was as if he was asking the crowd to come to a conclusion. He used to think things out with the crowd. People in minority groups and blue-collar workers found a common bond with him.'

Adams: 'Would he have won the nomination and the presidency?'

Clarke: 'Yes.'

Adams: 'What a different world it would have been.' (Sirhan Sirhan, a Palestinian angered by Bobby Kennedy's support of Israel, shot him in a passageway off the kitchen of the Ambassador Hotel in Los Angeles just after midnight on June 5, 1968, and Kennedy died 26 hours later. Vice-president Hubert Humphrey won the Democratic Party nomination but was beaten by Republican Richard Nixon in the presidential election. Sirhan Sirhan was still in jail in 2010, 42 years later.)

Chapter Twenty-one: **Adams' Artifacts — His Ghostly Friends**

Phillip Adams owns Australia's largest private collection of artifacts but he didn't have any interest in collecting until he was walking down Bond Street in London with Barry Humphries in 1972. Humphries seemed to believe that American Express would make him use the card all the time and he rushed into expensive stores buying a monocle in one, a scarf in another and then, in another, a Cecil Beaton hat from a little man who looked like the villain Uriah Heap in Charles Dickens' *David Copperfield*, grovelling in front of him. Uriah Heap told Barry, "Sir, that hat is a bargain" and Humphries replied, "I abhor a bargain. I insist on paying extra," and flashed his Amex card. Adams left them to it and wandered off down Bond Street until, in the window of a shop with 'By Royal Appointment' over the door, he saw a little blue amulet about the size of a fingernail with a card on it saying it was Egyptian, four thousand years old and cost ten pounds. He didn't know until then that he could buy things so old so cheaply. He bought it and still has it in his office in Sydney. It sat on a shelf to my left whenever I had tape-recording sessions with him.

Within a few years the little amulet had been joined by thousands of friends, totalling 4,100 objects stored in various places. As catalogued by Consulting Arts, they included: 1,512 antiquities; 546 pre-Columbian artifacts; 347 from Europe; 299 from Asia; 128 from Australia (including Wes Walters' portrait of Adams, which won the 1979 Archibald Prize); 90 American artifacts, 50 tribal artifacts, 31 Near and Middle Eastern items, 46 others and 30 fakes and questionable objects. (Consulting Arts, which spent 18 months cataloguing the collection, said: 'Every museum and major art collection has forgeries.')

Adams told me, 'Your attitude to antiquity changes dramatically as you become an antiquity yourself. When you're in your twenties and collect pieces of Egypt, you still feel on top. When you're past seventy, you realise the pyramids have won. They will be still here when you've gone. So your sense of triumph in obtaining a piece of ancient Egypt is mitigated by the realisation that you don't actually own it but you have it for your brief lifetime. It's almost like you rent it.'

Adams has a special affection for Egyptian art because of its serenity — 'People say Khmer culture is serene, but Egyptian is more so. In Eastern art, the eye line is downcast and inward looking. In Roman art, the beginning of modern portraiture, the eyeline is directly looking at you. In Egyptian art, the eyeline is beyond you and beyond the horizon because the Egyptians looked to eternity.' Adams collected items that intrigued him, so the collection grew and grew and is undisciplined. He only occasionally sells items because he falls out of love with them or they become suspect. He has not bought anything for quite a while. In the past, he bought from dealers in Australia, New York City, Los

Angeles, Amsterdam or London, often from Sotheby's. Once, when he opened the Phillip Adams Antiquities Gallery in Toorak in Melbourne, he phoned Graham Geddes, a local antique dealer, to try to borrow some Spanish tables. Geddes came around to his shop and said, 'What's all this crap?' He knew nothing of antiquities as distinct from antiques but Adams believes Geddes is now one of the world's biggest antiquities dealers.

After Adams moved to Sydney in the 1980s and while he was taking part in the Bicentennial telecast on January 1, 1988, the pro-Nazi National Front raided his 1840s house in Darlinghurst, spray-painted the sandstone walls with choice words such as 'Adams is a multi-racial cunt' and was starting to smash his artifacts collection when the police arrived. So he moved his collection to several safer locations.

These days, Egypt and most other countries ban antiquities exports, in contrast with the days when archeologists filled their own or national galleries with relics stolen on Tutankhamen or other digs. Diplomats still steal relics in diplomatic bags. So do international pilots. Street markets are full of relics stolen not by Europeans but by locals. Soldiers' and locals' mass looting of relics in Iraq after the US invasion could have been avoided if the American Defence Secretary Donald Rumsfield had not been more intent on knocking over statues of Saddam Hussein than on saving 5,000-year-old antiquities.

Once when Adams walked into a dealer's shop in Rodeo Drive, Los Angeles, and asked a salesman the price of an item, a voice called out from the office above, 'Is that

Phillip Adams?' He could tell the voice was Australian, he had never met Adams but guessed it was him because Adams was well known as a collector. Ironically, most antiquities are not expensive. Adams' are valued at from $100 to $1million each and average $4,988, according to his catalogue. Egyptian antiquities are the most valuable, averaging $8,373 followed by European art (averaging $5,314), Near and Middle Eastern art ($1,839) and Oriental art ($1,242). The biggest numbers of items are statues and sculptures (1,404 items), household items (618), paintings and wall and floor art (378), funerary and religious equipment (243), jewellery (103), arms and armoury (83), furniture (69), musical instruments (61), numismatics and philately (45) and books and manuscripts (17).

The world antiquities market goes up and down and many items don't gain in value. When Adams went to the Nelson Rockefeller exhibition at the Museum of Modern Art in New York City, he found it cost more to buy a Rockefeller replica than the original item. He said the Egyptian Museum in Cairo is 'a wreck, and I love it.'

He told me a story about William Matthew Flinders Petrie (1853-1942), one of the greatest Egyptologist in history and connected by family to the Matthew Flinders, who circumnavigated Australia from 1801 to '03. Petrie was digging near Cairo in 1903, at a time when no image existed of Khufu (known as Cheops), who was the Pharaoh of Egypt from 2589 to 2566 BCE and who built the Great Pyramid of Giza, the tallest building in the world until the Eiffel Tower was built in 1889. Petrie was digging when one excited archeologist rushed up to him with the base of an ivory statuette

7.6cm high, carrying Cheops' name but without the head. Petrie's archeologists searched like demons and found the head after three days and, stuck together with glue that has dribbled down the side, the statuette is in a glass case in the Cairo Museum, where Adams found it on a trip to Egypt. As he was admiring it, one of the tourist police came up and asked, 'You like it?', to which Adams replied, 'I'll give you 12 Egyptian pounds (a few Australian dollars) for it.' The man looked around, went away and came back with a screwdriver, apparently planning to pick the lock. Adams had to persuade him that he had been joking.

The five-week trip to Egypt in January 2009 with his partner Patrice Newell and their daughter Rory was Phillip's eighth but Rory's first. She was 17 and Adams wanted her to have a comprehensive experience of one of his favourite places. They travelled from Abu Simbel in South Egypt to Alexandria in the north and had a great time in the Library of Alexandria, whose curator once appeared on Late Night Live when he was in Sydney. Behind the Egyptians' engaging smiles was mounting concern about how they would feed their families as the world financial crash hit tourism, which provides about eighty per cent of Egypt's income, concentrated into a few weeks every winter.

Adams saw people he originally met more than 30 years ago. The Adams family bounced around in everything from camels to hot-air balloons and went through hundreds of security doors with metal detectors that didn't work. Every Egyptian tomb has a false door with hieroglyphics on it, through which pass the spirits of the dead, but since a terrorist massacre at a temple 12 years ago stopped tourism in its tracks, Egypt has been filled with false doors containing what are supposed to be metal detectors. About a third of Egyptian workers are involved in 'securit' but Adams said guards carrying AK47s would do anything for you if you gave them five Egyptian pounds. It was so much like Monty Python's Flying Circus that he expected to meet John Cleese at any moment.

His favourite artifact is the Spink Head, the limestone head of a nobleman from Memphis, the ancient site of the Great Sphinx. The arrogant-looking fellow was sold in London in the 1920s at Spink, a famous auction house, but was blown to pieces in Berlin in the last days of World War 11. Adams bought the fragments and had them put together by Peter Wighton, whose credentials for the job were that he was a panel beater, and panel beaters are good at curves and shapes. The Spink Head now sits behind Adams' desk in his Sydney office with the academic cap from one of his honorary degrees on it.

Adams had no interest in Aboriginal relics, and the fact that some of them are ten times older than the Egyptian pyramids, until he visited a museum in Munich. He was visiting it because it displays Hitler's favourite art works, and the museum also had an exhibition of plaster reproductions of Aboriginal cave paintings that astounded him.

Chris Fischer, who catalogued his collection, said in his report that the antiquities portfolio (from the onset of civilisation to the Middle Ages) is the largest, representing almost half of all Adams' artifacts. The portfolio is dominated by two Etruscan objects: 1) A painted ceramic Etruscan funerary plaque with two Amazons on horseback, made in Etruria, Italy, in the Fifth Century BCE and 2) A painted polychrome figure of a standing bull, also made in Etruria, between 449 and 350 BCE. Fischer said, 'These represent a unique insight into the funerary customs of a civilisation still largely cloaked in mystery. 'We are not aware of any other objects similar to these in any other private collection throughout the world.'

The catalogue of antiquities also lists for special mention: a marble figure of the goddess Aphrodite bathing, from Greece in the Fourth Century BCE; a painted ceramic figure of a naked dancing satyr from Fourth Century Greece; a painted ceramic Fifth Century BCE Greek urn lid on which is a muscular naked man reclining on his elbow; a Second Century CE Imperial Roman marble figure of the god Eros as a child, with a portly body, thick fleshy thighs and a large potbelly and holding a goose; a marble figure of the demi-god Hercules as an elderly man standing over the slain five-headed Hydra, from Second or Third Century Imperial Rome; a coffin for a woman, with on the top a carved pear-shaped face wearing a false wig and broad collar, from Egypt between 1069 and 747 BCE; and a marble figure of an Imperial Roman senator from the Second Century BCE.

The highlights of Adams' European art collection are: 20 first edition Goya etchings from the Los Caprichos series; a group of marble statues from between the 17th and 19th Centuries (particularly the portrait bust of a nobleman that combines the artisan's skill to mimic classical Roman portrait busts); a wooden-framed piano from

England between 1800 and 1809; a 1634 oil portrait of Henry Daleebret, King of Navarre, Spain; and a 19th Century marble horse head that is a direct copy of the Horse of Selene, part of the Elgin Marbles in the British Museum.

Adams' Near and Middle Eastern art collection dates from the Middle Ages to the present day. The item highlighted by Consulting Arts is a colossal figure of the seated Buddha made of painted wood and inlay in Burma between 1850 and 1949.

The pre-Columbian collection comes originally from North and South America between the onset of civilisation and the mid-16th Century. It is dominated by objects made from ceramic (the preferred material due to its abundance, malleability and durability) such as vessels and figures from Mexico, including fine small figures from Colima, Nayarit and Vera Cruz. The highlights are a Colima standing duck; a painted ceramic plate with legs shaped like open-mouthed dragons, from Costa Rica between 950 and 1150; a painted ceramic figure of a kneeling woman wearing a short skirt, decorated cap and ear discs and holding a small child on her lap, from Mexico between 100 BCE and 250CE; and a ceramic standing figure of a nobleman Mexican ball player made between 350 and 950.

Adams' 46 prehistoric artifacts from around the world before civilisation include stone and animal bone tools produced in Africa or Europe from the Neolithic period to the start of agrarian culture in mainland Europe, especially a European stone axe head dated about 240,000 years BP (Before Present); a stone triangular United

Kingdom hand axe or knife from 250,000 BP; and a stone Egyptian axe head from 240,000 BP.

The Tribal Art collection highlights, according to Consulting Arts, are: a selection of 20th Century musical instruments ranging from a leather and bamboo drum from Indonesia to an African xylophone; a Nigerian wooden throne carved with figures of men, women and leopards; and an African xylophone made of wood, rope and gourd.

One oddball item in Adams' collection is a postcard written by George Bernard Shaw (1856-1950) to the Australian cooking author Edna Walling, of Mooroolbark in Melbourne, on which Shaw says in handwriting: 'Don't ask me to read anything. I have more writing on my shelves than I can hope to get through in the few days (perhaps hours) left to me.' He died not days or hours but three years later and his sentiments are similar to Adams' when he is sent manuscripts that the authors ask him to read and criticise.

Adams bought items that particularly appealed to him, mostly years ago. He said in the oral history that the National Library recorded in 1994 the collection was 'a metaphor for loneliness, for needing, something quiet I could do at home.' Now, his unique and valuable collection seems to have faded into the background of his life, although it gives him many memories as he sees the artifacts all around him at his Sydney office and in secure places elsewhere. Asked by the National Library whether he had any plans for it, he said he tried to give it to the National Gallery 'but I had a very strange run-in with the then director. It will finish up being disbanded and probably handed out to a dozen different galleries.' The collection is now so large that if Uriah Heap came to his door with a priceless item going cheap, he would probably bid him goodbye.

Chapter Twenty-two: **What Drives Phillip Adams**

Phillip Adams has left his mark on many people. He has his own touch. His imperative is to do things continuously. He responds to enthusiastic people and he is driven by ideas, and by his justifiable ego, although he denies he has an ego, which shows he doesn't fully understand himself. He also does not accept criticism, and that is a fault. He cares a great deal about society and he has a genuine love of people, although he is prone to fall out with some of them. The Australians who scare him are those who never have a moment of intellectual engagement and who do nothing much with their time — most of them.

Adams sincerely wants to improve people's lives, either personally or through his column and program. He says he is driven by an awareness of mortality, which he has had since he was very young. It gives him a great sense of urgency to do all he can in his remaining years: 'You want to do all you possibly can in the miserable time you're allotted.' Using Adams' figures, we have 175,000 hours to do anything in our lives, or 4,375 forty-hour weeks. In the total lifetime of humans on this planet, the life of Adams or anyone else is like a bird flying across a room, and Adams is aware of this more than most people.

He often talks about his unpleasant childhood — perhaps too often, as it is now so long ago. And he does admit that many other people had a much more unpleasant childhood than he did. As he says, people don't choose their childhood or their DNA. It chooses you. When he says he is still working very long days, he doesn't by any means have to do so; he chooses to, and many of the things he does are not work at all. I phoned him at his Paddington pad one weeknight at 7.30 p.m. When he answered, he'd obviously been asleep, and having catnaps is one way he makes up for being an insomniac.

Adams' days are largely unplanned except for the imperative of fronting his microphone at 10.05 p.m. four nights a week, fronting the few remaining organisations he gives his time to and meetings and conferences he agrees to chair. He's just as scared of falling off the media landscape as falling off the planet. He says he's amazed how many people waste so much time in their lives. He doesn't seem to understand that most people just live day to day or even hour to hour. It's a pity they do, but that's people. Adams claimed to me, 'I'm amazed how little I've done,' but this is in reality a scene of a play — the humble front he puts to people. He has achieved many, many times more than most people and more than most pillars of society, business or industry achieve. Some of his weeks are much busier than almost any other 71-year-old could handle.

'You need stamina to do it,' he told me. 'It's not a moral venture; it's predetermined by your genes. These days I'm not chairing seven organisations like I used to. I'm still in half a dozen organisations but I used to be in twenty. That was a sort of madness.' He used to endure hundreds of boring meetings but hardly ever goes to meetings now. He avoids the company of bigots, racists and bores — often the same people. He has no real complaints about life, except sometimes about his ageing body.

Adams would be devastated if he lost *Late Night Live* or his *Weekend Australian Magazine* column. The program standard is as good as ever, partly because, in spite of his ageing voice, he is as good as ever at presenting it and also because its producers put a lot of effort into preparing the background material and arranging interviews around the world. The column is sometimes as good as it was years ago, often not. Adams seems to think he can just bash it out at weekends year after year at his farm — he says it takes him hardly any time at all — and still maintain the quality. To maintain an even quality it needs more research and thought, more new topics and fewer revived ones.

Adams overstates most things, which works well when he exaggerates the importance of a person he's interviewing. But although his contribution to society has been huge, it has a dubious effect on politicians. They might listen to some of his broadcasts and read some of his columns, but politicians usually have strong opinions about what should be done, so they do what *they,* rather than *he,* believe. Adams' views would be more likely to change the thoughts of the hundreds of thousands of ordinary, uninfluential people who read or listen to him every week.

It is paradoxical that he believes in his own importance but (his friends say) he does not take himself too seriously. His self-depreciation on-air wins him many listeners. It is also paradoxical that he helps many people, both in what he says and also personally. Some of his friends worry about his health and lack of exercise, just walking to and from his car. Like his friends, I tell him he should look after himself better. He doesn't take any notice.

Adams is passionate about people but a self-proclaimed anti-social who likes to say he hasn't been to a dinner party for years. But if he is in a group of people, he likes to be the centre of attention, which he usually is. He has 'presence'. There is no-one like him, certainly in Australia and perhaps in the world. He gets his own way, as do most influential or powerful people. And if he doesn't get his own way with someone, he is likely to cross them off his list. In the tussle with the ABC over it wanting him to identify himself with every broadcast, he won. On the other hand, he does not, in print or on-air, criticise Rupert Murdoch, who pays him for his *Weekend Australian Magazine* column, although when the magazine editor reduced its size, he protested loudly and got others to do so, but in the end put up with less space than he had previously, but a more prominent position. He certainly enjoys his work and the attention he gets when, for example, chairing functions. He has an attractive voice both in person and on-air. Few people have a brain like his. The other side of the coin is that he is abrupt when he doesn't want to continue a conversation and he sometimes agrees or offers to arrange things and never gets around to it.

He can match word for word the people he interviews, including professors from around the world. When he has a *Late Night Live* conversation with an enthusiastic person he knows and likes about a subject he also likes, it is great radio. When he reads what his producers have given him and the person on the other end of the phone in Quito or Addis Ababa is not good at being interviewed, the result is naturally less gripping. But he never sounds bored, and he sounds as if he is talking just to *you*. He admits he is sometimes already exhausted when he arrives at the ABC studios, but when he faces the microphone, his adrenalin takes over and he's off and away with another program, spoken in correct but colloquial English, showing warmth to his guests and his listeners, enjoying his own whimsy and jokes but sometimes, as he grows older, rambling a bit too much.

Adams is always on the go and thinking of the next thing to do. Now that he has passed 70, this puts a strain on his body, which he fears is falling apart. He should not keep saying on-air that he's old; it's obvious anyway, and saying so doesn't impress anyone. None of us can help getting old. He enjoys having two places to live, Paddington and Elmswood; if he didn't have Patrice Newell to care for and feed him over his long weekends at Elmswood, his health would suffer, and he admits he and she would tear each other apart if they lived together all the time. Some of his friends believe he has never quite forgiven himself for leaving Rosemary, although he would say it was what he had to do after he met Patrice and was charmed by her when both their marriages were already on the rocks.

In spite of his radio interviews, chairing of meetings and circle of friends, Adams is essentially a loner. His friendships with people quoted in this book are typical of male friendships and unlike intense, intimate female friendships. Apart from Paul Keating and Barry Jones, Adams and his other friends don't talk often or at length but would help each other readily if help were needed. They re-open phone conversations where they left off months or years previously.

Adams has a reputation for being a gossip, but not in a destructive way. The stories he tells about well-known people are usually affectionate, with rare exceptions, such as his stories about Bob Hawke. Even there, his gossip is not poisonous. One of Adams' oldest friends, the composer Peter Best, told me Adams talks a lot about Paul Keating, who he really admires. But it is always good natured gossip. For example, Adams once said Keating had been seeing some woman. Adams asked Keating, 'Are you playing doctors and nurses?' Keating got quite huffy and replied, 'We've only been out a couple of times.' Peter Best thought how charmingly old-fashioned that was. Adams sometimes told him some light gossip about the Labor Party leadership. He would tell Best, 'I've been trying to persuade them to do this or that.'

Adams has a diverse mind and a huge curiosity about almost any subject from technology to wombats. In fact, he has a soft spot for wombats: the *Late Night Live* theme music until January 2011 was 'Russian Rag', by the Uzbekistan-born Sydney pianist and composer Elena Kats-Chernin, but Adams called it 'The Waltz of the Wombats'. Wombats abound at Elmswood, via Gundy near Scone in the Hunter Valley of NSW, but Adams looks and acts more like a city person than a country landowner. He had no previous rural connections apart from living as a lonely boy with his maternal grandparents on their poverty-stricken little flower farm in the suburban streets of East Kew in Melbourne. Patrice Newell's only rural experience had been growing a pot plant at her flat in King's Cross in Sydney, although she had a burning desire to quit presenting television and to grow organic meat and fruit and vegetables. Adams told me he has no idea whether their farm makes a profit or not. Obviously the prolonged Australian drought has made farming profits harder to make, but the fortune Adams and his partners made when they sold Monahan Dayman Adams, plus his steady and good income from writing his column and presenting his program, means he has remained wealthy.

Adams enjoys himself on and off-air. Almost all his friendships are work-related. His personality is passionate engagement. On-air, he grabs people he has never met and knows only from his producers' briefings. He talks to them across thousands of kilometers by phone or radio cable as if they're across his desk at the ABC. He is good at understanding people. He understood some points of my personality the first day we met, although if he believed I would write only complimentary things about him and not apply honest writing to him as the subject of a biography, he was mistaken. He likes enthusiastic people with a lot of energy and those, like himself, with a love of humanity and a concern for its future. Even if he doesn't like a person, he can like their enthusiasm. He finds Alan Jones, the right-wing 2GB breakfast presenter, politically appalling but says his output is fascinating and he has been so successful as a broadcaster because he does a great deal of his own research, and he's unstoppable — his relentless energy jumps out of the radio and chases people around the room.

Adams himself worked flat-out from when he left school at 15 until he was 45, which was when he left Rosemary, went to Sydney and started his relationship with Patrice Newell. He was tired and at a low ebb, in spite of having a new romance with a challenging intellectual woman. He started again. Kerry Packer had just bought 2UE, which phoned him and asked him to do a breakfast program. Neither 2UE nor Adams liked his program and he was switched to late night. He didn't do well with commercial talkback and 2UE did not renew his contract, which was just as well because in 1990 the ABC managing director Brian Johns phoned him and asked him to do *Late Night Live*, and he's been there ever since.

He now has a life that suits him. He slams the advertising industry, which made him wealthy, but it is very rare that anyone succeeds well in both business and a creative occupation like broadcasting and writing. He has given up the ad business; he has been either shown the door or has walked away from an infinite number of government committees; he's walked away from the film industry; few other journalists have had, for 40 years, the luxury of being able to write about anything they like. He still keeps busy, but now with less pressure.

He has a huge collection of awards and appointments (listed in the next chapter), which shows how, once people are on the awards gravy train, the awards rain down, often largely to the benefit of the organisations making the awards.

He regrets not giving his first family enough attention, when he was ludicrously busy. He regrets not being more formally educated, although Phillip Adams with a university degree might have lost his attractive common touch. He is disappointed that he won't leave a monolithic work, although he has a bigger audience of listeners and readers than any Australian author.

Chapter Twenty-three: **Appendix — Awards and Appointments**

This information was supplied by Phillip Adams:

Honours:

Phillip Adams was made a Member of the Order of Australia (AM) in 1987 for services to film and television.

Officer of the Order of Australia (AO) in 1992 for services to the arts and journalism.

Chosen in a National Trust opinion poll to be one of Australia's One Hundred Living National Treasures.

Received the film industry's highest award, the Raymond Longford Award, for services to the industry in 1981.

Senior ANZAC (Australian and New Zealand Army Corp) Fellow in 1985.

Humanist of the Year in 1987.

Henry Lawson Australian Arts Award in 1987.

His campaign for the United Nations International Year of the Disabled Person won the Golden Lion award at the Cannes film festival in 1982.

His feature films have received ten Australian Film Institute awards, including two Best Film: *Jack and Jill: A Postscript* in 1969 and *Lonely Hearts*, directed by Paul Cox, in 1982.

The Adelaide-Auckland International Film Festival awarded *Jack and Jill: A Postscript* its Grand Prix, the Golden Southern Cross, in 1970.

Responsibility in Journalism Award at the University of New York in 1996.

Awarded Honorary Doctorates by Griffith University in 1996, by Edith Cowan University in Perth in 2003, by the University of South Australia in 2004 and the University of Sydney in 2005.

International Astronomical Union named a minor planet orbiting the Sun between Mars and Jupiter the Phillipadams in 1997.

A painting of Adams won the Archibald Prize in 1979.

Received a Walkley Award for journalism in 2005.

A Pater Award for excellence in radio.

A Television Logie.

The Celebration of Ability Media Award in 2000.

United Nations Media Award in 2005.

In October 1996, when a poll of 200 prominent academics was conducted to identify Australia's Most Influential Public Intellectuals, Adams was in the top five with Robert Manne, Henry Reynolds, Tim Flannery and Noel Pearson.

Republican of the Year in 2005.

Fellow of the Academy of Humanities of Australia.

Fellow of the Royal Society of the Arts.

Appointments: Adams has served as:

Chairman of the Australian Film Commission.

Chairman of Film Australia.

Chairman of the Australian Film Institute.

Chairman of the Australia Council International Committee.

Chairman of the Australia Council Research Committee.

Chairman of the National Australia Day Council.

Foundation Chairman of the Commission for the Future.

Foundation Chairman of the Film, Television and Radio Board.

Foundation member, Film Victoria.

Foundation Chairman of the Independent Feature Film Producers' Association President of the Victorian Council of the Arts.

President of the Australasian Academy of Broadcast Arts and Science.

Chief Executive Officer of Southern Cross Film Productions Pty Ltd.

Chief Executive Officer of Double Head Productions Ltd.

Chief Executive Officer of Longford Productions Pty Ltd.

Chief Executive Officer of Adams Packer Films Pty Ltd.

Foundation director of the Australian Caption Centre.

Foundation director of the Australian Children's Television Foundation.

Representative, arts and film industries, Taxation Summit, 1982.

Member of the Children's Television Committee for the Nine Network.

Member of the Australian Governments Committee on the Centenary of Federation Member of the Aboriginal Treaty Committee.

Member of Amnesty International.

Member of the National Museum of Australia Board.

Member of the Museum of Victoria Board.

Member the National Council of the Australian Opera.

Member of the Sydney Opera Company Board.

Member of the Greenpeace Australia Board.

Advisor, Victorian Sesquicentenary Committee.

Board member, Interim Council for a National Film and Television School.

Member of the CARE Australia Board.

Member of the National Federation Centenary Committee.

Member of the Australian Labor Party Arts Committee.

Member of the Federal Government Committee on the French Bicentennial.

Member of the Landmark Committee of the Victorian Government.

Member of the Joan Sutherland Sculpture Committee of the City of Sydney.

Member of the Queen's Birthday Reference Committee, Government of NSW.

Member of Advisory Committee, Institute of Multicultural Affairs.

Member of the Council of Victoria.

Examiner, Swinburne Film School.

Convenor, Friends of The Age.

Member of Wallenberg Committee Board.

Life Member, National Trust of Australia (NSW).

Foundation Chairman, Ideas at the Powerhouse.

Foundation board member, Don Dunstan Foundation, University of Adelaide.

Member, Australian International Documentary Conference.

Currently, Adams is:

Chairman, Advisory Board, Rights Australia Inc.

Chairman, Advisory Board, Centre for the Mind, University of Sydney and Australian National University.

Member, Advisory Board, Architects Without Frontiers.

Member, Convocation of the Australian Film, Radio and Television School.

Member, Australian International Documentary Conference.

Member of the Board, Anti-Football League.

Editorial Advisory Board, the Council for Secular Humanism, New York.

National Council member of the Adelaide Festival.

Advisory Board, Adelaide Festival of Ideas.

Board member and Australian representative, Index on Censorship, UK.

Board member, Families in Distress Foundation.

Foundation member, Independent Scholars Association of Australia.

Member, Australian International Organising Committee for the Restitution of the Parthenon Marbles.

Member, Council for Media Integrity, New York.

Board member, Festival of Ideas, Adelaide.

Board member, Festival of Ideas, Brisbane.

Board member, Ausflag.

Board member, National Heritage Committee.

Board member, Montsalvat Artists' Colony.

Ambassador, Council for Aboriginal Reconciliation.

Ambassador, Australian Capital Territory.

Patron, Manning Clark House.

Patron, Australian Humanists.
Patron, Australian Skeptics.
Patron of Defense for Children International.
Patron, the Trade Union Education Foundation.
Patron, Freedom From Violence Australian Inc.
Patron, the Humanist Society.
Patron, the Dorothea Mackellar Society.
Patron, the Strzelecki Society.
Patron, Youth Challenge Australia.
Patron, Jannah, SIEV-X Memorial.
Vice-Patron, United Nations Association.
Fellow, Royal Society of the Arts.
Co-Founder, The Voltaire Society.

Feature Films:

Jack & Jill: A Postscript (with Brian Robinson). Winner Best Film, AFI Awards, winner Grand Prix, Adelaide-Auckland Film Festival.
The Naked Bunyip (with John Murray).
The Adventures of Barry McKenzie (with Bruce Beresford and Barry Humphries).
Don's Party (with Bruce Beresford). Winner six AFI Awards.
The Getting of Wisdom (with Bruce Beresford).
We of the Never Never (with Igor Auzins). Winner of five AFI Awards.
Abra Cadabra (with Alex Stitt).
Grendel Grendel Grendel (with Alex Stitt).
Lonely Hearts (with Paul Cox). Winner, Best Film, AFI Awards.
Fighting Back (with Michael Caulfield). Winner of AFI Award.

Kitty and the Bagman (with Donald Crombie). AFI Award winner.

A Personal History of the Australian Surf (with Michael Blakemore), Peter Sellers

Award, UK. Most Popular Film at Melbourne Film Festival, 1982.

Adams played the role of God in the feature film *The Road to Nhill.*

Documentaries and Television:

Hearts and Minds (with Bruce Petty): The first Australian documentary on then Vietnam War.

Comedy sketches for The Mavis Brampton Show .

Death and Destiny (with Paul Cox): A study of Macquarie University's excavations near the Step Pyramid at Sakkara.

Be Back After This Break: a Seven Network series on the history of Australian advertising.

The Big Questions (with Professor Paul Davies): An SBS series on quantum mechanics, cosmology and theology. *More Big Questions:* A sequel

Two-Shot, Series 1 and 2: Adams interviewed Paul Keating, Professor Allan Snyder, Richard Butler, etc.

Short and Sweet: Two six-part ABC series of short films.

Adams' Australia (with Ben Lewin): The BBC's contribution to the Bicentennial Celebrations

See It My Way, ABC: Personal view of our attitude to death.

Face The Nation, SBS, including the first interview with three surviving prime ministers, Bob Hawke, Gough Whitlam and Malcolm Fraser.

Australian Bicentennial telecast: Adams was a co-presenter of Peter Faiman's largest live television program ever undertaken, with 100 locations across Australia and the world.

Compere, Australian Film Institute Awards telecasts.

Compere, Australian Tourism Awards.

Adams was featured in the ABC series *The Peripatetic Philosophers.*

Adams played Pope Innocent X1 in the world premiere of Accademia Arcadia Cantatas at the Arcadian Academy: *A Dialogue of Love and Power* in the Melbourne Festival, 2004.

Journalism:

Adams is the longest-published columnist in *The Australian.* Previously his columns have been published in *The Age, The Sydney Morning Herald*, the Brisbane *Courier Mail*, the Adelaide *Advertiser* and the Launceston *Examiner.* His columns have also appeared in *The National Times, Nation* and *Nation Review*, *The New York Times*, London *Financial Times*, *Index on Censorship* (London), *The Sunday Times* (London) and have been broadcast by the BBC. Two of his columns appeared in *The Columnists* (Penguin, UK).

Speechwriting:

Phillip Adams has written speeches for The Queen, Pope John Paul II, Mikhail Gorbachev, President Reagan, President Mitterrand, Helmut Kohl, Deng Xiaoping and the Prime Minister of Japan, Australian prime ministers and premiers. He has worked on Labor Party state and federal election campaigns.

Books:

Adams has written more than 20 books, including:

Adams With Added Enzymes (Sun Books).

The Unspeakable Adams (Thomas Nelson Australia).

More Unspeakable Adams (Nelson).

The Uncensored Adams (Nelson).

Adams Versus God (Nelson).

Classic Columns (ABC Books).

Harold Cazneaux: the Quiet Observer (with H. Ennis), National Library of Australia.

The Big Questions (with Professor Paul Davies), Penguin.

More Big Questions (with Professor Paul Davies), Penguin.

A Billion Voices — impressions of Indian life and politics (ABC Books).

Kookaburra (edited by Adams) — *a journal of political satire* (Penguin).

The Retreat from Tolerance (edited by Adams) — essays on the Pauline Hanson phenomenon.

Talkback (with Lee Burton), Allen & Unwin.

Mass Media Review (edited by Adams).

Collected Documents — The Art of Place.

Adams' Ark (Viking Penguin).

Adams was a contributor to:

Two Nations (on the Hanson phenomenon).

The Last Rite, the Penguin Book of Death (on voluntary euthanasia).

Speaking Their Mind — Portraits of Australia's Public Intellectuals (Robert Dessaix).

Life With Gough (Barry Cohen).

As The Twig Is Bent (Terry Lane).

The Best Australian Humorous Writing 2008 (Melbourne University Publishing).
The Best Australian Politician Writing 2008 (MUP).
Well May We Say — The Speeches That Made Australia (Black Inc).

His collections of jokes (with Patrice Newell) include:

The Penguin Book of Australian Jokes (1994).
The Penguin Book of More Australian Jokes.
The Penguin Book of Jokes from Cyberspace (1995).
What a Joke! (with Terry Denton), 1998.
The Penguin Book of Schoolyard Jokes.
The Penguin Book of World Jokes (2004).

Audio Books:

New Trends in Mass Media (*The Age*).
The Big Questions (with Paul Davies).
More Big Questions (with Paul Davies).
The Penguin Book of Australian Jokes.
A Billion Voices: The Elements of India.
Conversations with Phillip Adams, Vols 1, 11 and 111.
Adams' Ark.
The Ideas Book (University of Queensland Press).
Two Nations Bookman.

Public Speaking:

Adams delivered the inaugural Freilich Lecture (ANU).
He has also delivered:
The Whitlam Lecture (Sydney, 1997).
The Oscar Mendelssohn Memorial Lecture (Monash University).

The Inaugural Charles Sturt Oration.

The Inaugural Harry Sorensen Business Ethics Lecture (Monash University).

The Queen's Pictures Lecture (National Gallery, Canberra).

The Walter Burley Griffin Lecture (ANU).

The Angus McMillan Memorial Lecture (Bairnsdale).

The National Press Club.

The Press Club, Melbourne.

The Foreign Correspondents' Club, Hong Kong.

Sydney Writers' Festival.

Adelaide Writers' Festival.

Brisbane Writers' Week.

Byron Bay Writers' Festival.

The Global Cultural Diversity Conference,

The Australian Institute of Jewish Affairs Conference.

The Museums Australia Conference.

The Queen's Trust Conference.

The Immigration Outlook Conference.

The Perth Press Club.

The Melbourne Press Club.

The Adelaide Press Club.

The Government Communications Conference.

The American Newspaper Publishers' Association Conference.

The Australasian Academy of Forensic Sciences.

The Royal Australian Institute of Architects.

The International Conference of Psychiatry.

The International Committee for Skeptical Inquiry Conference, New York.

The University of Potsdam, Germany.

The Australian Chamber of Commerce, Hong Kong.

The Armenian Genocide Commemorative Lecture.
The Louvre Exhibition of Ancient Egyptian Art (Australian National Gallery).
The Picasso Exhibition (Art Gallery of NSW).

Cultural Delegations:

Adams has led delegations to China and Russia and as Chairman of the Australian Film Commission led the Australian contingent to the Cannes film festival for many years. He presented a series of lectures on Australian politics in Berlin at the Foreign Affairs Department's request.

Business:

Adams was a partner in Monahan Dayman Adams, which grew from a small Melbourne office into the largest Australian-owned advertising agency with an annual turnover approaching $1 billion and offices throughout Australia, New Zealand and Asia, London and New York. Adams' best-known campaign (in collaboration with Alex Stitt) was "Life. Be In It." He also devised the "Care for Kids" campaign for the International Year of the Child and the "Break Down the Barriers" campaign during the International Year of the Disabled Person. It won the Gold Lion at the Cannes film festival. Adams also developed campaigns attacking racism, urging Aboriginal employment, and on breast cancer, cervical cancer and skin cancer — "Slip Slap Slop."

Miscellaneous:

A painting of Phillip by Wes Walters won the Archibald Prize in 1979. A portrait of Adams by Larissa Mackay was a finalist in the Portia Geach Memorial Prize in 2008. A portrait of Adams by Peter Smeeth won the People's Choice in the Salon des Refuses in 2008.

Collection:

Adams has Australia's largest private collection of antiquities, more than 4,000 items, including Egyptian, Hellenistic, Roman, Etruscan, Cypriot, Luristan, Sumerian, Hittite, Persian, Minoan, Anatolian, Babylonian, Assyrian and Chinese pieces and others from African, Inuit, New Guinea and Trobriand Island cultures.

Index

In some cases, an entry continues on pages following the nominated page.